SIDECOUNTRY

ALSO BY JOHN BRANCH

Boy on Ice

The Last Cowboys

SIDECOUNTRY

Tales of Death and Life from
the Back Roads of Sports

JOHN BRANCH

W. W. NORTON & COMPANY
Independent Publishers Since 1923

For information about special discounts for bulk purchases, please contact
W. W. Norton Special Sales at specialsales@wwnorton.com or 800-233-4830

Manufacturing by Lakeside Book Company
Book design by Ellen Cipriano
Production manager: Julia Druskin

Library of Congress Cataloging-in-Publication Data

Names: Branch, John (Sports reporter), author.
Title: Sidecountry : tales of death and life from the
back roads of sports / John Branch.
Other titles: Newspaper columns. Selections.
Description: First edition. | New York, N.Y. : W.W. Norton & Company, [2021]
Identifiers: LCCN 2021004053 | ISBN 9781324006695 (hardcover) |
ISBN 9781324006701 (epub)
Subjects: LCSH: Sports—United States. | Sports—Social aspects—United
States. | Newspapers—Sections, columns, etc.—Sports.
Classification: LCC GV707 .B7195 2021 | DDC 796.0973—dc23
LC record available at https://lccn.loc.gov/2021004053

ISBN 978-1-324-02188-9 pbk.

W. W. Norton & Company, Inc., 500 Fifth Avenue, New York, N.Y. 10110
www.wwnorton.com

W. W. Norton & Company Ltd., 15 Carlisle Street, London W1D 3BS

1 2 3 4 5 6 7 8 9 0

To those daring enough to share their stories with me,
in these pages and elsewhere.

CONTENTS

INTRODUCTION

There was a term that came up a few years ago, when I was reporting what ultimately became a story called "Snow Fall," that I had never heard and that I have never forgotten.

Sidecountry.

It is a place just outside the controlled parts of a ski area—not quite the backcountry, but beyond the ropes and wild enough. It seduces the daring with its illusion of safety, thanks to its proximity. It is an adventure within reach, but still out of bounds.

It occurs to me now why I found this word so evocative: it is exactly where I like to go with my reporting and writing. Somewhere on the edges, away from the crowds, exploring worlds known only to a few.

"Snow Fall," the first story in this collection, is all about the sidecountry. But so are all the others, in their own way. They're just a few steps from the familiar, fresh but imaginable.

When people learn that I am a sports reporter for *The New York Times*, they invariably ask what sports I cover or what kinds of stories I write.

They imagine that I go to big games, hang around locker rooms and interview renowned athletes. I've done a lot of that, and still do. But I sometimes go months between games and I don't cover a specific sport.

I don't find people interesting just because they're famous. I don't find games fascinating just because they have a big audience. I tend to find more meaning in smaller stories.

I'm used to the reaction: a mix of doubt and disappointment. *Wait a minute—what kind of sports reporter are you?*

Over the years, I've settled on this murky explanative shorthand: I try to write stories you didn't know you wanted to read.

In 2020, I covered the death of Kobe Bryant—there's the flicker of name recognition people seem to want—but the story that stuck with me was not really about him. It was about the pastor and the congregants at the little church near where Bryant's helicopter crashed.

The hope is to give readers something different, something unexpected. They would never ask for it, because they wouldn't know to ask. My quest is to provide the unforeseen pleasure—always the best kind.

They don't know that they might want to read a story about a deadly avalanche, or about two climbers hoping to be the first to scale 3,000 feet of famed granite a particular way. No one told them that they might fall for the endlessly losing Lady Jaguars, or the eternally running Hopi boys, or the faithful workers living the last days of a famed horse track. They know nothing of the dead men left high on Mount Everest or their grieving families in India. Maybe they've never heard of abalone or speedcubing or competitive dog grooming. They would never think to ask me about a girl on my daughter's soccer team, no matter what happened to her mother.

My job can feel like a dare: Can I get this story into the *New York Times* sports section?

<hr/>

These stories are some of my favorite dares. Many don't seem to be about sports at all.

A good number of these are adventure stories. All of them are adventures of the spirit—people pushing themselves in some way, toward perfection, toward acceptance, toward closure.

That is what all these stories have in common—what all good stories have in common: they are about ordinary people tangled in something extraordinary. They are people pushing their own limits, with no quest for fame or money. The people in these stories want to dare, to persist, to brave, to venture, to confront, to believe—just because. The rewards are internal. The risks can be real.

We could all imagine ourselves stepping through these gates, whether pulled by adventure or pushed by circumstance.

When reporting "Snow Fall," I told people that I was working on a story about an avalanche. I knew that was not quite right. It was about people caught in an avalanche. And if I needed a reminder of the difference, it came on a late spring day, when I went searching for the memory of an avalanche hidden in the emerald green nooks of the Cascade Mountains.

The day before, I had wandered into the woods alone and thought I found it. I came across the bulky end of a snowslide runout, like the fat head of a skinny snake that slinked uphill and out of sight through a thicket of trees and shrubs. The pile was about ten feet tall, maybe forty feet wide.

Somewhere nearby was a stream called Tunnel Creek, heavy with spring runoff. I could hear it. I tried to climb to the top of the snow pile. It was slushy and slick, but there were things to grip and step on, like fir boughs and thick, broken logs and a million pine needles. It was as if the pile had eaten a Christmas tree lot. I could smell the needles and sap. The pile was full of rocks, too. The ice was like Grandma's holiday Jell-O, holding together a salad of pieces frozen inside.

That's when I realized that an avalanche carries a lot more than snow. It is not the puffy, whooshing plume familiar from videos taken from a distance. At ground level, it is a scouring pad. It is mass times velocity, a force unleashed, usually by humans, that flows downhill on the strict laws of gravity and momentum. It scrubs the earth—the vegetation, the rocks, even the animals and people unlucky enough to be in the way.

Like liquid cement, the ice flow hardens when it stops, gripping and suffocating everything inside. Hope for life rests in good fortune or the fast action of rescuers. Otherwise, extraction comes naturally, if at all, in the warming days of spring. That was what I had discovered, alone in the woods one spring day, atop the melting mound of a winter avalanche.

It was weeks before I started writing. It was months before the story had a title. It was a year before it won a Pulitzer Prize.

It was the wrong avalanche.

I learned this the next day, when I returned with a snowboarder named Tim Carlson. He had been one of sixteen people swept up in the stoke of a February morning who formed a loose group that met at the base of nearby Stevens Pass. They took a chairlift up, then another. Once at the upper reaches of the ski area, they took off their skis and boards and hiked through the boundary gate to the summit of a ridge called Cowboy Mountain. Below them was nothing but fresh powder.

This was the sidecountry—an adventure within reach, if you dare.

Carlson was there when the group whooped and glided down the steep ravines toward Tunnel Creek. And he was there at the bottom, having lost track of most others by taking another route, when he saw it: a massive pile of snow with a single ski pole sticking out of the top like a flag. His electronic avalanche beacon chirped. He was the first to start digging. He was the first to find a body.

That was winter. Now it was spring.

We didn't make it as far as the avalanche debris pile I'd found the day before. Carlson cut uphill before we got there. He led me into a vast meadow, a gentle rise nearly impassable because of thick willows blooming green with spring leaves. The meadow was backed by a steep mountain gouged by what looked like near-vertical ravines shaped by spring runoff. They were like squiggly rain gutters of a giant fortress that stretched thousands of vertical feet into the day's low clouds.

We kept going, higher and higher. The ground was soaked from melted snow. Our boots were encased in mud. My jeans were wet and heavy. We bushwhacked our way through the willows. Carlson stopped. This is where the pile was, he said. This is where I saw the ski pole.

There was no snow. There was nothing there but spring growth and mud. We kept going. We crawled toward the mouth of a ravine. The walls were twenty or thirty feet high. This was the flume, the narrow spout of a funnel that had carried tons of snow, ice, trees and bodies and spit them out into the meadow months before.

We clawed ourselves up the mountain along the right edge of the ravine by holding onto the bendable branches of the growing willows or the brittle limbs of conifers. Some branches along the ravine's edge were gone, broken or sheared off. Some trees had their bark stripped by the avalanche. Others were gone entirely, their trunks snapped near the base. There was a squiggle of snow and ice down the center of the ravine. There was a sound of rushing, crashing water below it, a river of runoff we could not see.

Midway up that unnamed gorge, as we clung to trees at the edges, Carlson spotted something on the snow below. He scrambled down the muddy banks, holding limbs and roots. When he got to the ice, he crawled, army-like, not wanting his body weight to break the ice shelf and drop him into the hidden river below.

It was exactly what he was afraid it was: a ski.

It had come off of Jonny Brennan's boot somewhere in his final moments of life. Maybe it came off when the avalanche first knocked him off his feet. Maybe it came off during the downhill tumble that pummeled his body and broke so many bones. Either way, it somehow stopped here, midway through the avalanche's journey, buried in snow in a ravine that only now was coming out of hibernation.

Carlson snared the ski and quickly retreated off the ice. He slouched on the bank. I could hear him below me, sobbing, over the sound of the cascading water. I can still see his shoulders heaving.

A day before, standing atop the runout of an avalanche that apparently no one else had noticed, I had come to realize the destructive power of falling snow, a marvel of science and nature. Now I realized that the story was not about an avalanche. The story was about people caught in an avalanche. There is a difference.

⎯⎯⎯◄⎯⎯⎯

I've written about two thousand stories for *The New York Times*, and I rarely go back and reread them. The metabolism of newspapers does not allow for much reflection. By the time a story is published, we're usually on to something else, and it is too late to get caught up in what people thought of it and too late to do anything about it.

The list of stories gathered in *Sidecountry* was mostly culled from memory. They are among the stories that have stuck with me more than others. Some became reader favorites, some won awards. Quite a few, I bet, are remembered only by me and the people whose stories they contain. I'm glad to give them a fresh audience.

There were some stories that came to mind and that I expected to include in this collection, but I did not love the words as much as I remembered. I sometimes winced at the missed opportunity and wished I could go back and rewrite, armed with hindsight and experience.

But there's a strange phenomenon among writers, and I know I'm not the only one to experience it. When I surf the archives for my work, the older the story is, in general, the more likely I am to like it. I suppose it's because I forget the pain of writing—the frustrations of reporting, the pressures of deadlines, the angst over words and tone, the dread of fearing that the piece doesn't match the hope I had when the page was blank. Now, deep in my career, I've learned to remind myself that the reader knows nothing of the writer's anxiety, but experiences each story fresh and open-minded. Maybe that is why I tend to enjoy my older pieces most: time hides the process. Still, even knowing that, I live in constant worry that my writing is getting worse.

The hardest part of writing is not what to put in; it's what to leave out. I often read about how editing and re-editing and editing some more are the keys to good writing. It's usually said by editors. I tweak stories, read them aloud to get the flow and to hear the words, and maybe shuffle a few things around. If there's time, I'll read it aloud again, and again. But if I tweak it too much, I start to doubt the entire thing. It feels overthought and gummed up. And I worry that I've turned a good idea and a free-flowing draft into something sticky and uninteresting, certainly not worthy of *The New York Times*.

And that's when I file. It usually feels like an act of surrender, not triumph—relief, not joy. If I had a camera on me at the moment I hit the Send button, it would probably capture me wincing and shaking my head. I hope to never see the piece again.

You forget that anguish over time. Gone, eventually, are all the things that you might have, should have, done differently. Forgotten are the internal doubts about structure and word choices.

It's strange, the mix of stories that came to mind here, and the differences in my memory of writing them. The first piece, "Snow Fall," became part of a massive multimedia effort that took most of six months. The last piece, "The Girl in the Number 8 Jersey," was a Facebook post I hammered out, emotionally, in one sitting. A *New York Times* editor saw it and asked to publish it on the front page of the paper.

Forgotten, by me, are most of the words. Left behind is the memory of the experience—not always the story itself, but the reporting of the story, like that day with Tim Carlson.

What I remember are the people telling me their stories, sometimes about the worst days of their lives. I remember where we were when we spoke, where I was when I wrote, and a million little images in between.

I couldn't have told you anything about the first lines of a story I wrote about alligator hunting, but I'll never forget trawling through the vast, mazelike bayou with a game warden in the middle of the night, shining flashlights into the dark shadows to capture the reflective eyes of lurking gators, and the tense interaction with two armed men mysteriously camping in a remote bog.

When I think of the story about wingsuit flying that was titled "Lost Brother," I remember meeting Dean Potter at a film premiere months earlier, and I remember hiking out alone on a chilly Yosemite evening to the cliff where he took his final leap.

I spent weeks with the Lady Jaguars of Carroll Academy, and yet my strongest memory is the first bus ride with them, giddily on their way to a basketball game that they would lose by fifty points.

For what became "Deliverance From 27,000 Feet," I think of the haunted families in India who welcomed us into their homes with tea and biscuits and a desperation for answers. I think of that dim basement morgue and the stiff frozen bodies, in faded and tattered climbing clothes, lying alone on the hallway floor. I think of the crematorium along the river, and being the only one in the room when the gates to the furnace closed behind Goutam Ghosh's body.

I think of "The Girl in the No. 8 Jersey" every time I pass that soccer field not far from home.

I'm hoping some of these stories will stay with you, long after you've read the last word, just as they do with me. Maybe these will become stories that you didn't know you wanted to read, but are glad you did.

PART I

CLIMBING
AND
FALLING

1

SNOW FALL

Stevens Pass, Washington

THE DAY A MOUNTAIN MOVED

The snow burst through the trees with no warning but a last-second whoosh of sound, a two-story wall of white and Chris Rudolph's piercing cry: "Avalanche! Elyse!"

The very thing the sixteen skiers and snowboarders had sought— fresh, soft snow—instantly became the enemy. Somewhere above, a pristine meadow cracked in the shape of a lightning bolt, slicing a slab nearly two hundred feet across and three feet deep. Gravity did the rest.

Snow shattered and spilled down the slope. Within seconds, the avalanche was the size of more than a thousand cars barreling down the mountain and weighed millions of pounds. Moving about 70 miles per hour, it crashed through the sturdy old-growth trees, snapping their limbs and shredding bark from their trunks.

The avalanche, in Washington's Cascades in February, slid past some trees and rocks, like ocean swells around a ship's prow. Others it captured and added to its violent load.

Somewhere inside, it also carried people. How many, no one knew.

The slope of the terrain, shaped like a funnel, squeezed the growing swell of churning snow into a steep, twisting gorge. It moved in surges, like a roller coaster on a series of drops and high-banked turns. It accelerated as the slope steepened and the weight of the slide pushed from behind. It slithered through shallower pitches. The energy raised the temperature of the snow a couple of degrees, and the friction carved striations high in the icy sides of the canyon walls.

Elyse Saugstad, a professional skier, wore a backpack equipped with an air bag, a relatively new and expensive part of the arsenal that back-country users increasingly carry to ease their minds and increase sur-vival odds in case of an avalanche. About to be overtaken, she pulled a cord near her chest. She was knocked down before she knew if the canister of compressed air inflated winged pillows behind her head.

She had no control of her body as she tumbled downhill. She did not know up from down. It was not unlike being cartwheeled in a relentlessly crashing wave. But snow does not recede. It swallows its victims. It does not spit them out.

Snow filled her mouth. She caromed off things she never saw, tum-bling through a cluttered canyon like a steel marble falling through pins in a pachinko machine.

At first she thought she would be embarrassed that she had deployed her air bag, that the other expert skiers she was with, more than a dozen of them, would have a good laugh at her panicked over-reaction. Seconds later, tumbling uncontrollably inside a ribbon of speeding snow, she was sure this was how she was going to die.

Moving, roiling snow turns into something closer to liquid, thick like lava. But when it stops, it instantly freezes solid. The laws of physics and chemistry transform a meadow of fine powder into a wreckage of icy chunks. Saugstad's pinwheeling body would freeze into whatever position it was in the moment the snow stopped.

After about a minute, the creek bed vomited the debris into a gen-tly sloped meadow. Saugstad felt the snow slow and tried to keep her hands in front of her. She knew from avalanche safety courses that outstretched hands might puncture the ice surface and alert rescuers. She knew that if victims ended up buried under the snow, cupped hands in front of the face could provide a small pocket of air for the mouth and nose. Without it, the first breaths could create a suffocating ice mask.

The avalanche spread and stopped, locking everything it carried into an icy cocoon. It was now a jagged, virtually impenetrable pile of ice, longer than a football field and nearly as wide. As if newly plowed, it rose in rugged contrast to the surrounding fields of undisturbed snow, twenty feet tall in spots.

Saugstad was mummified. She was on her back, her head pointed downhill. Her goggles were off. Her nose ring had been ripped away. She felt the crushing weight of snow on her chest. She could not move her legs. One boot still had a ski attached to it. She could not lift her head because it was locked into the ice.

But she could see the sky. Her face was covered only with loose snow. Her hands, too, stuck out of the snow, one still covered by a pink mitten.

Using her hands like windshield wipers, she tried to flick snow away from her mouth. When she clawed at her chest and neck, the crumbs maddeningly slid back onto her face. She grew claustrophobic.

Breathe easy, she told herself. Do not panic. Help will come. She stared at the low, gray clouds. She had not noticed the noise as she hurtled down the mountain. Now, she was suddenly struck by the silence.

TUNNEL CREEK

The Cascades are among the craggiest of American mountain ranges, roughly cut, as if carved with a chain saw. In summer, the gray peaks are sprinkled with glaciers. In winter, they are smothered in some of North America's deepest snowpack.

The top of Cowboy Mountain, about seventy-five miles east of Seattle, rises to 5,853 feet—about half the height of the tallest Cascades, but higher than its nearest neighbors, enough to provide 360-degree views. It feels more like a long fin than a summit, a few feet wide in parts. Locals call it Cowboy Ridge.

To one side, down steep chutes, is Stevens Pass ski area, which receives about 400,000 visitors each winter. To the other, outside the ski area's boundary to what is considered the back of Cowboy Mountain, is an unmonitored play area of reliably deep snow, a "powder stash," known as Tunnel Creek.

It is a term with broad meaning. The name is derived from the Cascade Tunnel, originally a 2.6-mile railroad tube completed in 1900 that connected the east and west sides of the Cascades, a boon for the growth of Seattle and Puget Sound. The mountain pass that it burrowed beneath was named for the project's engineer, John Frank Stevens, who later helped build the Panama Canal.

In late February 1910, ceaseless snowstorms over several days marooned two passenger trains just outside the tunnel's west portal. Before the tracks could be cleared, the trains were buried by what still stands as the nation's deadliest avalanche. It killed 96 people.

Bodies were extricated and wrapped in blankets from the Great Northern Railway, then hauled away on sleds. Some were not found until the snow melted many months later.

To skiers and snowboarders today, Tunnel Creek is a serendipitous junction of place and powder. It features nearly 3,000 vertical feet—a rarely matched descent—of open meadows framed by thick stands of trees. Steep gullies drain each spring's runoff to the valley floor and into a small, short gorge called Tunnel Creek.

The area has all of the alluring qualities of the backcountry—fresh snow, expert terrain and relative solitude—but few of the customary inconveniences. Reaching Tunnel Creek from Stevens Pass ski area requires a ride of just over five minutes up SkyLine Express, a high-speed four-person chairlift, followed by a shorter ride up Seventh Heaven, a steep two-person lift. Slip through the open boundary gate, with its "continue at your own risk" warning signs, and hike ten minutes to the top of Cowboy Mountain.

When snow conditions are right, the preferred method of descent used by those experienced in Tunnel Creek, based on the shared wisdom passed over generations, is to hopscotch down the mountain through a series of long meadows. Weave down the first meadow, maybe punctuate the run with a jump off a rock outcropping near the bottom, then veer hard left, up and out of the narrowing gully and into the next open glade.

Another powder-filled drop ends with another hard left, into another meadow that leads to the valley floor.

Tunnel Creek is, in the vernacular of locals, a "hippie pow run"— breezy and unobstructed, the kind that makes skiers giggle in glee as they descend through a billowing cloud of their own soft powder and emerge at the bottom coated in white frosting.

Despite trends toward extreme skiing (now called freeskiing), with improbable descents over cliffs and down chutes that test the guile of even the fiercest daredevils, the ageless lure of fresh, smooth powder endures.

But powder and people are key ingredients for avalanches. And the worry among avalanche forecasters, snow-science experts and search-and-rescue leaders is that the number of fatalities—roughly 200 around the world each year—will keep rising as the rush to the backcountry continues among skiers, snowboarders, climbers and snowmobilers.

The backcountry represents the fastest-growing segment of the ski industry. More than ever, people are looking for fresh descents accessible by helicopters, hiking or even the simple ride up a chairlift.

Before 1980, it was unusual to have more than ten avalanche deaths in the United States each winter. There were thirty-four last season, including twenty skiers and snowboarders. Eight victims were skiing out of bounds, legally, with a lift ticket. And many of the dead were backcountry experts intimate with the terrain that killed them.

"It's a cultural shift, where more skiers are going farther, faster, bigger," said John Stifter, the editor of *Powder* magazine, who was a part of the group at Tunnel Creek in February. "Which is tending to push your pro skiers or other experienced, elite-level backcountry skiers that much farther, faster and bigger, to the point where there's no margin for error."

No one knows how many avalanches occur. Most naturally triggered slides are never seen. Those set off by humans are rarely reported unless they cause fatalities or property damage.

But avalanches occur in Tunnel Creek regularly. Its slopes, mostly from 40 to 45 degrees, are optimal for avalanches—flat enough to hold deep reservoirs of snow, yet steep enough for the snow to slide long distances when prompted. The long elevation drop means snow can be fluffy at the top and slushy at the bottom. Temperatures, wind and precipitation change quickly, and something as welcome as a burst of sunshine can alter the crystallized bonds deep inside the snow. And because Tunnel Creek is outside the ski area, it is not patrolled or specifically assessed for danger.

In March 2011, a University of Washington student was caught in an avalanche in Tunnel Creek. Having been carried into a stand of trees, he was unburied by friends within minutes and found dead. Three others were partially buried about an hour later when the ski patrol's arrival set off a second avalanche.

Many of the most experienced locals view Tunnel Creek with a mix of awe and fear.

"I've always been a naysayer of Tunnel Creek," the snowboarder Tim Wesley said. "I've seen a big avalanche back there before. It has about 2,600 vertical feet. Not typical. The snow changes a lot in that distance.

That's the reason I always have a second thought about Tunnel Creek. In Washington, there's a saying: If you don't like the weather, wait five minutes. And it's true. You'll be on the chair and it'll be freezing, and then all of a sudden there's a warm breeze that smells like the ocean."

Even those who are not leery of Tunnel Creek on the best days heed the pass-it-on warning of the experienced: stay left.

To head straight down to the bottom is to enter what experts call a terrain trap: a funnel of trouble and clumsy skiing, clogged with trees and rocks and confined by high walls. Few go that way intentionally.

Chris Rudolph, the effervescent thirty-year-old marketing manager for Stevens Pass, knew the preferred route down. Tunnel Creek was his favorite at-work diversion. Earlier that weekend, he mentioned plans for a field trip to Tunnel Creek to a select group of high-powered guests and close friends.

The operations manager for Stevens Pass agreed to pick up the group in one of the ski area's trucks at the end of its descent. From the bottom of Tunnel Creek, it is about a half-mile trek through deep snow to U.S. 2, then a four-mile ride back to Stevens Pass.

At 11:32 a.m. on Sunday, February 19, heading up the mountain, Rudolph sent a text message to the operations manager.

"A big posse," Rudolph wrote.

A PLAN IN MOTION

Like many ideas that sound good at the time, skiing Tunnel Creek was an idea hatched in a bar.

It was Saturday, February 18, the afternoon light fading to dusk. Outside the Foggy Goggle, a bar at the base of the ski area, the snow continued to fall, roughly an inch an hour. By morning, there would be 32 inches of fresh snow at Stevens Pass, 21 of them in a 24-hour period of Saturday and Saturday night.

That was cause for celebration. It had been more than two weeks since the last decent snowfall. Finally, the tired layer of hard, crusty snow was gone, buried deep under powder.

Rudolph promoted Stevens Pass with restless zeal. In seven years there, he helped turn a relatively small, roadside ski area into a hip destination.

He unabashedly courted ski journalists and filmmakers to take a look. They, in turn, gave Stevens Pass star turns in magazines and popular ski movies, raising the area's cool quotient.

Rudolph was the oldest of three children raised in California's Bay Area by outdoors-minded parents. The young family pulled a pop-up Coleman camper around the West and skied the areas around Lake Tahoe. The grown siblings continued to vacation with their parents, climbing peaks like Mount Whitney in California and Mount Rainier in Washington.

Rudolph peppered his language with words like "rad" and "stoked." But he was no simple-minded ski bum. He was an Eagle Scout with a marketing degree. When he applied at Stevens Pass years earlier, he sent a video of himself speaking, skiing and mountain biking. He included a bag of popcorn for the viewer. He got the job.

Children knew Rudolph because he kept his pockets full of Stevens Pass stickers. He starred in self-deprecating webcasts promoting Stevens Pass. He wrote poetry on his blog and strummed a guitar. He drank Pabst Blue Ribbon, the unofficial beer of irony and the hipster generation.

Tunnel Creek was where he took special guests. And it is where he wanted to take the tangled assortment of high-caliber skiers and industry insiders who, as if carried by the latest storm, had blown into Stevens Pass that weekend.

Many of them happened into the Foggy Goggle on Saturday night. Among them were professional skiers like Saugstad, thirty-three, a former champion of the Freeride World Tour. There were reporters and editors from *Powder* magazine and ESPN. There were executives from ski equipment and apparel companies. There were Stevens Pass regulars, some with broad reputations in the niche world of skiing, glad to spend time with the assortment of guests.

"It was a very, very deep, heavy, powerful, strong group of pro skiers and ski industry people," said Keith Carlsen, a photographer and former editor of *Powder*.

Rudolph was the connecting thread. Some visitors, like Saugstad, were at Stevens Pass for a promotional event aimed at expert female skiers sponsored by Salomon, the ski equipment maker. Rudolph skied with the group all day Saturday. He organized and hosted a catered dinner for the women later that night in Leavenworth, a serious outdoors town dressed as a Bavarian village, thirty-five miles downhill to the east.

Powder had come to spotlight Stevens Pass for a feature article on night skiing. When the magazine's editor, John Stifter, arrived by train at Leavenworth two days earlier, he found Rudolph's car waiting for him. Inside were keys to the car, keys to a slope-side cabin and two Pabst Blue Ribbons in the cup holders.

At the bar, Rudolph mentioned an idea to a few people: Tunnel Creek on Sunday. Invitations traveled in whispers and text messages, through a knot of friendships and slight acquaintances.

Meet at the fire pit, on the stone deck at Granite Peaks Lodge, at eleven. Rudolph thought his Sunday morning staff meeting would end by then.

As darkness enveloped Stevens Pass on Saturday night, stadium-style lights flooded the slopes in white light, and snowflakes fell in cotton-ball clumps.

Rudolph and those with the Salomon event left for dinner in Leavenworth. Stifter, twenty-nine, and Carlsen, thirty-eight, headed outside to work on their article for *Powder*.

"I skied just off the trail, not out of bounds, but in the ski resort, to shoot some of these night shots I took," Carlsen said. "And in tree wells I was, like, neck deep—easily nipple deep, wading around in snow, trying to get my angle. There was so much new snow."

With the daytime crowds gone, the nighttime atmosphere was festive and the faces were familiar. Families played in the deepening snow. More serious skiers and snowboarders sought the freshest powder.

There are no public accommodations at Stevens Pass, only a parking lot available to a few dozen campers and recreational vehicles. As the evening wound down, several of those with loose plans to ski Tunnel Creek the next morning huddled in the RV lot around a fire. Carlsen continued taking photographs. Stifter and others ducked inside one camper to watch homemade videos of others skiing Tunnel Creek over the past couple of decades.

"So it's something they skied often," Stifter said. "Not something like, 'We're going to go ski Tunnel!' Not like a once-a-year deal."

The flames in the fire died to orange embers. The last beers were sipped empty, and people slipped into the night. The campers were blanketed with snow.

Beyond the lights glowing from the ski area, snow still fell over the ridge, too, in the vast darkness of steep meadows and narrow gullies just past the western edge of Stevens Pass.

Each snowflake added to the depth, and each snowflake added to the weight. It might take a million snowflakes for a skier to notice the difference. It might take just one for a mountain to move.

TO THE PEAK

Dawn cracked with the intermittent sound of explosives near the top of Cowboy Mountain. Stevens Pass ski patrollers, called to duty whenever more than a few inches of snow fell, had arrived to check and control the ski area's 200 inbounds avalanche zones.

After getting the latest assessment from the area's full-time avalanche forecaster, more than a dozen patrollers filled their backpacks with 2.2-pound emulsion charges, shaped like cartoon dynamite. Chairlifts rumbled to life, ferrying the crews up the dark mountain.

Three two-person teams assigned to Cowboy Ridge removed their skis and filed through the boundary gate. They took turns plowing a path through the fresh snow with their bodies. Their boots forged an icy stairway to the top of the skinny ridge.

Back on their skis, facing down into the ski area and with their backs to Tunnel Creek, they spread across the ridge to stamp and destroy wind-swept cornices, small balconies of crusty snow.

They removed the charges from their packs. Like party poppers that spew confetti, charges have a pull-wire, an ignition that lights a 90-second fuse. The patrollers lobbed the lighted charges into the many steep chutes below them. With muffled booms, heavy waves of snow tumbled harmlessly into the recesses of the empty slopes below, clearing danger for the day's thousands of inbounds customers.

The lines for the ski lifts began forming about 7 a.m., two hours before they were to open. When the gathering skiers and snowboarders heard the explosions echo down the mountain, they cheered. It signaled a powder day.

In Leavenworth, Chris Rudolph awoke in his two-bedroom house on Ash Street, the one that he and his girlfriend, Anne Hessburg, painted a rich blue and accented with a garden out front.

"Chris was so mad that he had a meeting," Hessburg said. "It was a pow day, and you couldn't tie him to his desk on pow days."

But he thought the meeting would end by eleven.

"He said, 'It's going to be so good, babe. I'm going to take some folks up to Tunnel Creek,'" Hessburg said. "Tunnel Creek, it was kind of like the holy grail for Chris. It was where he wanted to show off for friends."

Among those who joined the 45-minute parade from Leavenworth, through tight Tumwater Canyon, past the Lake Wenatchee turnoff and up to Stevens Pass, were Dan Abrams and Megan Michelson. They planned to marry in March.

Michelson, thirty, was the freeskiing editor for ESPN.com. Abrams, thirty-four, was a founder and the president of Flylow, maker of apparel marketed to backcountry users.

The couple lived in Seattle, but had come to Stevens Pass on Saturday for the Salomon promotional event. Michelson and the other women stayed at a Leavenworth hotel. Abrams slept in a spare bedroom at Rudolph's house. He and Michelson drove to Stevens Pass together.

"I said to Dan, 'Do you think Tunnel will be safe today?'" Michelson said. "He said something along the lines of, 'Yeah, those guys know the best route down.'"

There were similar conversations elsewhere. In the slope-side cabin at Stevens Pass that Rudolph arranged—he had cleaned it on Friday as he spoke to his mother on the phone—the journalists from *Powder* magazine, Stifter and Carlsen, contemplated the day's plans.

"We started asking questions," Carlsen said. "'Where are we going? Out of bounds? Didn't it just snow nonstop for two days? How much snow?' That's when John pulled up the avalanche report, and he read it aloud."

Mark Moore, director and lead meteorologist of the Northwest Weather and Avalanche Center, had set that day's forecast on Saturday afternoon. A sixty-four-year-old with graying hair pulled into a short ponytail, Moore had a feeling it could be a busy weekend.

The avalanche center, based in Seattle, is one of about twenty regional avalanche forecasting centers in the United States, most run by the Forest Service. During the winter, one of its three employees arrives in the middle of the night, analyzes weather maps and computer models, and examines data—snowfall, temperatures, wind, humidity and so on—from forty-seven remote weather stations scattered across the mountains, including five in the vicinity of Stevens Pass. They take calls from ski patrollers and highway crews.

The biggest storm of the season increased avalanche concerns. But it was not just the new snow that concerned Moore. It was what lay nearly three feet beneath—a thin layer of perfectly preserved frost called surface hoar. The frozen equivalent of dew, created on crisp, clear nights, it features fragile, featherlike crystals that grow skyward.

On the surface, they glimmer like a million tiny diamonds. When frosted and protected by soft blankets of fluffy snow, they are weak stilts supporting all that falls on top. When they finally give way, falling like microscopic dominoes on a steep slope, they provide an icy flume for the snow above.

A shot of rain or above-freezing temperatures, both common in Cascade winters, usually destroy the fragile crystals, melding them into the snowpack. But five days of dry, cold weather, from February 3 to 7, created a perfect, sparkly layer of surface hoar. Sporadic light snow, never more than an inch or two a day, delicately shrouded it over the next ten days.

By the weekend, as snow fell heavily over the Cascades and powder-hungry hordes took to the slopes, the old layer was long out of sight, and mostly out of mind.

Not to Moore.

"Snowpack is never static," he said. "It's changing, even once it's buried."

Changes in temperatures, precipitation, humidity and wind can turn a benign snowpack into a deadly one, and vice versa. Sometimes weather is enough to start an avalanche. But "natural" avalanches rarely kill. The majority of avalanche fatalities are in human-triggered slides—usually of the victims' own making.

"Every skier, everyone who hits the slope, changes the structure of the snowpack," Moore said. "Even though they don't know it."

In the rugged area of the Cascades that includes Stevens Pass, Moore deemed the avalanche danger "high"—the fourth degree out of five—for slopes above 5,000 feet in elevation facing north to southeast.

For everything else, the danger level was deemed "considerable," defined as "dangerous avalanche conditions" with "human-triggered avalanches likely."

The top of Cowboy Mountain is nearly 6,000 feet. The Tunnel Creek terrain descends off its southwest side to roughly 3,000 feet. Officially, the danger was "considerable."

"In avalanche forecasting terms, 'considerable' is a really weird forecast," Saugstad said. "Because it's this gray area. It's a hard one to predict. It can mean, well, you're not going to see any activity. Or, if something goes, you're going to be screwed. It's hard to work with that one."

Moore's forecast offered more specifics.

"Although decreasing light showers and decreasing winds are expected Sunday, cold temperatures should slow stabilization of existing wind slabs and help maintain the threat of further human-triggered avalanche activity, especially on previously wind-loaded terrain showing no evidence of recent avalanche activity," Moore wrote.

Spotty afternoon sunshine, he added, could raise the danger, especially on south-facing slopes.

The snow had stopped at Stevens Pass by the time the lifts opened Sunday morning. The runs were quickly doodled with curvy lines.

Stifter sat in the cabin and examined the forecast on his laptop.

"I have this image burned in my head," Stifter said. "I had a coffee cup in my right hand, I was reading e-mails, and I read the Northwest Avalanche Center report. And it said 'considerable to high' was the avalanche danger. And I read it out loud to Keith. And he listened, and I read it again—I read it twice—and looked at it. Huh. I've skied enough to know that when it snows a lot, which it did, up to two feet, there's always going to be instability, with that much weight on an older snowpack."

Stifter left Carlsen behind and headed to the lifts. He found Jim Jack. If anyone could judge terrain and snow in the backcountry, it was Jim Jack.

The license plate on Jack's Subaru Brat as a teenager read "IM JIM." To family and his closest friends, he was Jimmy, sometimes J.J. To most everyone else, he was Jim Jack, blended into one name, accent on the first syllable: JIM-jack.

Jack was the head judge and former president of the International Freeskiers Association, which oversaw a world tour of competitions. At forty-six, he was a sort of Peter Pan of the ski world, a charismatic, carefree boy who never grew up, beloved by like-minded skiers and snowboarders half his age.

He spent winters traveling the world, spreading the gospel of freeskiing, professing the beauty of finding improbable ways down precarious slopes with grace, nerve and flair. He had been a competitor on the tour, distinguishable from a great distance by the silkiness of his loose form, until he landed hard and took his own knee to his face, shattering the bones around his right eye. You could feel the screws when you touched his face.

He was a party accelerator with a penchant for streaking. He did drama in high school and never declined the stage as an adult. On Halloween, his costumes played off his name: Jack on the Rocks, Jim Jack in the Box, Cracker Jack, Jack Frost.

Wearing lederhosen, Jack starred in a cheeky promotional video

for Leavenworth. He was a sure-handed shortstop for the team from
Uncle Uli's, a bar and restaurant in the heart of town. A grilled chicken
sandwich on the menu, smothered in spicy sauce, is named the Napkin'
Slappin' Jim Jack.

Jack shared a bungalow off the highway, near the Howard Johnson, with his longtime girlfriend, Tiffany Abraham. They danced late
at night in the kitchen and built bonfires in the backyard. The covered
front porch held a pile of ski gear and a futon couch, perfect for watching the world go by, beer in hand.

Jack drove a 1994 Chevy pickup with 216,000 miles on it, topped
by a Wilderness camper that he added for $350. Widely recognized on
the highways and in ski area parking lots around the West, it was held
together largely by duct tape and bungee cords. The radio's volume
was stuck on high. If it's too loud, Jack told passengers, just roll down
the window.

Jack and his camper rolled into the RV parking lot at Stevens Pass
on Friday night. On weekends, when the snow was good, the lot filled
with dozens of pickup campers and motor homes.

"I woke up on Saturday in my RV," said Tim Wangen, a fifty-three-
year-old former commercial diver who lived in a cabin at nearby Lake
Wenatchee. "When I wake up, I look outside to see who is next to me. I
saw that Jim Jack was next to me. I thought, cool, I got a great neighbor
this week."

Jack and Wangen had skied a couple of runs Sunday morning by
the time Stifter caught up to them. Wangen knew Tunnel Creek as well
as anyone, having skied it since he was a boy. Jack traveled the world,
scouting courses for extreme skiing. He knew how to avoid danger.

Stifter asked Jack about the avalanche report.

"He's like, 'Yeah, not to worry,'" Stifter said. "'We'll just do it slowly
and safely and just stay in the trees.'"

"GEAR UP?"

The fire pit sits at the center of the bustle on busy days. At the corner of the patio, in front of the lodge, it is a crossroads for people coming and going. Some pull up chairs and relax, facing the bowl of ski runs strung before them. When the clouds lift, Cowboy Mountain dominates the view high to the right. It can feel close enough to reach and touch.

By midmorning, the fire pit began attracting a growing but confused band of expert skiers. Some were local, some were visitors. Some knew others, some did not, but most knew either Chris Rudolph or Jim Jack. They traded nods and handshakes, unsure if others were headed to Tunnel Creek, too.

"We didn't know why everyone was there," said Dan Abrams, there with Megan Michelson. "We wondered if everyone was meeting up for the same reason. But it's like when you find out where the extra keg is at the party. You don't go tell everybody."

Joel Hammond, the thirty-seven-year-old regional sales representative for Salomon, had teamed with Rudolph to organize the previous day's women's event. He did not intend to ski Sunday until he awoke in Leavenworth and could not resist the lure of the fresh snow. He drove to Stevens Pass and sent a text message to Rudolph, still in a staff meeting.

"Chris was like, 'Meet at the fire pit, where everybody meets. Then we're going to rally up,'" Hammond said.

Hammond told Jack that he had the latest model of skis in his truck, then left to retrieve a pair for him to try. Stifter bought coffee, a couple of Americanos, from the stand for himself and Jack.

Tim Carlson and Ron Pankey, both thirty-seven and childhood friends from Vermont, had spent the morning on the inbounds side of Cowboy Mountain, navigating near-vertical chutes and rock outcroppings. During a break, they spotted familiar faces near the fire pit.

Pankey was a former competitor on the Freeskiing World Tour, so he had known Jack since the mid-1990s. Like Jack, he eventually worked competitions around the world, including the X Games.

Carlson was a snowboarder, not a skier, and a regular at Stevens Pass. Earlier that week, he competed at Washington's Crystal Mountain. Jack worked the event, and Carlson slept several nights in Jack's camper.

When Carlson and Pankey arrived at Stevens Pass that Sunday, they joined Tim Wesley, known to most as Tall Tim—a lanky thirty-nine-year-old snowboarder from Leavenworth. The three merged with those waiting for Rudolph.

Another arrival was Wenzel Peikert, twenty-nine, an off-duty Stevens Pass ski instructor from Seattle. Skiing over the weekend without his wife and infant daughter, he hung around the Foggy Goggle and the RV lot on Saturday night. He, too, sent a message to Rudolph on Sunday, confirming the plan.

"I wrote, 'Gear up?'" Peikert said. "And he wrote, 'Yeah, for sure.' So I went into the ski school and grabbed my pack, with my beacon, probe and shovel. I went to the fire pit and I met the whole group. You could tell they were a different level of skier by how they acted and how they dressed."

Among the strangers he saw was Rob Castillo, a forty-year-old father of two and former competitive skier. He had exchanged text messages with Jack.

Castillo and Jack lived together in Alta, Utah, for several years in the 1990s. They went helicopter skiing in Alaska and skied down mountains they had climbed in Washington.

"Tunnel Creek at 11," Jack wrote.

"Perfect," Castillo thought. "That's just what I wanted to do."

At the fire pit, Castillo considered the others.

"It was kind of like, all right, this group is getting bigger," Castillo said. "I wouldn't pop in with a bunch of no-names, necessarily, and trust any of them, but the ones I knew were definitely qualified to go. And they're not going to bring people out who aren't."

More than anything, Castillo wanted to ski for the first time all season with his two best friends at Stevens Pass—Jack and Johnny Brenan.

In the RV parking lot, a few hundred yards away, Johnny and Laurie Brenan convened in their motor home for an early lunch with their daughters, Josie, ten, and Nina, seven, members of the Stevens Pass ski teams.

Brenan, forty-one, grew up comfortably in the Seattle suburbs, not far from Jack. He followed his passion for skiing to Breckenridge, Colorado, working as a ski patroller in the winter and a carpenter in the summer. A burly man whose five o'clock shadow arrived by noon each day, he eventually opened a business that he named for home: Cascade Contracting.

"I met Johnny at the Gold Pan in Breckenridge," Laurie Brenan said. "It was Thursday night, 25-cent beer night. He was sitting on the pool table, and he had an open spot next to him. And I said, 'I'm going to go sit next to that cute guy.'"

They married in 1997 and moved to Leavenworth. Brenan worked as a cabinetmaker, then resurrected Cascade Contracting. On the strength of Brenan's amicable personality and no-fear creativity, it blossomed with custom homes and expansive remodels.

The Brenans bought a deteriorated hundred-year-old farmhouse on a hill in an apple orchard. Johnny Brenan lifted the structure on jacks, rebuilt the foundation and gutted the inside, intending to resell it as a bed-and-breakfast. The Brenans kept it for themselves to raise their family.

Brenan zipped from one construction site to another in his truck. He coached soccer teams. He held Monday night poker games in the garage, which Nina always helped prepare. He built a chicken coop in the yard.

"Johnny and Josie bought five chickens, and they called the business Eggs, Ink," Laurie Brenan said. "They had signs and business cards. Then they bought thirty more chickens. It's like, she's five years old. But the more the merrier for Johnny, even with chickens."

Sunday began perfectly for Brenan. The family RV was parked in space number 3, where the satellite dish picked up the best television reception. Brenan was at the front of the lift line at dawn.

He offered to fetch coffee for those behind him, a trick he used to keep his place while he helped Laurie get their daughters fed and dressed. He returned to the line, excited for an increasingly rare chance to ski with old friends like Jack.

"I dropped the kids off for ski team about 8:45," Laurie Brenan said. "I remember looking down and Johnny was yelling at Jim Jack, doing something with his hands, something crazy. They were like little boys in a candy store. They were so excited."

Back with his family for lunch, Brenan ate an egg sandwich and discussed a business deal on the phone. It was after eleven, and he was afraid he would miss the Tunnel Creek run.

But Rudolph sent a couple of people text messages at about 11:15. He apologized for running late, and said he would be out in about ten minutes.

Brenan had time. He made a pact with Josie.

"Josie, be ready at two," Brenan said. "I'm going to come back and we'll go on a powder mission. Be here, because I'll be here."

Brenan strapped on his avalanche beacon, also called a transceiver, a device that emits a silent signal for others to detect your location in case of burial. A friend in the RV noted that its batteries were dead. Brenan replaced them with fresh ones.

"What's that, Papa?" Nina asked her father.

Brenan paused to show her how it worked.

"He explained it," Laurie Brenan said. "It was understood that avalanche beacons were really for body recovery. Not many people survive avalanches. He would say that."

Brenan gathered his things and headed toward the fire pit to join his friends.

"I said, 'Are you sure it's safe?'" Laurie Brenan said. "He looked me right in the eye and said, 'Of course. I wouldn't be going if it weren't.' I said OK because I knew that was true."

At about 11:30, Rudolph burst through the doors of the lodge at Stevens Pass. He was surprised by the size of the group waiting for him, but he barely broke stride.

"Get me out of here before another spreadsheet finds me," he said.

The group, jolted into action, scattered to gather gear.

"We all rallied up, jumped on the lifts," Castillo said. "I remember seeing some other buddies of mine later, like, 'Oh, I wanted to go out so bad with you guys that day. It looked like such a fun crew.'"

THE BACKCOUNTRY BECKONS

Stevens Pass opened in the winter of 1937–38 with a rope tow on Big Chief Mountain. A lodge and five new tows were added in the 1940s, including a mile-long T-bar that pulled people up the side of Cowboy Mountain. The ski area took shape in the bowl below the crescent-shape ridge that connects the two mountains.

Seventh Heaven, a two-person lift up a steep wall of Cowboy Mountain, changed the complexion of Stevens Pass when it was built in 1960. It opened a high swath of expert terrain, now marked as double diamond—experts only—on posted signs and the ski map.

It also provided easy access to the top of the high ridgeline. Back then, few people dared to remove their skis and hike the few hundred extra feet to the summit. "When I was younger at Stevens, no one skied off Cowboy—maybe just a few locals," said Wangen, who has skied the area for nearly five decades. "But the last twenty years, it's gone ballistic."

Now there is a steady procession of expert skiers and snowboarders through the boundary gate next to the top of the lift. Most drop off the left side of the ridge, back into the resort, through the rocky and narrow chutes.

Those who drop away from the ski area, toward Tunnel Creek, are simply following a much wider trend into "sidecountry"—backcountry slopes easily entered by lifts and, sometimes, a short hike.

"I don't like the term 'sidecountry,'" Moore, the avalanche forecaster, said. "It makes it sound like 'backcountry light.'"

The rise of backcountry skiing can be credited to a collision of factors.

Ski areas that once vigilantly policed their boundaries, from Jackson Hole, Wyoming, to Squaw Valley, California, have gradually opened their gates to the territory surrounding them. While that has led to wrangling over liability issues and raised debate over search-and-rescue responsibilities, most areas note that they are carved out of public land. They really cannot keep people from going there.

But ski areas also see the potential to attract more ticket-buying customers, and more influential ones, by blurring the boundary lines. Many areas slyly promote not just the terrain inside their borders, but the wilder topography beyond, using the power of media and word of mouth—as Rudolph did for Stevens Pass.

Skiing adjacent to ski areas, however, can numb people to risk. Easy access, familiar terrain and a belief that help is just a short distance away may lead people to descend slopes they might avoid in deeper wilderness.

While most backcountry users would not consider entering known avalanche territory without a beacon, one study last winter at Loveland Ski Area in Colorado found that fewer than 40 percent of people who passed through a boundary gate wore one.

Equipment advances have emboldened people. Intermediate powder skiers have been turned into expert ones thanks to fatter skis and the "rocker" shape of their tips—design advances borrowed from snowboarding. Popular ski bindings now temporarily detach at the heel, allowing skiers to glide up rises like a cross-country skier, then reconnect so they can descend like a professional downhiller.

Snowboards have borrowed from skis, too. Some models can be quickly split into two pieces, allowing users to stride up short hills in pursuit of bigger descents.

Similar advances in safety gear, like easy-to-use digital beacons and air bags, have helped make the backcountry feel less dangerous. Beacons help rescuers find people buried under the snow, while air bags deploy a large balloon meant to help keep the skier closer to the surface of an avalanche. A leading American manufacturer of safety gear is named, appropriately, Backcountry Access.

Companies, including Salomon and Flylow, have marketed heavily to ride the backcountry trend. They are keenly aware that many buyers will never ski the backcountry but want to dress the part.

Those marketing shifts have coincided with a generation raised on the glorification of risk. From X Games to YouTube videos, helmet cameras to social media, the culture rewards vicarious thrills and video one-upmanship. This generation no longer automatically adheres to the axiom of waiting a day for safer conditions. The relative placidness of inbounds skiing is no match for the greater adventure of untamed terrain.

Among avalanche forecasters and the growing cottage industry of safety instructors, there is pride in noting that the number of fatalities has risen at a slower rate than the number of backcountry users. But they see themselves as part of a difficult race between the coming hordes and the tools to protect them.

"You could argue that skiers have never been this educated or safe,"

Stifter, the *Powder* magazine editor, said. "There's been a huge emergence and emphasis on avalanche classes. Then you also have this life-saving technology. But if you go to Jackson or Utah, you'll see people who are not educated, who are just going out there because they see it in the movies and they see it in magazines like *Powder*: there's fresh tracks and, man, it looks like fun."

At the top of Seventh Heaven, the members of the group took off their skis and snowboards. Directly to the right of the lift's unloading ramp was a narrow trail that disappeared up through a clog of trees.

"Read this," one sign read in all capital letters. "Ski Area Boundary. Minimum of $1000.00 rescue fee! Do you have a partner, beacon, probe and shovel? Explosives may be used in this area at any time. Continue at your own risk."

A smaller sign read, "Stop. Ski Area Boundary. No ski patrol or snow control beyond this point."

To the right was a small gray steel box. It was labeled, "Avalanche Transceiver Check Station."

"You walk by and it goes beep, beep," Rob Castillo said. "So as we were going through, you heard it going all the way, right on everyone. Beep. Beep. Beep."

While there are no laws dictating what equipment people carry into the backcountry, there is a code. Carry a beacon (for sending and receiving signals), a probe (for poking for victims in the snow) and a shovel (for digging them out).

"When you go in the backcountry, you're trusting your life in the hands of everybody else and they're trusting their life in you," Michelson said. "If I get buried and my ski partner doesn't have a beacon, shovel or probe, it's my life on the line."

One member of the party did not elicit a beep: Erin Dessert, a thirty-five-year-old snowboarder who was early for her afternoon shift as a Stevens Pass lift operator. Wesley had invited her along. She thought everyone was riding off the front side of Cowboy Mountain, back into the ski area.

The group marched single file along the narrow ridge for a few minutes until it reached a wider area to convene. Tracks dropped back over a steep edge and into the ski area to the left.

To the right was nothing but deep powder, hidden by thick trees, like a curtain to the big attraction.

THE DESCENT BEGINS

There were sixteen people, although no one thought to count at the time. Their ages ranged from twenty-nine to fifty-three.

"This was a crew that seemed like it was assembled by some higher force," Dessert said.

It was about 11:45. The storm had passed. A low, pewter sky hid the surrounding peaks. Castillo glanced around at the others, wearing helmets and rainbow hues, a kaleidoscope of color amid the gray surroundings, like sprinkles on vanilla ice cream.

"I was thinking, wow, what a bunch of heavies," he said.

There was loose banter and a few casual introductions. Not everyone met everyone else. Someone pulled out marijuana to smoke, and passed it.

Wesley, the snowboarder known as Tall Tim, saw the size of the assembled group. More than a dozen, he thought.

"That never happens," he said. "And it's basically the legends of Stevens Pass standing up there."

There was little doubt that those with Tunnel Creek experience knew the way. About half the group had been down dozens of times each, if not hundreds. The others would follow.

There was no broad discussion of the route down. Pockets of the group talked about staying left, not being too greedy by going too far down the meadow before cutting across.

"That run, it's not that it's supersteep, or there are cliffs, or that it's a really rowdy run," Carlson, one of the Stevens Pass regulars, said. "It's that if anything goes wrong, it's a terrain trap. If somebody happens to set off even a slough slide and you're below them in Tunnel, it all bottlenecks and really adds up superfast. That's the reason that run is heavy. It's notorious."

Unspoken anxiety spread among those unfamiliar with the descent. The mere size of the group spooked some. Backcountry users of all types—skiers, snowboarders, snowmobilers and climbers—worry about how much of a load a slope can absorb before it gives way. They worry about people above them causing an avalanche. When it comes to the backcountry, there is usually not safety in large numbers.

That is not only because of the physical impact on the snow. It is because of the complicated dynamics that large groups create. Deadly avalanches are usually the product of bad decisions—human nature, not Mother Nature.

"If it was up to me, I would never have gone backcountry skiing with twelve people," Michelson, the ESPN journalist, said. "That's just way too many. But there were sort of the social dynamics of that— where I didn't want to be the one to say, you know, 'Hey, this is too big a group and we shouldn't be doing this.' I was invited by someone else, so I didn't want to stand up and cause a fuss. And not to play the gender card, but there were two girls and ten guys, and I didn't want to be the whiny female figure, you know? So I just followed along."

Others suppressed reservations, too.

"The whole thing felt rushed to me, and it felt kind of like this covert operation," Stifter said. "Which it kind of was, because you're going out of bounds. It's obviously acceptable, especially when you're going out there with all these locals and the director of marketing. It's not illegal or anything. It just had this rushed feeling from the time Chris walked out of the office, and he's like, 'All right, let's go.'"

Carlsen, Stifter's *Powder* colleague, was uneasy. He tried to convince himself that it was a good idea.

"There's no way this entire group can make a decision that isn't smart," he said to himself. "Of course it's fine, if we're all going. It's got to be fine."

After a few minutes, the small talk faded. Worries went unexpressed.

"When you're up on top of a peak like that, it's usually hang out for a second, and then it's momentum," Castillo said. "You just kind of feel it. Everyone's like: 'OK, we're not here to hang out. Let's start going.' So I saw people starting to slide, get going, and I was like: 'Hey, Johnny, partner up. Buddy system. Let's go. Me and you.' And at that point, it clicked. Everyone's like, yeah, partners, partners, partners."

It is a tenet of avalanche safety, and the command snapped the group to attention.

"Someone said, 'Partner up'—everyone should grab a partner," Carlsen said. "Immediately I thought, we're in a somewhat serious situation. It wasn't just grab a partner so you don't get lost. It was grab a partner so you . . .

"It just felt bigger all of a sudden."

Rudolph, the Stevens Pass marketing director, teamed with Saugstad, the professional skier.

"I was really excited about that," Saugstad said, "because he's just such a cool guy and I thought, wow, cool, he wants to be my partner. A very trustworthy guy that's an amazing skier."

Jack, on borrowed Salomon skis, paired with Joel Hammond, the Salomon representative. Carlson looked at Pankey, his childhood friend.

"Dude, you're coming with me," he said.

Wesley gave a little whistle to Carlson and Pankey and nodded downhill. He wanted to be first. The conditions were too good to waste time, and he did not want to be slowed by the huge pack.

With little warning, Wesley dropped straight through the large cluster of trees, using firs as a slalom course. Pankey and Carlson followed.

Rudolph, always up for competition, sped around the trees, not through them. He curved around a banked C-shape turn that dropped him a couple hundred feet into the broad meadow below.

He arrived just in time to see Wesley, Pankey and Carlson burst from the trees into the open powder. Rudolph pointed his ski poles and playfully shouted invectives as their tracks crossed.

Wesley laughed, and his two friends followed him left and over a small rise.

Rudolph headed straight down the mountain.

"I remember looking back at where he was going and being confused," Wesley said. "Like, 'Where is he going?'"

All the locals in the group presumed they knew what the others were thinking. They did not.

"When you know an avalanche is not very likely, that's a great way to go," Wesley said of Rudolph's choice to ski straight down farther. "It's three open glades of awesome powder."

Earlier that morning, Wesley and Carlson had skied the opposite side of Cowboy Mountain, in the ski area. It had been cleared of avalanches by the ski patrol at dawn, but the two still triggered several slough slides—small, shallow avalanches that washed at their feet and petered out before snagging victims.

"That's why, when they said we're doing Tunnel, I was like, ooh, dicey," Wesley said.

Pankey and Carlson followed Wesley and looked back, too, wondering why Rudolph and the others were not following them toward relatively safer terrain. Within a minute, long enough to be well out of sight of the group they left behind, the three men found something that made them stop.

"We were right on top of a knoll, a little rollover, where we were about to make some really fun turns, and we saw that the face had already slid," Carlson said. "It was pretty large."

Alarmed, the three decided to go farther left. They crossed through trees and avoided big meadows and steep pitches. They soon found evidence of another avalanche, this one cutting through the forest.

"I'd really never seen anything slide in the trees like that," Carlson said. "And that was definitely like, 'Holy cow, we shouldn't be back here, Ron. Let's go left. Let's go hard left.'"

Wesley had disappeared in the pale light. He left nothing but a track through the deep snow that the others tried to follow.

"I just went, and didn't really stop," Wesley said. "I went all the way down. But I've never taken a run where I looked uphill more times in fear."

"I GOT EYES ON YOU"

Rudolph stopped on the left edge of the upper meadow, above a cluster of trees. Others filed behind him, spilling down the mountain in plumes of spraying snow.

Erin Dessert did not follow. She was confused. She was once a Tunnel Creek regular, until a nonfatal avalanche captured five friends in 2002 and scared her away.

"Chris Rudolph's, like, totally all about safety protocol and mountain awareness and wisdom," she said. "That guy knows the conditions like an animal. He has instincts. It didn't register, even for a second, that he might be bringing this group to Tunnel Creek. It wasn't logical. I thought we were doing the front side."

She headed hard to the right, away from the others. The other snowboarders she knew, Carlson and Wesley, were gone in the opposite direction. Some in the remaining group noticed Dessert heading away in the distance and dismissed her as an oblivious backcountry rookie. She dipped out of sight in a lonely panic.

"I've been riding Stevens Pass since I was three years old," Dessert said. "I can tell circumstances, and I just felt like something besides myself was in charge. They're all so professional and intelligent and driven and powerful and riding with athletic prowess, yet everything in my mind was going off, wanting to tell them to stop."

Rudolph and the others, now a group of twelve, were focused down-hill. It was 11:52 a.m. Rudolph did not wait for the back of the pack to arrive before continuing to demonstrate the way.

"So Chris Rudolph went first, and then he pulled into the trees and we waited for a sec," said Castillo, who was near the front of the group, wearing a helmet camera. "He goes out of sight and behind the trees. So I said, 'OK, Megan, go ahead, spoon those tracks, and you'll see Chris on the left.'"

It was not Megan Michelson. It was Elyse Saugstad.

"I thought it was Megan," Castillo said. "I said, 'Are you Megan?' She said, 'No, no, I'm Elyse.' That's when I met Elyse. It was right there. And she made these turns that were like: 'Aah, I think I know who that is. I've seen her name. Those are pro turns.' She ripped the hell out of it."

She traced through the knee-deep snow just to the right of Rudolph's elongated S-shaped tracks. She dipped through trees at a pinch in the meadow and disappeared out of sight. She crossed over Rudolph's tracks and giggled. After about thirty seconds, she was back at Rudolph's side, having cut left into a notch of the trees again.

"We skied to an area that was probably about five hundred feet down or so from where we started," Saugstad said. "And where we skied to was an area of old-growth trees. You know, several-hundred-year-old trees. A very good indication that this is a safe place. Things don't happen here."

Castillo and Brenan teased each other about who would go next.

"Finally, he's like, 'Go ahead, I got eyes on you,'" Castillo said.

From where Rudolph and Saugstad stopped, they could not see the subsequent skiers approach. Castillo went past and cut left. His camera recorded Rudolph and Saugstad whooping their approval as he stopped in a shower of powder, about forty feet below them.

But just before he stopped, Castillo was jolted by a weird sensation.

"A little pang, like, ooh, this is a pretty heavy day out here," Castillo said. "Thing's holding, but I remember having a feeling."

Castillo stopped above two trees. He nestled close and pushed his right ski tight against them.

"A lot of people think you should be below trees, but I stand above them," Castillo said. "I'm like, I'd rather get pinned against this than taken through."

His helmet camera showed that fourteen seconds after Castillo stopped, Brenan appeared through the trees above Rudolph and Saugstad. Brenan had hugged the tree line on the left, avoiding the open meadow, then slalomed through the patch that the others used for protection. He stopped in a spray of snow a few feet from Rudolph and Saugstad.

"That was sick!" someone shouted.

Castillo silently took note of the terrain.

"I was downhill from them—skier's right from them," Castillo said. "But the trees that they were behind, I didn't think it was a bad spot to stop. They were huge. Giant old-growths that three of us probably can't put our hands around."

But he knew the direction of the slope did not follow the meadow. It dipped harder left into the trees, down toward a gully. And there were still a lot of skiers above them.

Saugstad was next to Rudolph. Brenan was a few feet away.

"We weren't straight across from each other, in a perfect horizontal line on the slope," Saugstad said. "We were peppered up and down, spread out."

Castillo kept his attention up the hill. Less than thirty seconds after Brenan stopped, he saw Tim Wangen cut through the trees above the earlier arrivals, gliding horizontally through the forest. Wangen had been taught how to navigate Tunnel Creek by his father. He knew that the farther down the mountain he went, the harder it would be to cut over the ridge and into the next big meadow. He crossed the shallow gully and rose up the other side.

"I could see the others when I cut over," Wangen said. "I thought, oh yeah, that's a bad place to be. That's a bad place to be with that many people. But I didn't say anything. I didn't want to be the jerk."

Wangen had told Peikert to follow his tracks, and Peikert was close behind. Castillo watched where they went.

"Want to cut over?" Castillo shouted to those above him.

SLIDING SNOW

The start of an avalanche is unlike any other force of nature.

A hurricane is foretold by wind and lashing waves. A tornado often is spotted before it strikes. Lightning is usually presaged by black clouds and rumbling thunder.

Avalanches rarely provide such a warning. Unlike waves or wind, tremors or storms, they are usually triggered by their own victims, who are sometimes unaware of what has been unleashed.

"If you swim out in the ocean, the ocean's always alive," Saugstad said. "You can feel it. But the mountains feel like they're asleep."

Back up the mountain, Jack never seemed worried. That was his nature. Here he was, a rare weekend off, skiing with some of his best friends from Leavenworth and people from *Powder* and ESPN and all over the industry, on an epic run on a perfect powder day.

Carlsen, the *Powder* photographer, had never been to Tunnel Creek. The first few easy turns gave way to a slope that fell steeply away, out of sight. He sidled up to Jack.

"I grabbed him, and I said, 'What is the move here?'" Carlsen said. "It was basically like, 'This is getting real, how do we handle it?' He's like, 'Oh, no big deal. We go out here, swing out, make a few pow turns, and get back in the trees.' I looked at him and said, 'Have a great run.' Gave him a fist, a knuckle-to-knuckle high-five thing. And that was it. I watched him swing out, way out, skier's right, and then dive into his turn left."

Jack flowed through the thick powder with his typical ease. He skied the way other people walked down a sidewalk, a friend had said.

Jack disappeared over the knoll, gliding through the trees in the middle of the meadow. Behind him, the five remaining skiers watched in silence.

"He looked like he was having a great time, the run of his life, in fact," Michelson said. "And he actually made, I remember, a little 'woo' sound, as he dropped in on his first or second turn because the snow was really good. It was deep and light."

Then the snow changed without warning.

Across the meadow, above Jack, loose snow seemed to chase him down the hill and out of sight.

Not everyone saw it. A couple did. They caught it in their peripheral vision and were unsure what to make of it.

"That was sketchy," Hammond said.

The five others listened. Not a sound. They stared for clues through the flat light below a murky sky. Nothing.

Silent seconds ticked. Finally, Hammond spotted the first sign of evidence. It came from a tree, one among thousands, far down the hill, almost out of sight. Only the top of it was visible, and it was covered in snow.

"I saw it moving," Hammond said. "Like something had hit the tree, and it shook. And I could see the powder falling off the tree."

BLUR OF WHITE

A few hundred yards down the mountain, a ghostly white fog rushed through the forest.

"I saw it," Saugstad said. "I saw it coming. But it was weird because it was coming through the trees. It was like snow billowing through the trees. Because it was such a treed area, I think for the first second I saw it I didn't believe it."

Wangen and Peikert had just traversed in front of its path. It did not miss them by much.

"I don't know if I'd even come to a stop when I heard it," Peikert said. "It was almost like wind and pressure more than noise. It literally felt like a freight train went over my tails. It wasn't a deep rumble. I could feel this rush of air."

It was a blur of white, its shattered pieces moving about 50 m.p.h., a powder cloud two stories tall.

Rudolph was the only one to scream.

"Avalanche! Elyse!" Rudolph shouted.

Saugstad tried to stride right, hoping to escape. She barely moved before snow flowed through her legs, dragging her down like a riptide.

She pulled the cord on her air bag. She was overwhelmed so quickly by the rising snow that she did not know if it inflated.

"I had no ability to control what was happening to me," Saugstad said. "I was being tossed over and over and over. It was like being in a washing machine and all my body parts flailing every way. I didn't know which way was up. I didn't know which way was down. I couldn't see anything."

She is likely to have tumbled just past Castillo. He groaned and turned his face away. He stuck his head between two trees, like a prisoner in a stockade.

For sixteen seconds, snow and ice pounded his back and washed over him. His shoulders were jammed against the trees. His face pushed into branches of pine needles. He could feel the barrage of snow lashing at his back.

Trees cracked around him. Some in the path were chopped in half—the stumps left in the soil, the rest carried away in the growing torrent.

The avalanche, a relatively small one, started with about 6,000 cubic meters of snow and collected 7,000 cubic meters more on the way down. It probably weighed about 11 million pounds.

The trees Castillo hugged in each arm swayed but held. He told himself that when he felt the flow slow, he would pop a hand in the air so that it might stick out of the snow and make him easier to rescue.

"Just as I had the thought about what I'm going to do, wondering if it was going to bury me, that's right when I could feel it," Castillo said. "It was like a wave. Like when you're in the ocean and the tide moves away from you. You're getting thrashed and you feel it pull out and you're like, OK, I can stand up now."

Castillo saw daylight again. His camera captured snow sliding past his legs for another thirteen seconds. The forest sounded as if it were full of sickly frogs. It was the trees, scrubbed of their fresh snow, still swaying and creaking around him.

Castillo turned to look back up the hill.

"Where there were three people, there was nobody," Castillo said.

A TICKING CLOCK

He did not know who or what set off the avalanche. He did not know how far down the mountain it went. All he knew was that about a dozen people had been above him a minute earlier, and that the gully below him descended another 2,000 vertical feet to the valley floor.

And he was alone.

"Johnny! Johnny Brenan!" Castillo screamed into the stillness, his voice escalating with panic. The scope of the disaster was too much to comprehend. He wanted to find his partner.

"So I'm screaming his name," Castillo said. "I'm screaming and screaming. Silence."

Streams of snow still flowed downhill as he scooted toward the heart of the slide path. It flowed into a wide gully, maybe one hundred feet across, that narrowed as it descended. Castillo turned his beacon to "search" mode, meaning he would receive signals of those buried but would not emit signals himself.

"I don't want to be in this gully because I don't know what's coming down next," Castillo said. "I don't want to be the next guy taken out. Now I don't even have a beacon on because I'm on search. They're not going to find me if anything happens to me."

Across the gully, unable to see anyone else, either, Peikert and Wangen had gone into search mode, too.

"I was like, if there's someone in that, the clock's ticking," Peikert said.

Chances of survival drop precipitously every minute. According to a recent study, the survival rate for individuals completely buried in an avalanche falls to about 40 percent after fifteen minutes of burial and to 25 percent after thirty minutes. About 75 percent of avalanche victims die from asphyxia or suffocation. The other 25 percent of fatalities result from trauma.

Castillo spotted Peikert and
were nervous about hangfire, the uns
an avalanche's path that can release at any h. They, too,

The avalanche had turned the gully into an o. edges of
with slick, high-banked walls.

"This gully's hard-core!" Castillo yelled. "They're in it!"

Wangen stayed mostly on the banks. Peikert and Castillo crossed
the gully a couple of times, reluctantly and quickly.

"What's your name again?" Castillo shouted at Peikert.

It was soon apparent that the victims, however many there were,
suffered one of two fates: they were hung up on the banks of the gully,
snagged by a tree or buried in snow, or they had been flushed to the
bottom, thousands of feet below.

If searchers spent too much time looking along the gully, they
might squander a chance at rescuing someone at the bottom. If they
rushed downhill, they might pass someone in need of saving.

"We started to ski down, hoping to find him in a tree well or hanging on or something," said Castillo, his focus on Brenan. "But I started
to realize all the trees were bent over, and I started thinking, this is
really fricking bad. And then I skied down to a point where I found
Johnny's ski, probably three or four feet up in a tree. Stuck."

Castillo called 911. It was 12:02 p.m. The avalanche occurred seven
minutes earlier.

"Hi, I'm at Stevens Pass resort, on the backside of Tunnel Creek,"
Castillo told the King County Sheriff's Department dispatcher. He
added, "We had a major avalanche, and we might have three or four
people missing, at least."

The dispatcher asked him to slow down. Castillo, occasionally shouting at others nearby, tried to explain where the avalanche
occurred. He was asked how many people there were.

"There's at least ten," Castillo said. "Between ten and twelve."

...ed if anybody was hurt.

...und them," Castillo said. "I found one ski. It rolled

...y heavy, man. I had partners right next to me and they're

...just found a ski about 1,000 yards down. Or 1,000 feet down."

...he call lasted four minutes. Castillo, carrying his friend's ski,

...urned down the mountain.

"THIS THING RIPPED BIG"

Near the top, the five skiers who planned to follow Jim Jack deciphered what happened through a series of increasingly blunt clues. Loose snow. A shaking tree.

Hammond was due to ski next. He took a couple of turns through the fine powder of the meadow and stopped. There was a sudden drop, nearly three feet deep. The fluffy snow was gone. A surface of bluish ice stretched down the hill, into the trees and out of sight.

"Once I had gotten to the edge, I was like, oh my gosh, this thing ripped big," Hammond said. "I could see the scope of it."

He shouted for everyone to go into search mode. The other four skiers moved quickly to see.

"We all skied up to it and were like, holy smokes," Stifter said. "From there all I remember was pulling out my phone. And I called Jim Jack."

Others started dialing numbers, too. They called Chris Rudolph and Elyse Saugstad. There were no answers. Hammond dropped onto the slick slide path. Another clue lay on the ice, pointing downhill.

"I hopped out there and made one or two turns, and I saw one of Jim's skis," Hammond said. "The only reason I recognized Jim's skis was that it was a pair of skis that he borrowed from me."

The realization that Jack had been carried away was a gut punch.

"In one respect, you're like, oh no, a ski—where's Jim?" Abrams said. "On the other hand, you think, OK, there's his ski. Let's find him."

Michelson called 911. According to sheriff's department records, it was 12:03 p.m.

Her voice was steady and sure. She patiently tried to explain where they were—"The backside of the ski area in the backcountry," she explained. "Tunnel Creek."

The dispatcher asked if people were buried.

"I believe so, yes," Michelson replied. "I don't know how many. We have a large group."

Word was relayed to the ski area. Chris Brixey, manager of the Stevens Pass Ski Patrol, had seventeen patrollers working on the mountain that day, two more in the aid room, and a dispatcher. Brixey is a regular at Johnny Brenan's Monday night poker parties. He did not know that a group of friends, including Rudolph, his Stevens Pass co-worker, had gone to Tunnel Creek.

"I happened to be walking through the aid room," Brixey said. "Our dispatcher handed me a note that said ten people are buried in Tunnel Creek. I called the 911 operator and got Megan's information. I called Megan directly. She said there's about twelve people and they were looking for eight people. I didn't know Megan. My gut feeling was that this was a group of inexperienced people who are now dealing with tragedy."

Brixey called the area's most seasoned patroller and put him in charge of the four-member first-response unit, called the hasty team, to follow the group's trail. He also enlisted other patrollers and a pair of avalanche rescue dogs.

Word of a large avalanche in Tunnel Creek soon echoed around Stevens Pass, from the patrol room to the RV lot, up the lifts and down the slopes. According to the Stevens Pass Ski Patrol log, the area closed public access to the boundary gate atop the Seventh Heaven lift at 12:19.

By then, the group that had started off together less than thirty minutes earlier was strewn up and down nearly 3,000 vertical feet. No one knew how many were missing.

Keith Carlsen was nearest the top, searching for Jack.

"I thought someone has to make sure he's not still up here," Carlsen said. "It wasn't likely, but his ski was there, and he got swept, and there's no sign of him, so maybe he got pummeled into the snow, into a hole, somewhere, right away."

The others headed down, scanning the path and its edges with their beacons. Carlsen methodically checked the upper meadow.

"I thought I was going to be the one to find him, and I would find him alone," Carlsen said. "And the bed surface at the top was rock hard. And I'm thinking: I'm going to get a signal, and this guy's going to be buried, and I'm going to have to somehow dig him out. I'm going to find Jim Jack."

Scared and alone, Carlsen's voice broke the silence.

"I'm saying, and I remember repeating this in my head: 'Jim, am I about to find you? Jim, are you underneath me? Jim, where the hell are you? Is this possible? Is he really underneath here? Am I about to dig Jim out?'"

Farther down, others followed the path into the gully. As it descends toward the valley floor, it carves deeper into the mountain. In some spots, canyon walls are twenty feet high. There were steep, icy drops that would become gushing waterfalls during the spring runoff.

"There are places it's so tight that I would stop and my skis would straddle the middle," Hammond said. "And I'd be elevated, like being on springs."

It was still clogged with rocks and trees that had not been fully scoured away. Where the ravine bent, the avalanche rode high on the outside wall, like a child on a water slide, sometimes breaking over the top of the bank and unearthing trees on the ridges.

"It was fear," Abrams said. "Fear that you lost someone, and fear that you're standing in an avalanche path. You're thinking, Don't get caught up on trees, listen for the beacons, where's my fiancée?"

It became increasingly evident that whoever was caught in the avalanche would be found at the bottom.

"I probably went down for one or two minutes and I got no signal," Michelson said. "I shouted, 'They've gone all the way down! The way this gully is, they've been flushed.'"

DISCOVERY

Tim Carlson and Ron Pankey, having split from the big group at the top, nervously negotiated the roundabout route to the bottom of Tunnel Creek. They could not catch up to Tim Wesley, but followed his snowboard track to the valley floor. It was 12:07 p.m.

They glided past the foot of a mound of chunky debris. One of the ravines had spewed a sizable avalanche, but there was no way to know it had occurred in the past few minutes.

"I looked up and I saw a ski pole sticking up," Carlson said. "It looked like someone stuck it in there. It was sticking up right at the very end of the pile. Handle up."

He shouted to Pankey.

"I was like, 'Dude, you need to turn your transceiver on,'" Carlson said. "'There's people in here.'"

Carlson clicked out of his snowboard bindings and climbed onto the pile. Pankey turned his beacon to search mode. It beeped immediately.

His skis off, Pankey climbed onto the debris pile, too. He saw the ski pole and two gloves. He was sucker-punched by dread.

"You figure someone who is fighting is going to have his gloves on," Pankey said. "If they're limp, yeah, their gloves are going to come off."

Then he noticed the brand.

"That was my thought: oh, God, those are Scott gloves. Jim Jack was wearing Scott gloves," Pankey said.

Their beacons shrieked.

"I probably searched for maybe a minute before I was on top of a signal," Carlson said. "Your signal goes 'beepbeepbeepbeepbeepBEEP-BEEPBEEPBEEPBEEP,' and it gets a little fainter, like oh, over here. I got a strong signal, traversed over, got a weak signal, went back, got a strong signal, went back and I was basically on top of a body.

"And, uh, the first shovel I dug in, I hit Jim Jack's arm."

The two men dug frantically.

"I saw Jim Jack's face," Carlson said. "Eyes open, just staring at me. We could see he wasn't breathing. Ron started giving him breaths and I was searching for his body, underneath his chest. I was like, 'What the hell is going on?' There was no body where you'd expect a body to be. And then I started digging around, and I could see he was folded up into this ball. His feet were above his head."

His body had been pummeled.

"There was no blood, but he didn't have his helmet on, he didn't have his backpack on, his jacket was pulled over his head," Carlson said. "He had some scrapes on his belly. And just pulling him out of the snow you could feel it and see it. Giving him a couple of breaths, it just came out so quick. And you push on his chest and it would just collapse. There was nothing there. And Jim Jack—we're all strong dudes, and there was just nothing left."

"I pulled his arm upright, and it was just really soft," Carlson added. "It was like pulling a wet towel. Pulled the other arm and it was the same feeling. And I pulled his legs out, and there was nothing connected to anything. It was completely crushed."

They turned off Jack's beacon and tried to lay him peacefully in the snow. Pankey pushed his eyelids closed.

He called 911 at 12:31 p.m. and told the dispatcher that Jack was dead.

Jack's phone chirped. It had survived the avalanche, and Pankey reached into Jack's pocket and pulled it out. It was a text message from

Jack's girlfriend, Tiffany Abraham. Rumors of a big avalanche in Tunnel Creek had reached the base area of Stevens Pass.

"Where are you?" it read. "You OK?"

Pankey looked over at the ski pole sticking straight out of the snow. It looked familiar. Pankey had noticed it on the hike up the ridge to Cowboy Mountain.

"That's the guy's in front of me," Pankey said. "He was hiking in front of me and Jim Jack was behind me, and he had these old Smith, corrective angle, curved poles. So I'm like, that's Johnny's pole."

"IT WAS JUST A BAD DREAM"

More than 100 yards away and out of sight, Elyse Saugstad waited in the silence, unable to move.

She did not know how long she had been frozen there—head pointed downhill, hands sticking out of the snow, face poking through the ice just enough to breathe and to see the breaking clouds trailing the weekend's storm.

Her hip ached. Her mind wandered. She wondered who else was caught in the avalanche. She wondered who was left to rescue them.

She felt herself getting colder. Her pink mittens, like those of a child, had strings that attached them to her jacket. When she had come to a stop, one of the mittens was on her hand. The other was off, hanging from her wrist.

Saugstad could not claw the hard-packed snow with her mittens on. She took them off and picked at the ice until her fingers ached. She put her mittens on again until they warmed up.

She had not spoken since the avalanche stopped. It had not occurred to her to cry for help. Someone would come. She hoped.

Finally, for the first time, she shouted.

"Help!" she screamed.

The face of Wenzel Peikert startled her.

Among those who skied down the gully, Peikert arrived first to the avalanche's final resting place. The walls of the ravine slowly fell away and opened onto a wide, sloping meadow. It was covered by an enormous pile of chunky ice cubes, some fit for a cocktail glass, others the size of couches. The debris was filled with dirt, rocks and shredded tree parts.

It stretched about 150 yards down what remained of the slope. It was ten or twenty feet tall, obstructing Peikert's view to the bottom. Peikert's beacon began its frantic chirping.

"I started getting a signal," Peikert said. "I marked it with one of my poles. That's what they teach, to mark where you start picking up a signal and keep working to where it gets stronger. I took my skis off because it was so hard to ski on that stuff. And as I got close to that signal, I saw two pink gloves sticking out."

Saugstad was about twenty feet downhill.

"Her feet were into the snow and her head was downhill, but I saw two pink gloves and her face," Peikert said. "I don't know if she uncovered her face or not, but it was just barely sticking out of the snow. And a little bit of orange from her backpack. I started digging her out, trying not to hurt her. I said, 'Are you OK?' And she said, 'I think so. My leg's kind of hurt.'"

Peikert pulled his shovel from his backpack and started to dig.

"For a pause, really quickly, I thought to myself: she's alive, she's breathing, her face is out of the snow," Peikert said. "I thought, let's go find others. But then I realized that more snow could come down. I found someone alive, and I needed to get her out of here."

Saugstad sensed his urgency.

"When he started unburying me, he flung his shovel and it went flying down the hill so far that he couldn't stop and go get it," she said. "And so then he had to start digging me out with his hands."

Peikert hurried, knowing that others were likely buried nearby.

"She was actually really hard to get out," he said. "One of her skis had stayed on, so it had kind of locked her into the snow. Even a ski boot gets locked in. I dug to get her ski off. It probably took five minutes of digging to get her out."

Finally, Michelson and Abrams arrived from above. They found Peikert and Saugstad on their feet.

"It didn't dawn on me that she had been buried," Michelson said. "I was relieved she was alive."

Over several minutes, others trickled down from above.

"Once we got to the bottom, when we got through the ravine and got to the mouth, I just remember saying, 'Oh, my God,'" Stifter said. "Snow chunks the size of boulders. That's when I realized the magnitude of everything. It looked like a war zone. It was chaos."

Michelson took charge as an impromptu site commander. No one was sure who was missing or how many victims there might be. Michelson used her beacon and pinpointed two spots for others to search, then continued sweeping the meadow to search for more.

"My numbers and directions were bouncing all over the place," Peikert said. "But Megan comes up and hers was right on it. Mine is a little bit older, but I don't know why it was bouncing around. I started probing, and I hit a spot where there obviously was something other than snow."

Peikert and Rob Castillo dug through the ice. It had been more than thirty minutes since the avalanche.

Johnny Brenan was discovered about three feet below the surface. He had been buried a few feet from Saugstad all along.

"I found his back first," Peikert said. "His head was really bent under. I tried to dig a hole through his armpit, to his head, thinking I might be able to get his face turned to give him CPR. There was blood. His chin was split open. His helmet was pushed back onto the back of his head and was filled with snow. One leg was off in a weird position, like he had a broken femur or hip or something. I finally got him out. He was cold. Blue."

Castillo, Brenan's longtime friend and ski partner, worked side by side with Peikert, at last getting his legs out.

"The muscles were just beat," Castillo said.

About twenty feet up the hill, Abrams, Wangen and Stifter zeroed in on a victim, too. It was the spot that Peikert had marked with his pole before he spotted Saugstad.

"We were still searching for the lowest signal," Stifter said. "And the lowest signal I got on the transceiver was 2.4, and it took me, like, half a second to realize, oh, that's six feet down because it's in meters. So I'm like, all right, this is our lowest reading. And I think on our third probe we struck something. I told Dan and Tim, 'All right, get the shovels out,' and we started digging."

Digging was nothing like scooping snowfall from a driveway. It was more like shoveling the chunky piles that snowplows leave along the side of a cleared highway, full of large pieces seemingly glued together.

"They're big mounds of snow and they're like concrete," Stifter said. "So you dig and dig, and then that person would rotate to the back and take a break and the guy who was second would start clearing snow out for the guy who is digging."

Quickly exhausted, they rotated frequently.

"It was just a bad dream," Abrams said. "I was standing there holding my shovel that I never intended to use, except maybe to get my car out."

Finally, they reached a victim: Chris Rudolph.

"He was lying face down, so it was hard to get to his face," Stifter said. "And it was hard because we couldn't move him because he was just encased in there. His feet were buried really deeply. Finally I was able to get to his face. His face was blue. And so finally I was like, 'We've got to get his feet out! We've got to get his feet out!' That took another good couple of minutes to get his feet free. Then we gently pulled him out by his backpack."

Stifter performed CPR on Rudolph: two breaths, thirty compressions, to the point of exhaustion.

Saugstad called 911. It was 12:40 p.m.

"I'm reporting an avalanche," she said, breathlessly.

Frantic voices behind her shouted encouragement: "Come on! You can do it! Come on, buddy! Take a breath!"

The dispatcher said there were "units on scene." Saugstad said they had not arrived and asked if they were coming by helicopter.

"Uh, we do not have a helicopter yet in the area because of the avalanche risk," the dispatcher said.

Hammond was the last to arrive from above and took over trying to revive Rudolph.

"I definitely believed that there was a chance," Stifter said. "My hope dissipated certainly after Joel got there and I was sitting there. We knew. We looked at each other."

Twenty feet downhill, the huddle around Brenan slowly came to the same conclusion. Peikert had been performing CPR for close to thirty minutes, with Castillo's help.

"I was hoping for a miracle then," Castillo said. "But I really kind of understood that he was probably dead."

An hour's worth of adrenaline dissolved to disheartened shock. A few other skiers had happened upon the scene, but no rescue help had arrived.

Saugstad walked around dazed, wearing her deflated air bag "like dead angel wings," Carlsen said. Castillo made his way to the bottom of the hill to learn that Jim Jack was dead, too. Erin Dessert, the snowboarder who had veered away from the group at the top, frightened by the direction everyone was headed, had cautiously made her way down and rediscovered the group. She cradled Rudolph's head as others tried their last attempts to resuscitate him.

"It's Chris Rudolph," she said. "You know? He's the knight in shining armor of Stevens Pass."

WORD SPREADS

Laurie Brenan and Tiffany Abraham, Jack's girlfriend, were both in the Bull's Tooth Pub and Eatery, on the second level of the Granite Peaks Lodge.

"I saw Tiffany sitting at the bar, and I sat a few seats away," Brenan said. "She says, 'I haven't seen Jim yet.' And I said, 'Oh, he and Johnny did Tunnel Creek.'"

The man next to Abraham, a neighbor from Leavenworth, overheard. There was an avalanche in Tunnel Creek, he said. Someone came into the restaurant a while ago and asked for volunteers to help search.

Abraham's heart sank. Normally a font of buoyant optimism, she had a sudden pang of dread.

"I downed my cocktail because I knew I'd need it," Abraham said. "The bartender was telling a story, and I was trying to be polite and listen, but I knew I had to get out of there. I got my lunch boxed up and walked down to the ski patrol office. I took the elevator, and it was the slowest elevator in the world."

She could tell immediately that bad news was waiting. She spotted a friend who was on his way to the scene.

"He grabs my hand and I screamed at him," Abraham said. "'What the hell is going on?'"

They went into the ski patrol room, on the ground level on the back side of the lodge. Inside is a first-aid room with beds for injured skiers. Beyond is a ski patrol break room, a couch against one wall.

Anne Hessburg, Rudolph's girlfriend, was sitting there, balled up in tears. She had skied all morning with a friend and taken an early lunch at the Iron Goat pizzeria. She walked up to the slope-side cabin that Rudolph had provided to the journalists from *Powder* magazine. Hessburg stored skis there. A friend received a call while she was there.

"Someone told him there was an avalanche in Tunnel Creek," Hessburg said. "He told me, and my stomach immediately dropped."

Hessburg rushed to the ski patrol room. She could tell by the way people were moving that it was something serious. She could hear the squawks on the walkie-talkies. Someone told her only that Rudolph was probably involved, as if to break the emotional fall.

Brixey, the ski patrol manager, confirmed it. Rudolph was dead. That was about when Abraham walked into the patrol room with her friend, noticing a broken Hessburg on the couch.

Abraham's friend turned to her, looked her in the eyes, and told her about Jack.

"Baby girl, he's gone," he said.

"I just lost my breath," Abraham said. "I lost it. I couldn't even be in my skin."

Laurie Brenan had no premonition. She watched Abraham rush out of the restaurant at the news of an avalanche and casually followed a few minutes behind.

"I thought everything was fine," she said. "But I'm going over to ski patrol. I felt like Johnny was probably using his skills, digging somebody out."

She tried to stay out of the way as people hurried in and out of the patrol room.

"Then I heard someone say something about Jim Jack, and I thought, oh my God, how can that be?" Brenan said. "I knew they were all in the same group. I start calling to see if I can get someone to get my kids safe, back to the RV, and get them a snack and put on a movie or something."

Brenan spotted Brixey, the patrol manager and Monday night poker player, and waited for an opening to approach.

"I said, 'So, Chris, there's been an avalanche in Tunnel Creek?'" Brenan said. "And he said yes. Anyone hurt? He said yes. Is anyone dead? He said yes. And I said, 'Do I know these people?' And he said yes. I said, 'Where's Johnny?' And he said, 'I haven't heard.'"

It was true. One 911 call from Tunnel Creek had reported the death of Jack. Another had reported the death of Rudolph. A third made mention of a third fatality, but the dispatcher never asked the name. Brixey did not learn about Brenan until his own patrol members reached the scene.

"I went outside, totally shaking," Laurie Brenan said. "I kept dropping my water bottle, again and again, because I was shaking so much. Then Chris Brixey comes and gets me."

Brixey's outward calm belied the turmoil inside. As a paramedic, he had told a lot of strangers that a loved one had died. But never a close friend.

"That was, by far, the biggest challenge for me, walking Laurie from outside back to my office," Brixey said. "Not knowing what I was going to say, but knowing what I had to say."

They walked past the empty beds, past Hessburg on the couch, past Abraham. In the office, he turned to her.

"He said Johnny was one of the people buried," Brenan said. "'He didn't make it.' I didn't want to believe it. I said, 'Have you seen him?' He said no. I said, 'Then you don't know. It's possible he's not there. You go back and get more information because that is wrong. Go. Go find him. You're wrong.' I remember thinking, He's got two kids. This was for fun. Johnny doesn't leave his responsibilities. Ever."

Brixey left. Brenan melted into shock. Finally, a friend from Leavenworth came in. He had gone to ski Tunnel Creek about twenty minutes behind the large group and happened upon the scene.

"He said, 'I can tell you it was him,'" Laurie Brenan said. "'I gave him CPR. We tried.'

"It really felt like I had died then," Brenan said. "And that I was reborn into a nightmare."

A GRIM VIGIL

Back on the other side of Cowboy Mountain, and down a meadow that had been turned inside out, weary huddles surrounded three dead men.

Hope had surrendered. Rescues became grim vigils. The survivors did not know what to do other than wait. The bodies and faces of the victims were covered in jackets because it seemed the respectful thing to do. Survivors introduced themselves to those they had not met.

A group of sixteen skiers and snowboarders, all of them experts, all of them unable to refuse the temptation of an hourlong excursion into steep powder, had been reduced by three lives.

"I'm so done with it," Stifter thought to himself. "I'm so done with skiing."

The first ski patrollers, along with an avalanche dog named Cava, arrived at 1:05 p.m., seventy minutes after the mountain gave way. They had started at the top and combed the entire path, following the funnel from the wide upper meadow through the flumelike ravine, searching for victims along the way. By the time they spit out of the mouth at the bottom, there was no rescue to be done.

The patrollers recognized faces in the huddles. They realized then that they had been searching for friends, not strangers. They stopped to find Rudolph and Brenan. Another patroller headed farther down to learn about Jack.

More patrollers began to arrive from below, on snowmobiles brought from the highway. A scene of quiet contemplation buzzed with activity and a second wave of despair.

"It just became this sea, getting merged into everybody else's shock," Dessert said. "When it was just us out there working on them, it seemed beautiful and spiritual, almost like an Indian burial ground."

The patrollers tried to revive the victims. It was useless.

A medical examiner determined that Jack's cause of death was "subdural and subarachnoid hemorrhage"—brain trauma. She also diagnosed a partially torn aorta; a broken neck, vertebrae, sternum and ribs; and lacerations of the liver, spleen and pancreas. She described "blunt force injury of the head, neck, torso and extremities."

Rudolph, with a "blunt force injury of the torso," sustained "rib fractures with right hemothorax and probably compressional asphyxia." Brenan had "blunt force injury and compression of the trunk," with "multiple rib and vertebral fractures with probable compressional asphyxia."

They were probably dead by the time the avalanche stopped, or shortly after.

Brixey, working by radio over the mountain at Stevens Pass, told all rescue units to stand down. A second surge of patrollers would assist in taking the bodies off the mountain.

The survivors were encouraged to make their way to the highway, where ambulances awaited. Saugstad, missing a ski, used the one of Jack's that had been found. Hammond had been carrying it on his back.

Stifter and Carlsen sat in the meadow, unable to pull themselves away.

"Everybody kind of skied down," Stifter said. "It seemed weird to me to leave the bodies."

As with other survivors, the quarrel with their own guilt began immediately, the first sign that avalanches swallow more lives than just the ones buried beneath the snow.

They wondered if their mere presence at Stevens Pass that weekend gave rise to the Tunnel Creek trip, a group of proud locals eager to show off for influential out-of-towners. They wondered why they recognized all of the danger signs, starting with the avalanche report that morning over coffee, but did not do enough to slow or stop the expedition. They wondered if they could have saved lives after the avalanche by speeding to the bottom rather than combing the path.

They wondered how so many smart, experienced people could make the types of decisions that turned complex, rich, enviable lives into a growing stack of statistics.

Activity disturbed the quiet again. A Sno-Cat, a large machine with treads to climb through snow-covered terrain, rumbled through the trees below and parked at the bottom of the debris pile. Ski patrollers solemnly marched up the hill, carrying gear to wrap the bodies.

It was one deadly avalanche among many, perhaps no more worthy of attention than any other. It was not the nation's deadliest avalanche of the season. And it was not at all like the one that killed ninety-six people near Tunnel Creek more than a century ago.

But some rituals do not change. The accidents end with an unrefined ceremony.

Some patrollers stopped at Jack and wrapped him in a crude bundle using red blankets and rope. Others hiked to where Stifter and Carlsen sat. They wrapped the bodies of Brenan and Rudolph, with quiet expediency and reverence.

"I remember they said, 'There's no easy way to do this,'" Stifter said. "And they started slowly dragging them down the hill."

POSTSCRIPT: *"Snow Fall" was awarded the 2013 Pulitzer Prize for Feature Writing and was widely praised for its innovative use of multimedia and digital design. It is still studied in avalanche-safety courses and in journalism schools. In the eight years following its publication, more than 200 people have died in avalanches in the United States.*

2
THE DAWN WALL

Yosemite National Park, California

I. "BATTLING" UP A SHEER YOSEMITE FACE, SEIZING A DREAM, NOT A ROPE

The tip of El Capitan, 3,000 feet above its base, glowed in late-day sunlight while a full moon rose at the other end of the Yosemite Valley on Saturday. In the shadows halfway up the sheer granite face were a pair of dots, the latest to attempt one of rock climbing's greatest challenges.

There are about one hundred routes up El Capitan, first summited from the valley floor in 1958. But these dots, climbers named Tommy Caldwell and Kevin Jorgeson, were trying something that had never been done. They were scaling the Dawn Wall—as smooth as alabaster, as steep as the bedroom wall, more than half a mile tall—without the benefit of ropes, other than to catch their falls.

"If they get it completed, it will be the hardest completed rock climb in the world," said Tom Evans, who first climbed El Capitan forty-eight years ago and has chronicled assaults on it for decades, through his camera lens and a blog. "This will be the climb of the first half of the twenty-first century."

After a week of slow, steady progress, and with good weather forecast for the next week, optimism was building that Caldwell and Jorgeson would complete a task they had worked toward—studying, training and failing on a couple of prior pushes—for several years with single-minded obsession.

Through his lens, Evans watched Caldwell complete the precarious fifteenth of thirty-two pitches, or sections, of varying difficulty and length. In the chilled twilight of the meadow below stood a few other photographers, a couple of friends of the climbers, and several tourists who had ambled into the scene, craning their necks. Evans led them in a whooping cheer that reached the climbers 1,500 feet above.

"Things have been going unbelievably well," Caldwell said during a phone interview on Sunday afternoon from a base camp, 1,200 feet up. "We worked on this so long, and it feels kind of like a different route this time. We're just more prepared, the weather is working out great, and it's been going super well. Having said that, this climb is never going to get done without some doubt and some moments like, oh, my God, are we going to be able to do this?"

Evans said that only about thirteen of El Capitan's climbing routes had been free climbed, meaning that moving upward is done only with hands and feet. The Dawn Wall, so named because its southeast orientation catches the first light of morning, is far harder than any of the others, climbers said.

"What makes the Dawn Wall so special is that it's almost not possible," the renowned climber Alex Honnold said. "The hardest pitches on the Dawn Wall are harder than I've ever climbed."

The wall's relentlessly smooth face has few cracks to penetrate or nubs to clench. One short section requires a sideways leap, feet and hands off the wall, to holds the size of matchsticks. There are overhangs. Water creeps through some of the few fissures, and ice periodically drops from above. A scale used to gauge difficulty ranks several parts of the Dawn Wall among the toughest to climb in the world.

"People have done single-pitch climbs rated harder," said the filmmaker Josh Lowell, whose Big Up Productions has chronicled Caldwell's attempts at the Dawn Wall for years. "But this number of pitches, it'll certainly be the hardest big-wall climb ever—by a mile."

Warren Harding and Dean Caldwell (no relation to Tommy) were the first to climb the Dawn Wall, in 1970, using ropes and countless rivets over twenty-seven days. Around 2008, Caldwell, from Estes Park, Colorado, began to seriously ponder whether the entire length could be free climbed in one push, meaning no relief or rest on the valley floor.

Part of the difficulty of such a quest is the cumulative effect on the mind and body. Climbing for days in a row can rub fingers raw. Sleeping in slings amid the elements can be taxing, if not dangerous.

Caldwell, now thirty-six, was not sure it could be done, or if he was the one most capable of doing it. Jorgeson, a thirty-year-old from Santa Rosa, California, heard of the quest and contacted Caldwell to see if he wanted a partner. The two have spent much of the past five years training on El Capitan, mapping out their strategy and practicing every Dawn Wall pitch, perfecting sequences, positioning and holds.

The best time of year to make the full attempt, they decided, was winter. With the rock fully exposed to the sun, the cold temperatures of the season help keep hands from sweating and maintain better friction between the rock and the rubber soles of the climbers' shoes.

Caldwell and Jorgeson tried to climb it all in 2010, but storms halted their progress about a third of the way up. Jorgeson broke an ankle during a 2011 attempt on the kind of fall that climbers occasionally endure during the most difficult maneuvers. Caldwell persisted but was stymied for a week by the fourteenth pitch, the toughest of the route, and went back down.

The men decided to try to master each pitch before attempting them

in sequence again. This fall, Caldwell completed the fourteenth pitch. In late December, the weather, dry and cool, was favorable. The push began.

Caldwell admitted that he felt a bit like Ahab, chasing a white whale.

"This is my Moby-Dick, for sure," he said. "For me, it's just a fascination with the epic journey. I've always been a fan of stories of big journeys. And it's a question of curiosity. I love to play with my physical and mental limits and see how far I can push them, and I just love to dream big. And this project fulfills all those things."

Late last week, Honnold, the renowned climber, visited Caldwell and Jorgeson, needing about an hour to go with ropes as high as the two had free climbed in several days. He brought shelled pistachios and dark chocolate.

Honnold lives in Yosemite but climbs all around the world. He has tried to get Caldwell to come with him, but Caldwell has demurred, focused intently on the Dawn Wall. Now he and Jorgeson are as close as they have imagined to completing it.

Climbing mostly in the late afternoon and into the night, using headlamps and the lights of the roped-in camera crew recording the expedition, Caldwell and Jorgeson moved steadily. On Thursday, each made it past the fourteenth pitch.

Back in Colorado, Caldwell's wife, Rebecca, waits for updates from her husband while caring for their twenty-month-old son, Fitz.

"I don't think it was a reality that this could really, really happen until Pitch 14," she said.

Numbers 15 and 16 are considered nearly as hard, and she was relieved to hear that Caldwell had navigated the fifteenth on Saturday night. Jorgeson made three attempts at it before calling it a night.

"Battling," he posted on Twitter.

On Sunday afternoon, Jorgeson was full of optimism.

"It's far from over, but you can't ignore the fact that it has gone well so far, and it does feel a whole lot different than previous attempts," he said shortly before attempting Pitch 15 again.

That tricky crux, as climbers call difficult maneuvers, could slow the itinerary, but the combination of good health, good spirits and a clear forecast gives the climbers wiggle room to complete the climb.

"Best case is seven days," Caldwell said of the finish. "Worst case is mid-February. Or not at all, I suppose."

Family members and friends are tracking the climb through text messages and social media. If things continue to go well, they will converge on El Capitan sometime in the coming days—not in the meadow below but atop the summit. They will ascend via a couple of hiking trails, for there are far easier ways to get to the top of El Capitan, but none of them are as meaningful.

II. HANGING OUT 1,200 FEET UP (YES, DOWNTIME)

The two men attempting to free climb the daunting 3,000-foot Dawn Wall route of El Capitan spent much of Monday morning in their tents, hanging 1,200 feet above the valley floor.

When Tommy Caldwell and Kevin Jorgeson are not climbing, they are doing all the things that ground-bound people might do on their couch: resting, eating, drinking coffee, talking on cellphones and surfing the Internet. One difference is that they often sand their battered fingertips. Another is that they go to the bathroom in a bag.

For people around the world following their ascent, the wonder of attempting what many consider the most difficult rock climb in the world is hard to comprehend. But to those who have never climbed so much as to their own roof, the logistics of spending weeks on a wall, in winter, thousands of feet above the ground, is something beyond the realm of imagination, too.

How do they charge cellphones? Where do they get the food? And bathroom in a bag?

Quick answers: Solar power, deliveries every five days, and yes— though one of them was spotted urinating off the cliff.

"If you could send a hot pizza up tomorrow," Caldwell jokingly suggested in a phone interview Sunday. "And we're almost out of coffee."

In the valley below the climbers Monday morning, Erik Sloan prepared about 150 pounds of supplies, including five days' worth of food, that he and another man would spend the day hauling up the sheer face.

Sloan, a longtime friend of the climbers whose yosemitebigwall. com site is a key source for route maps, had "haul" bags filled with twelve gallons of water, pasta, chili, fresh vegetables and fruit, trail mix and a small bottle of Bulleit whiskey "to take the edge off." Alas, no hot pizza.

There are anchor points in the wall about every 150 feet. Sloan and his partner climb to the anchor points, then use a pulley system and their own body weight to drag each bag up, one section at a time. It takes about ten trips, and several hours, to get the bags to the camp.

The camp consists of three portaledges, basically four-foot-by-six-foot hanging cots with aluminum frames and clips that connect to bolts in the mountain. There is one for Caldwell, one for Jorgeson and one for the rotating members of a film crew chronicling the attempt. (The photographers, who are not free climbing, go down every couple of days to charge batteries and download their images.)

"Once we get most of the hardest pitches down, which is about 300 or 400 feet above us, we'll move our whole camp up about 500 feet, and we'll base out of there for a day or two," Caldwell said Sunday. "Then it'll be more traditional wall-style, where we'll climb and haul each day with us for a couple of days until we get to the top."

Part of the climbers' scouting work the past couple of years has been to insert bolts, where deemed necessary, to support the climb—to hold ropes and gear. It is a common practice, unless someone climbs without ropes at all, because there is nowhere else to fasten to a rock this size. But it pales in comparison to the hundreds of bolts used by Warren Harding and Dean Caldwell (no relation to Tommy) on the first ascent of the Dawn Wall, with aid, in 1970. Harding was widely criticized, and a rival, Royal Robbins, spent weeks cutting and removing much of the hardware left behind.

Caldwell and Jorgeson have spent years training for the climb, practicing individual pitches, or sections, again and again, memorizing and recording the best ways to move—this hand to this tiny nub, this foot splayed to this one, one move at a time. The quest now is to send, or complete, all thirty-two pitches, in sequence, to the summit without returning to the ground, whether chased off El Capitan by weather, injuries, fatigue or moral defeat.

On Monday, Caldwell wrote on his Facebook page, he had navigated Pitch 16, the "dyno," by circling around one portion that Jorgeson plans to tackle by leaping horizontally, body off the wall for a moment, and catching himself with his fingers and toes.

Jorgeson is not there yet. After two days of struggle on the sideways traverse of Pitch 15, he took Monday to rest and let his split fingertips heal. The dry, cold conditions are good for gripping, but fingers take a beating. Between attempts, climbers sand their fingers to remove the dead skin, and they apply lotion to them several times a day. (Caldwell's left hand is missing half of an index finger, severed by a saw accident years ago.)

Between climbs, they are captive in their camp. Each has a compact stove to heat meals and boil water. Making the climb in winter, where the temperatures have risen to 50 degrees during the day and fallen well below freezing at night, is ideal for more than climbing; it solves any refrigeration issues.

A few days ago, Caldwell posted a photograph on Twitter of a sandwich he was eating: salami, cucumber and avocado on a bagel.

Each has a toilet—essentially a bag with deodorizers, placed inside another bag.

Most of the climbing is done in the late afternoon and evening, when the temperatures are cool and the sun does not beat on the rock and cause sweaty hands and slippery soles. That leaves a lot of downtime for plotting the next advance, reading, texting, updating social media and talking on the phone. (The wall of El Capitan, inexplicably, might have the best cell reception in the Yosemite Valley.) Phones and electronic devices are charged by portable solar panels. The men usually put their phones in "airplane" mode to help save the battery.

Being stuck on the side of El Capitan can be both freeing and confining—not unlike a lazy day on the couch, minus the cold, the occasionally brutal winds, the periodic chunks of ice that fall like meteors and the stress of preparing to continue one of the great climbing expeditions.

That is why they do so-called ledge yoga, performing poses to stay limber. For as much exhilaration as the men get from climbing, and as much downtime they have between surges, there is one thing they desperately miss from the horizontal world that many might not imagine: a place to take a few steps and merely walk.

III. ABDUCTION. LOST FINGER. NOW, THE TALLEST HURDLE.

Whatever part inside of Tommy Caldwell that made him attempt the seemingly impossible—a free climb of El Capitan's Dawn Wall—might have been born in 2000 when he and three others were kidnapped by militants while climbing in the Pamir-Alai range of Kyrgyzstan. They escaped after six days on the run when Caldwell shoved an armed guard over a cliff.

Or it might have come shortly after, when Caldwell severed his left index finger with a table saw during a home renovation.

As with a concert pianist or a surgeon, the index finger is a useful digit for a world-class rock climber, and some worried that Caldwell's career was over.

Instead, his biggest climbs have been performed with nine fingers.

But to his parents, Caldwell was hard-wired against giving up from the beginning.

"As a kid, he'd draw a dragon, and he wouldn't draw just one," Mike Caldwell, Tommy's father, said from his home in Estes Park, Colorado. "He'd draw twenty, and they'd look almost identical. He once dug a hole so darn big, we could have used it as a foundation for a small house."

Tommy was three when Mike, a climber himself, attached a rope to his son and led him up the 200-foot Twin Owls formation in Rocky Mountain National Park, winning him over with the promise of flying a kite at the top. (They tried, but it was too windy.)

Tommy Caldwell is thirty-six now. For more than a week, he and his climbing partner, Kevin Jorgeson, have been scaling the Dawn Wall, trying what some believe is the hardest rock climb in the world. On Tuesday night, Caldwell completed the last of the trickiest sections, Pitch 16, giving him a clear shot toward the top, while Jorgeson continued to struggle to complete the sideways traverse of Pitch 15 and was saddled with battered fingers.

The question increasingly becomes whether Caldwell waits for his partner or continues upward, hoping Jorgeson catches up with him later. Caldwell called the day "bittersweet," adding, "Let's all send Kevin good skin healing vibes."

But while this push began on December 27, when the two men last touched the floor of Yosemite Valley, it took root nearly a decade ago. The Dawn Wall, so named because its sheer face catches the morning sun, was first climbed in 1970 by Warren Harding and Dean Caldwell (no relation to Tommy). They drilled hundreds of bolts and pulled themselves up ropes to reach the top.

The idea of free climbing the 3,000-foot rock formation—to use nothing but hands and feet to move upward, relying on ropes only to stop falls and pull equipment—was thought to be virtually impossible. Caldwell thrives on the virtually impossible.

"I have a very distinct goal all the time that I'm working toward, and I love the way it makes me live," Caldwell said Sunday from the mid-cliff camp that he and Jorgeson have, 1,200 feet up El Capitan. "Most of the days of the year I wake up with this on my mind, thinking, What am I going to do today to get one step closer? It gets me outside every day in the mountains in beautiful places, pushing myself. It makes me live at a higher level, having this as part of my life."

When he first considered the Dawn Wall, Caldwell and his wife at the time, the professional climber Beth Rodden, rappelled its vertical face, exploring if it could be free climbed despite its featureless surface.

That he is still working on it ten years later does not surprise Rodden.

"I'd say, 'That kind of sounds like Tommy,'" Rodden said Tuesday.

Caldwell had plenty of rocks to climb while growing up in Estes Park, at the edge of Rocky Mountain National Park, and his parents, Mike and Terry, were supportive of his pursuits. When Caldwell was seventeen, he went to watch a national sport-climbing competition in Utah. He entered the amateur contest and won it, earning a spot in the main event the next day. He won that, too. Sponsors called, and he has been a professional climber since.

"He went from diddly squat to red hot in one day," said Mike, now a retired middle school teacher working as an outdoors guide, from snowshoeing to fly-fishing. "You tend to enjoy things that you're good at. Unfortunately, Tommy became good at something that was totally impractical."

He has built a résumé of first ascents since, including many on El Capitan. He was one of National Geographic's adventurers of the year for 2014–15, recognized as "arguably the best all-around rock climber on the planet." In February, he and Alex Honnold conquered the seven razor-edge summits of Patagonia's Fitz Roy massif in four days.

Still, he receives less mainstream attention than climbers like Honnold, who is known for his free-solo (no safety rope) pursuits, and Chris Sharma, with his combination of first ascents and surfer good looks.

Caldwell is the understated sort, about 5 feet 9 inches and 150 pounds, with a big-toothed grin and a sneaky sense of humor. He does not stand out in a crowd unless that crowd is full of climbers, who know exactly who he is.

"He's definitely not this showy, big-ego guy," Rodden said. "But he's one of the most influential climbers of our time. He just keeps on pushing the limit in all these different realms."

Rodden was Caldwell's girlfriend when they, along with John Dickey and Jason Smith, were climbing in Kyrgyzstan. Rebels from the Islamic Movement of Uzbekistan kidnapped them, then spent days shepherding them through the mountains while caught in gunfire-filled chases with the Kyrgyzstan army.

As first detailed in an *Outside* magazine article by Greg Child, the group did not expect to survive. But when they found themselves hiking with just one armed guard, they saw an opportunity. Caldwell grabbed the soldier by the gun slung over his shoulder and shoved him over a cliff, presumably to his death.

The tale became international news—the group, for a time, declined to name which of them had pushed the guard—and some debated its accuracy. The guard was later found alive, and he confirmed the story.

The episode haunted Caldwell. Mike Caldwell recalled that when Tommy was a young wrestler, he nearly had a boy pinned, but let the opponent win after the boy started to cry. As a swimmer, he sometimes slowed down to let others pass him, if he thought it meant more to them to win.

The thought that he had killed someone, even a captor, was nearly too much to bear.

"It's still a huge part of him," Mike Caldwell said. "For the first year after that, Tommy was almost nonverbal, he was so shaken by it. We couldn't do anything offbeat enough to get his mind off it. Then the information came that the guy survived. That totally changed Tommy, that he didn't kill somebody."

Friends close to Caldwell say his ability to endure suffering is legendary, and part of that probably stems from what he and the others endured in Kyrgyzstan. Obstacles in climbing cannot compare.

"When he's up on a wall, it's almost first nature to him," said Rebecca Caldwell, Caldwell's wife since 2010. "The first time I was with him on a wall, I was like, 'You're almost more natural up here than you are on the ground.' He is so comfortable in places where most people would be entirely uncomfortable."

In 2008, the filmmaker Josh Lowell was working on a climbing movie called *Progression*. He asked Caldwell if he had any big ascents in the works.

"He said, 'There is one thing: I've started playing around on the Dawn Wall,'" Lowell recalled. "'I still don't know if it's possible.'"

The film, released in 2009, included a sequence of Caldwell's quest to eventually free climb the Dawn Wall. Jorgeson, a climber from Santa

Rosa, California, saw the film and was struck by the quest. He contacted Caldwell and asked if he wanted a partner.

It has been their undertaking since, devouring much of their time and effort.

A 2010 attempt was aborted because of storms. In 2011, Jorgeson broke his ankle in a fall on the Dawn Wall. Caldwell continued, using others on belay, including his wife and his father, but could not get past Pitch 14, perhaps the hardest section of the climb.

"His third year on it, he said if it doesn't happen this time, this is it," Rebecca said. "Then he came down at the end of the season and said, 'I think I'm going to go back.'"

No one was surprised. The next two autumns, Caldwell and Jorgeson continued scouting the climb, mapping sequences and practicing individual pitches.

In November Caldwell successfully navigated Pitch 14 for the first time.

"Oh my goodness!!!" Caldwell wrote on Facebook on November 18. "After six years I finally sent this beast of a pitch. Inspired by Kevin's fight to the death near miss. This officially means all the hard individual pitches have been redpointed. I am so psyched my hands are shaking!"

Energized and optimistic, determined to string all thirty-two pitches together in one push, the climbers waited for a favorable long-range forecast, a couple of weeks of dry, cool weather. It came in late December. Caldwell left Rebecca and their twenty-month-old son, Fitz, and returned to Yosemite.

Fitz, too, is growing up in Estes Park, with a father who tries to show him that mountains are obstacles, meant to be conquered.

"I am always thinking about the kind of dad I want to be," Caldwell wrote on Facebook, posting a photograph of him hugging Fitz. "I know that the best way to teach is to show by example. For me the Dawn Wall is the perfect venue for some of the most important values I want to show

Fitz. Optimism, perseverance, dedication and the importance of dream-
ing big. But leaving Becca and Fitz at home is never easy. I love you guys!"

Should Caldwell and Jorgeson finish the Dawn Wall, it will
cement their status in climbing lore. But Rebecca Caldwell wondered
if the exhilaration might be mixed with emptiness. Her husband, who
called the Dawn Wall his Moby Dick, admitted to wondering the same
thing.

"I'm a little bit worried what's going to happen if we do this because
it'll be like the end of a big long relationship, you know?" Caldwell said.

He laughed. The horizontal world was 1,200 feet below. Another
1,800 feet of El Capitan granite soared overhead.

"Hopefully I'll be able to fly high for a few months, and then figure
out something," he said. "Through climbing I've learned to find goals
and work toward them. That's just the way I love to live. This is just an
especially big and long one of those goals."

IV. AFTER BRUTAL TRAVERSE, CLIMBER LOOKS UPWARD

About two hundred miles away from Yosemite Valley and El Capitan,
Jacqui Becker got a text message and a photo from her boyfriend, the
climber Kevin Jorgeson. The photo was of him smiling in front of a wall
of granite. The text announced that he was not stopping now.

"I'm not holding this train up," Jorgeson wrote.

Jorgeson and Tommy Caldwell are trying to become the first people to free climb El Capitan's Dawn Wall. For six days, though, Jorgeson
could not get past Pitch 15, a brutally difficult sideways traverse with
almost nothing to hold.

Caldwell was already through twenty of the route's thirty-two
pitches, including all the most difficult ones. He could not wait indef-

initely. The climbers had reached a now-or-never point in their years-long partnership to reach the top.

On Friday, now won.

Jorgeson, desperate to reach the summit after six years of work detailing and practicing the route, with his fingers battered by the sharp rocks, clipped his safety rope into a fixed bolt after making it across Pitch 15 on Friday afternoon. A cheer rose from the small crowd in a meadow below El Capitan, about 1,500 feet below.

Jorgeson soon sent a text to Becker. Full of adrenaline, he joked that he would climb straight to the Wino Tower, at the top of Pitch 20, pulling even with Caldwell.

If nothing else, Jorgeson's success brought relief to the expedition, and settled, for now, any uncomfortable questions about how long Caldwell would wait before moving to the summit by himself.

Pitches 14 and 15 were rated as the two most difficult parts of the climb, with matching 5.14d grades—meaning they are among the toughest in the world to climb without aid. (Free climbing means to climb upward only with hands and feet, using ropes and equipment solely as safety devices.)

When Caldwell and Jorgeson breezed through the lower sections of the ascent after starting on December 27, then completed Pitch 14 on January 1, they celebrated with announcements on social media.

"Tonight, I sent the hardest pitch of my life and the hardest on the Dawn Wall!" Jorgeson wrote on his Facebook page. "Best of all, Tommy sent right after me! Pitch 14 (the first traverse) is in the bag!"

But Pitch 15, about 70 feet of horizontal sidestepping across a stripe of pinkish granite, became Jorgeson's albatross.

"There are tiny little holds, but they're far apart and facing different directions," said Josh Lowell, a filmmaker who has been chronicling the pair's attempts at the Dawn Wall for several years. "Some you grab in awkward ways, sometimes barely by your fingertips, sometimes cocking your wrist in weird angles."

The route goes that way because the rock is too smooth above and below it. The stripe has just enough of a sandpaper texture to cling to. The holds can be as sharp as razor blades.

During Jorgeson's run of difficulties, Caldwell tried to explain just how difficult the task was. On his Facebook page, he called the Pitch 15 traverse "some of the smallest and sharpest holds I have ever attempted to hold onto. It's crazy to think that the skin on our fingertips could be the limiting fact towards success or failure."

The men sand and file their fingers at night, and set an alarm so they can apply lotion every few hours.

Jorgeson failed in three tries at Pitch 15 last Saturday, and was unsuccessful on several more nights during the week, between days when he rested to allow his fingers to heal. One post showed his battered fingers as he tried to grip the rock.

"On my 4th attempt, around 11 pm, the razor sharp holds ripped both the tape and the skin right off my fingers," Jorgeson wrote Thursday night. "As disappointing as this is, I'm learning new levels of patience, perseverance and desire. I'm not giving up. I will rest. I will try again. I will succeed."

In making it past Pitch 15 on Friday afternoon, Jorgeson split one finger in five places. But he immediately moved on to Pitch 16, rated 5.14c, with a "dyno" crux—a move requiring the climber to leap sideways several feet to the left to an out-of-reach hold.

He managed that acrobatic maneuver but fell before completing the pitch, which turns straight upward. He said late Friday that he planned to start the pitch at the beginning on Saturday, to try to complete it in one attempt even though the unwritten rules of climbing would allow him to restart from after the dyno because he had reached a perch where he could stand without using his hands.

"My plan is to try to repeat the dyno," he said in a message late Friday, with a photograph of his bloodied hands. "But if it doesn't go quickly, I will probably take it from the stance in order to minimize further damage to the body. It's a violent move."

Caldwell had made it past Pitches 15 and 16 earlier in the week—climbing a longer route down and around the sideways "dyno" move. He did Pitches 17 and 18 one night, and 19 and 20 to reach the Wino Tower, a rare ledge on the face, on Thursday. Then, two climbing days from the top, he waited for Jorgeson.

It was unclear how long he would wait. Had Jorgeson not succeeded on Friday, it is possible that the two would have agreed for Caldwell to move forward alone.

That could still happen, depending on Jorgeson's fortunes as he tries to catch up. But Jorgeson's family and friends in Santa Rosa, California, are ready to come to Yosemite to meet him at the end of his long climb. It is not over yet.

V. CLIMBER YEARNS FOR THE SUMMIT, AND A SHOWER

Inside Kevin Jorgeson's living room, his smiling, bearded face popped up on the screen. His hair, two weeks since a shampoo, stuck straight up.

He spoke as if it were just an ordinary day and an ordinary circumstance.

He said hello to his girlfriend, Jacqui Becker, and his mother, Gaelena Jorgeson. But his eyes shifted uneasily as his portaledge, a hanging tent hooked halfway up El Capitan, lifted and swayed in Sunday's gusty winds.

In a few days, he hoped, he would be home through the front door, not through FaceTime.

Jorgeson, thirty, and his climbing partner, Tommy Caldwell, thirty-six, are trying to become the first to free climb El Capitan's Dawn Wall, a 3,000-foot vertical route of barely dimpled granite in Yosemite National Park.

After it happens, or even if it does not, Jorgeson will return here. He was born and raised in Santa Rosa, about an hour's drive north of San Francisco, four hours to the heart of Yosemite. He has a deep family connection there; a great-grandmother worked for the concessionaire in Yosemite a century ago, and the family has a photograph of her standing on the famed "diving board" atop Yosemite's Half Dome in 1916. (She hiked, not climbed, in a skirt.)

Jorgeson showed an early aptitude for climbing. His parents learned that when their toddler seemed to vanish, they should look up. At three, he climbed most of a two-story ladder at an aunt's house before he was spotted. As he grew older, he often disappeared into the garage rafters or was found atop the chain-link backstop at a baseball field.

"It probably scared other parents more than us," his father, Eric, said.

Eric Jorgeson worked for Santa Rosa's Recreation and Parks Department and had a love for the outdoors that he passed on to Kevin and his younger brother, Matt. Kevin Jorgeson's first exposure to climbing came at a wall inside a Santa Rosa sporting goods store. When Vertex Climbing Center opened shortly after, when Jorgeson was about eleven, his father gave both boys beginning lessons.

"It got him hooked," said Eric Jorgeson, who, divorced from Gaelena and remarried, now lives in Idaho. "And it told me that it wasn't the sport for me. But it got him through the teenage years without any of the typical teenage problems."

By sixteen, he was competing in international climbing contests and had his first sponsorship, from Marmot, the outdoor apparel and equipment maker based near Santa Rosa in Rohnert Park. He took his wall-climbing pursuits outdoors.

Jorgeson became one of the world's best at "highball" bouldering, which features extremely difficult, relatively short ropeless climbs. He was the first to ascend Ambrosia, near Bishop, California, one of his favorite climbing areas.

Beyond his physical abilities, Jorgeson seems wired for climbing blank faces of rock, where precision and patience are as important as strength and flexibility.

"It's a mental thing—he's really good at memorizing sequences," his father said, recalling Jorgeson's ability to rehearse taekwondo moves or the best moves down a river in a kayak. "I bet after this climb, if you sat with him and said, 'What's the fifth move on Pitch 12?' he could tell you. That may be an exaggeration, but he probably could do it for Pitch 15."

Yes, Pitch 15. Should Jorgeson complete the free-climb ascent in the coming days, his struggle with the sideways traverse of Pitch 15 will be the heart of the story.

"I'll always remember that battle," he said.

Over the course of a week, he fell on ten attempts, always on the same spot, shredding the skin from his battered fingers as he clung desperately, and vainly, to sharp, pebble-size holds on the wall. Caldwell made it past Pitch 15 and continued checking off pitches up the wall as Jorgeson lagged behind.

After Jorgeson failed on several attempts in the middle of last week, he texted one word to Becker, his girlfriend: "Devastated." His next text said he did not want to be known as the man who almost climbed the Dawn Wall.

He rested his fingers, waiting for his skin to heal over two days, before embarking on another attempt on Friday afternoon. In the back of his mind, he knew that if he failed again, he would most likely end his quest in deference to Caldwell.

"That would have been my call," Jorgeson said Sunday. "It definitely crossed my mind briefly, but I didn't linger there too long. Answering that question wasn't going to help me."

He added, "I'm not going to lie. I did feel a lot of pressure that day."

By then, Jorgeson had studied footage of each of his failures—how he pinched the rock on this hold, how he cocked his wrist on that one. He found that each fall had to do with a single foot placement.

"A millimeter change in the angle of my right foot on the exact same piece of rock," Jorgeson said. "Before, it didn't match the contour of this tiny little pebble I was trying to step on."

It worked.

"It clicked," he said. "I reached this balance where I could do this pivotal move and unlock the next sequence."

Jorgeson made it past Pitch 15 as a crowd in the El Capitan meadow cheered in the chilly twilight. By Saturday night, he was through Pitch 17. After a rest day on Sunday, he reached the top of Pitch 20 on Monday, pulling alongside Caldwell on the ledge of the Wino Tower.

From there, the final dozen pitches, extremely difficult by rock-climbing standards but not as difficult as what Caldwell and Jorgeson have completed, might be done in two days of climbing.

And then Jorgeson will come home.

"A shower," he said of the first thing he wants after more than two weeks hanging on El Capitan. "There's so many things. I can't let my head go there yet, though."

Jorgeson and Becker met at a resort in Anguilla three years ago. Jorgeson knew the manager, who had an opening for a fitness and climbing instructor. Becker was living in New York and teaching hula-hoop lessons as an executive for a fitness company. Friends called them "Hoops and Rocks."

Jorgeson contradicts the "dirtbag" reputation of climbing, showing that the sport's credibility need not stem, in part, from a vagabond, grungy devotion.

Becker quickly recognized that Jorgeson was different from any stereotype. "We had a meeting with clients, and he was dressed up and sophisticated and had a killer taste in whiskey," she said. "It caught my attention."

Part climber, part businessman, he started a company called Pro Climbers International to represent climbers and expand the sport through training, workshops and events.

But there were times in the past few years, as he devoted months to the Dawn Wall, that Jorgeson wondered whether he was being selfish—spending too much time on an individual goal and not enough doing things that would promote the broader climbing community.

As it turned out, the Dawn Wall push in the past couple of weeks, and the attention it received, forwarded both goals more than he had imagined.

The idea of free climbing the Dawn Wall—using only hands and feet to move upward, relying on ropes only in case of falls—belonged to Caldwell, dating back a decade. In 2009, Jorgeson asked if he wanted a partner.

Since then, for several months each fall and winter, Jorgeson has been consumed by the task of the Dawn Wall when he could have been expanding his business. Both men admitted that it often dominated their daily lives, filling their thoughts when they woke and keeping them awake at night.

Two years ago, after a seventeen-year wait, Eric Jorgeson finally received a permit to raft through the Grand Canyon on the Colorado River. Kevin Jorgeson anguished over whether to go with his father or meet Caldwell at the Dawn Wall. He eventually chose the nineteen-day raft trip, afraid he was letting Caldwell down.

The quest has taken an emotional toll, not only from the implausibility of the pursuit but also from the loss of friends to climbing over the years. Most haunting to Jorgeson was the loss of Brad Parker, a top climber also from Santa Rosa, who fell to his death in Yosemite in August.

Jorgeson had a deep conversation with Caldwell about it in September, and Caldwell opened up about the hurdles he had faced—a kidnapping in Kyrgyzstan and a divorce among them. Jorgeson committed to at least another year on the project. Maybe the next attempt would be the one.

In August, Jorgeson and Becker rented a small house outside Santa Rosa. A pair of sheep live in a field outside, and a seventeen-year-old cat, Monkey, clambers about inside. The living room includes Jorgeson's childhood piano, a wood-burning fireplace, hula hoops and a large mirror used as a message board. ("House needs" include four stools, a kitchen island and "art for walls.")

They considered moving to more familiar climbing meccas— Caldwell lives in Estes Park, Colorado, at the doorstep of Rocky Mountain National Park—but Jorgeson preferred to be close to home, within reach of the ocean.

While there are no rocks to climb within view of his home, his quiet getaway is less than an hour away—the above-the-ocean climbs of Goat Rock at Sonoma Coast State Park. His post-climb plans with Becker include swing dance lessons, furnishing the house and a trip to Europe.

Those must wait. Jorgeson is still a bit tied up.

"This is pretty awesome to watch," Gaelena Jorgeson said to her son on Sunday. He was hanging on El Capitan; she was hanging out in his house. "You're awesome."

He smiled through a shaggy beard. He said he would see everyone soon.

VI. PURSUING THE IMPOSSIBLE, AND COMING OUT ON TOP

On the nineteenth day of their climb, Tommy Caldwell and Kevin Jorgeson, both now bearded, reached the summit of El Capitan's Dawn Wall, completing a quest that included years of planning and that many considered the most challenging rock climb in the world.

Dozens of family members and friends greeted the climbers when they reached the top at 3:25 p.m. Wednesday, a cloudless day. After Caldwell hugged his wife and Jorgeson hugged his girlfriend, they were given sparkling wine. Jorgeson sprayed his. "That's the first shower you've had in a while," Caldwell's wife, Rebecca, said.

Jorgeson said of their feat, "I hope it inspires people to find their own Dawn Wall, if you will. We've been working on this thing a long time, slowly and surely. I think everyone has their own secret Dawn Wall to complete one day, and maybe they can put this project in their own context."

It was the first ascent of the 3,000-foot Dawn Wall in a single expedition with the use of only hands and feet to pull climbers up—a challenge long considered impossible. Ropes were merely safety devices to break the occasional fall.

The sunset view at the top was stunning. What was less clear was just what Caldwell and Jorgeson had achieved.

El Capitan is hardly unassailable. Its face was first rock-climbed in 1958, and it has been crisscrossed by countless climbers using roughly one hundred known routes. With its summit a mere 7,569 feet above sea level, it is no Everest or Denali. Thousands of visitors from around the world hike the eight steep miles to its top each year, including several who left before daybreak Wednesday to greet the climbers.

But that was part of what made this expedition monumental—El Capitan's familiarity. It is one of the best-known pieces of granite in the world, majestic and monolithic, causing crane-necked, open-mouthed gawkers to stand at its base and drivers in Yosemite Valley to veer off the road.

That accessibility was key to building fascination with the quest.

"I think the larger audience's conception is that we're thrill-seekers out there for an adrenaline rush," Caldwell said. "We really aren't at all. It's about spending our lives in these beautiful places and forming these incredible bonds."

The entire climb was visible to anyone who wanted to watch through binoculars or long camera lenses while standing in a nearby meadow. And in recent days the assembly grew, some bringing camp chairs and nibbling on meats and cheeses, as history unfolded high above. From the wall, the climbers communicated through text messages and social media. Fans cheered success, and the climbers could hear it a moment later.

That was the magic that turned the quiet quest of two quiet men into a worldwide spectacle—an event both unimaginable and watchable. There was no mystery, but there was plenty of suspense.

"This is just amazing, really beautifully amazing, like a four-minute mile or a sub-two-hour marathon or Tiger Woods destroying every single major for a year or something, just off the charts awesome," Will Gadd, an elite mountain sports athlete, said in an email message Tuesday.

For Caldwell, a thirty-six-year-old from Estes Park, Colorado, it was a goal that he could not shake since he first seriously conjured the idea a decade ago. It became his life-bending quest, a personal Moby-Dick. Could every inch of the blank, vertical face of the Dawn Wall be climbed with nothing more than bare hands and rubber-soled shoes? He was not sure. He never was, really, until Wednesday.

"From the outside it was starting to look like a Hemingway novel or something, an unresolvable quest," said Gadd, who has known Caldwell for many years.

Jorgeson, thirty, from Santa Rosa, California, learned about Caldwell's vision in 2009 and asked if he wanted a partner. Each year since, the two have spent weeks and months, mostly in the fall and winter, attached to the Dawn Wall, scouting holds, practicing pitches, imagining how to do it all in one push from the valley floor.

El Capitan is the height of three Empire State Buildings stacked atop one another, but with many fewer, and smaller, things to hold on to on the way up. The climb is divided into thirty-two pitches, or sections, like way points on a dot-to-dot drawing. When one pitch was successfully navigated, the climbers stopped and prepared for the next. Much of the work was done in the cool of the evening, when hands would sweat less and the soles of their shoes had better grip.

Some pitches were well over 100 feet straight up the rock, while others were sideways shuffles to connect two vertical pitches. One required a dyno, a jump from one precarious hold to another. Falls were not unusual; Jorgeson needed seven days and ten attempts to navigate the horizontal traverse of Pitch 15, unexpectedly slowing the expedition, which was blessed by an uncharacteristic stretch of dry weather.

Two pitches were rated at 5.14d on climbing's scale of difficulty, making them among the hardest sections of rock ever climbed. Nearly all were rated at least 5.12. To many rock climbers, completing one such pitch would be a career highlight. Few can fathom the difficulty of stringing together nearly three dozen of them without returning to the ground.

The Dawn Wall, sometimes called the Wall of the Early Morning Light, was first climbed in 1970 by Warren Harding and Dean Caldwell (no relation to Tommy). But their ascent was a virtual siege, using more than 300 bolts and hundreds of feet of rope to pull themselves up over twenty-seven days.

Storms pinned them to the wall for long stretches, but the men refused rescue attempts, dropping notes to the valley floor and, at one

point, greeting would-be rescuers on the wall with an offer of wine. When the men reached the top, they were greeted by a crowd of seventy and enjoyed champagne and fried chicken.

Their assault was widely criticized by those in the climbing community who preferred a quieter, more minimalist ascent. Royal Robbins, a rival of Harding's, went up the Dawn Wall and cut many of the bolts sprinkled up the rock.

Few, if any, thought the Dawn Wall could be free climbed, using just strength and guile—not ropes and equipment—for upward propulsion. Earlier attempts by Caldwell and Jorgeson had been aborted by bad weather, injuries and an inability to get past certain pitches.

Not this time.

When Harding reached the top of the Dawn Wall in 1970, he was asked why he had done it and said, "Because we're insane!"

Why did Caldwell and Jorgeson do it?

"For me, I love to dream big, and I love to find ways to be a bit of an explorer," Caldwell said. "These days it seems like everything is padded and comes with warning labels. This just lights a fire under me, and that's a really exciting way to live."

Jorgeson said the Dawn Wall "was the biggest canvas and the most audacious project I could join and see to the finish."

"Like Tommy," he added, "I don't know what is next."

After a summit celebration, they were eager to return to the valley floor for a bigger celebration, and the chance to soak in both a warm shower and whatever adulation awaited once they returned to the view of anyone who wanted to watch.

Soon, they would be back over the edge, headed down, and the top of El Capitan was alone and quiet again.

POSTSCRIPT: *The last of these stories, published over 10 days, was filed from the top of El Capitan as a swarm of television trucks clogged the valley floor below. The climb was the subject of a critically acclaimed documentary, The Dawn Wall. Caldwell and Jorgeson continue to climb and raise families. In the five years since their achievement, only one other climber has repeated it: Adam Ondra, the subject of a long story I wrote in 2020.*

3

LOST BROTHER

Yosemite National Park, California

fternoon gave way to evening, and the parade of restless clouds and the occasional bursts of rain had moved on from Yosemite Valley. In their wake was the empty quiet of Taft Point, 3,000 feet above a famous green valley going gray in late-day shadow.

There were no tourists, only a raven, black and unhurried, circling at the edge of the cliff. It spiraled upward, a silent signal of rising air. A good sign for BASE jumping and wingsuit flying.

Dean Potter, a forty-three-year-old professional climber and jumper, considered one of the world's best in a wingsuit, stood a few feet from Graham Hunt, twenty-nine, his apprentice and flying partner.

About 20 feet to their right was Jen Rapp, Potter's longtime girlfriend, and the couple's dog, Whisper. Rapp held a camera. She framed the photos so that El Capitan, across the valley toward the setting sun, was in the background.

BASE jumping is illegal in the national parks. But that does not keep people from surreptitiously doing it, at the risk of being caught, especially in Yosemite, where the sheer cliffs make it the best place on the planet to do it, some believe.

"Anywhere else you go is a compromise," Potter would say.

The men had jumped from dozens of spots around Yosemite Valley, but they knew this route well. At the end of a 1.1-mile downhill trail from a small parking lot on Glacier Point Road, Taft Point is marked by a railing meant to keep tourists from falling. Potter and Hunt preferred to jump from an edge about 100 yards left, to the west. They would drop hundreds of feet with their arms and legs spread, the webbing between their limbs and the baffles inside their suits filling with air until falling turned to soaring.

They would fly right, toward the heart of the valley. There is a sloping rib of a ridge there, a relatively unremarkable feature called Lost Brother. It is not marked on the park maps handed to visitors. It juts downward into the valley before it ends abruptly into a vertical wall known mostly to climbers. In that ridge is a notch, a V like a rifle sight.

Potter and Hunt had made the jump many times, sometimes together, sometimes not. Hunt had done it without Potter several days before. He would usually steer himself through the notch. Potter had been through the notch a couple of times, but he usually went around the ridge to the left. It depended on how well they maintained altitude once they began to fly.

The men were zipped into their suits. They did not wait for the full cloak of dusk. A breeze from behind caught their attention but did not send a strong enough warning to pause. It was 7:25 on May 16.

YOSEMITE'S BASE-JUMPING CULTURE

"I don't mind if I'm on the record," Potter wrote in an email in March, discussing the decades-long fight to legalize BASE jumping within National Park Service sites, and especially at Yosemite, with its unique valley of sheer cliffs.

"I've been flying in the park since 2003 and the NPS knows it, but they haven't been able to catch me or prove anything," he added.

Potter offered a tour of the BASE jumping culture at Yosemite, allowing himself to be captured on video leaping, illegally, from the cliffs at dusk or dawn and landing before being detected.

"There are at least 10 local guys who are regularly BASE jumping in Yosemite and probably 50 to 100 others annually traveling to Yosemite from around the world to experience the birthplace of big-wall BASE," he wrote.

Potter knew the long history of enforcement at Yosemite. Robin Heid was arrested and charged with jumping off El Capitan in 1979, which helped lead to a midsummer trial run for legal parachuting there in 1980, aborted after six weeks of unruliness. BASE jumping took hold in the global extreme sports culture of the 1990s, and stories of Yosemite rangers hiding in trees and using night-vision goggles became legend.

In 1999, Frank Gambalie drowned in the Merced River after trying to escape rangers. Months later, in a protest of park policy and enforcement, Jan Davis fell to her death from El Capitan without her parachute ever opening; she wore a borrowed rig, not wanting her own gear confiscated. In 2010, Ammon McNeely was caught and subdued with a stun gun.

In between, dozens have been arrested, jailed and subjected to thousands of dollars in fines and have had their gear confiscated. Several have gone to court to challenge the National Park Service rules banning the activity, ultimately to no avail.

It made no sense to Potter, and plenty of others, that climbing was legal, and that falling was legal, but that stopping a fall with a lifesaving parachute was illegal, a result of the application of an arcane law banning the delivery or retrieval "of a person or object by parachute, helicopter or other airborne means."

But it was 2015. Potter was hopeful. He believed he could be both renegade and diplomat.

"The NPS and the law enforcement have changed a lot in the past

year or two," Potter wrote in March. "Most all of the lead positions in the park service are now held by people who either don't have a huge problem with BASE or are quite lenient when it comes to catching and prosecuting jumpers. For sure the rangers enforce the law. If they see us, they pursue, but for the most part, they are not hunting us as before and there seems to be a lot more respect on both sides."

A sport that began as a rebel offshoot of sky diving had evolved into a popular and respected derivative of rock climbing. Places in Switzerland, Norway and Italy welcomed BASE jumpers. And Yosemite, the best place—maybe the safest place, with its vertical cliffs and grassy landing areas—had only six known BASE jumping deaths in its history, and none since 1999, despite thousands of jumps since.

INTO THE DUSKY VALLEY

Potter jumped. Hunt followed, like a shadow. Rapp clicked photographs. The men fell out of the frame before her lens caught them falling away, soaring with wings spread.

Hunt quickly passed Potter. His suit was made for speed. Potter had set records for long flights and preferred loft. He had been in Canada working on a design to allow him to land on his belly on glacial ice, no parachute necessary.

"He's low," Rapp thought to herself. "Why is he going toward the notch?" She saw Hunt veer left, as if to go around the ridge, then quickly back to the right. Potter held his line for the notch. They disappeared into the hole that led to the dusky valley.

Rapp heard a thwap. Her mind tried to tell her that it was the familiar sound of a parachute deploying. It was followed almost immediately by a duller, heavier sound.

Rapp waited alone on the cliff's edge for more clues from below. None came.

She clicked through her camera to retrace the flight paths in the photos. In two dimensions, without depth perception, it was hard to tell what had happened to the shrinking specks in the frames. There was Hunt, who disappeared into the grayness of the rocks. There was Potter, who made it through the leading edge of the notch, a downward halfpipe, and fell out of sight.

Somewhere far below was Rebecca Haynie, Hunt's girlfriend of a few months. She had been on a hike when Hunt called saying that he and Potter planned to jump at Taft Point. Meet at the meadow at 7:30, Hunt said. She aborted her hike and went to the lodge area in Yosemite Valley to get a drink and pass the time.

She did not see a text message that Hunt sent at 6:55 until about 7:25 because of spotty cellular service in Yosemite. He had asked her to turn on her two-way radio so they could communicate. She quickly texted back that she would in a few minutes. She drove around the darkening, forested roads for ninety minutes, waiting to hear from Hunt again.

"I was putting my faith in a lot of irrational places," she said. "Even though I knew what probably happened."

In the dwindling light, Rapp rushed back up the trail to the parking lot. She drove her car the thirteen miles or so back to Wawona Road, made a right and headed the ten miles down to the floor of the valley.

She went to El Capitan Meadow, but there was no one there. Her phone had no text messages. Unsure of what to do or where to go, she drove to the rented house that she and Potter shared in Yosemite West, a cluster of homes back up Wawona Road, past the Glacier Point turn-off. The couple had recently bought thirty-one acres nearby and had plans to build their own home. That day, rainy and cool, had been spent clearing trees and brush, and Hunt was there to help, until the clearing skies led to the idea of making an evening jump off Taft Point.

The house was dark and empty. Mind racing, Rapp studied the photos and scrolled through various outcomes in her head. Maybe the sounds she heard were Hunt crashing. Maybe Potter saw it happen and was searching for his friend. Maybe Potter crashed and was hurt. Maybe they were both OK but were hiding from rangers. Maybe they had been arrested.

Her mind was a tug of war with hope. Maybe they would pull up to the house any minute. A car came at 9:30. Out stepped Haynie. She was alone.

DISCOURAGING THE SPECTACLE

A little more than a year earlier, in March 2014, one of Potter's best friends and flying partners, Sean Leary, was killed BASE jumping at Utah's Zion National Park. It was only the second known BASE jumping death at Zion, but the first had come just over a month earlier.

Leary, alone, had apparently jumped off a sandstone tower called West Temple and tried to fly through a gap in the Three Marys, a set of statue-like formations resembling chess pieces. Leary was missing for days, and Potter was among those who rushed to Zion to help find him.

Potter and a few other climbers reached Leary's body, but the park service would not allow them to bring it down. Rangers packaged the body, and a helicopter, borrowed from Grand Canyon National Park, lifted it out.

"There are places within the United States that one can BASE jump, but not in Zion," the park's then-superintendent said in a news release. "There are many reasons for this, from resource protection, to visitor and employee safety, to Wilderness mandates. BASE jumping is not congruent with the founding purpose of this park."

Ray O'Neal, a longtime ranger at Zion, said that the problem with BASE jumping in national parks was not necessarily one of safety or rescue costs, as many jumpers presume.

"The reason we would like to discourage it is not so much because of the danger of it, but the spectacle of it," O'Neal said at the park's Emergency Operations Center. "We like to think that people come here to enjoy the scenery, and not the spectacle of people jumping."

Scott Gediman, a Yosemite park spokesman, agreed. On average, fourteen Yosemite visitors die each year—from falls or drownings, car accidents or natural causes. Rarely are they BASE jumpers.

"We're not against BASE jumping as a sport," Gediman said while sitting on a bench at Yosemite, where a rappelling accident had killed a climber the day before. "But we have to look at the big picture and its appropriateness in the park."

The frustration for Potter and other BASE advocates has been the apparent lack of consistency in park policies. It is generally legal to catch a fish but not to pick flowers. Horses are allowed on many trails, but mountain bikers are not. The Merced River is a jumble of colorful rafts carrying tourists; El Capitan is a dot-to-dot slate of climbers and ropes; and Yosemite even allows hang gliding on a limited basis off Glacier Point, not far from Taft Point. Potter was allowed to string tightropes between formations. But if he fell, it was illegal, in theory, to prevent his own death with a parachute.

In 2006, the last time the National Park Service updated its management policies, individual park superintendents were allowed the discretion to pursue approval of BASE jumping. None have. (The exception in the national park system is the annual Bridge Day at New River Gorge, in West Virginia, where hundreds take part in a one-day jumping celebration that dates back nearly forty years.) Potter thought times were changing. He pondered ways to devise a permit system, to limit the number of BASE jumpers and to ensure that only well-trained jumpers would leap into the valley. He did not have that part figured out yet. But it was his goal. He wanted nothing more than to BASE jump and fly wingsuits legally in Yosemite, the place he loved more than anywhere else.

SEEKING FAMILIAR FACES

The women drove back into the black valley. They looked for people they knew—climbers camping or hanging around the village and the bar. There were no familiar faces. At about 10:30, they showed up at the door of Mike Gauthier, Yosemite's chief of staff, a conduit between park bureaucracy and the climbing community.

A call to the Yosemite dispatcher quickly deflated hope that Potter and Hunt were in custody. There were no reports of BASE jumpers caught by park rangers.

A late-night search was called. Rangers and volunteers from Yosemite Search and Rescue were told that a pair of BASE jumpers were missing off Taft Point. It was not until they saw Rapp that they realized that one of the men missing was Dean Potter. Everyone knew him.

"I hoped he was just hurt," Rapp said. "Maybe he had two broken femurs. Maybe he was bleeding to death. We just needed to get up there."

She tried to leave the searching to the experts. But at 4 a.m., helplessly waiting, she took binoculars and headed to the base of the canyon below Lost Brother. She scanned the darkness for movement or color. She screamed into the black void above her. She got no response.

There were still no answers from above by daybreak. A helicopter took off and headed over the top of Lost Brother. Two bodies were quickly spotted. Neither man had deployed a parachute.

Hunt had cleared the base of the notch, but having most likely entered the downward funnel on a diagonal path, he had crashed into the right wall.

"Turns out the sounds I heard, I think, were the sounds of Graham hitting a tree and then the wall," Rapp said.

Potter was found several hundred feet farther into the notch. Speculation began immediately that maybe the sight of Hunt, or the air disturbance caused by his maneuvers, had affected Potter's concentration or control. Neither man was wearing a GoPro video recorder, contrary to some news reports, but Potter had jumped with a smartphone strapped to his head. It was heavily damaged, but park service investigators have it, along with Rapp's photos, hoping to mine them for clues.

Rapp returned to Taft Point three days after the accident. By then, there was a memorial at the cliff's edge, where Potter and Hunt had made their final jump. El Capitan sits across the valley a little to the left; Yosemite Falls can be seen a little to the right, over the top of the brown, down-sloping ridge with the notch. The memorial included feathers, a beer can, Tibetan prayer flags and a photograph of Potter.

Rapp sat alone on a rock. A raven appeared. Unflinchingly, it approached and patiently ate a piece of salami out of her hand. It had never happened to her before.

"The way the raven looked at me, so intently, so . . .," Rapp said, the thought drifting, unfinished. "Yeah, it was Dean."

POSTSCRIPT: Illicit BASE jumping still occurs in Yosemite Valley, and jumpers still push to be allowed to do it in American national parks. Rapp continues to climb, paraglide and skydive, but does not do BASE jumping. In 2020, she got engaged in El Capitan Meadow.

PART II

WINNING
AND
LOSING

4

ON LEAGUE NIGHT, A 300 GAME LIVES

Ravenna, Michigan

N ews of Don Doane's death on October 16 traveled the world, if only for the peculiarity of its timing. Short accounts—man bowls his first perfect game, then dies—appeared in newspapers and across countless computer screens. On a table at Ravenna Bowl on Thursday night, a temporary shrine held two such blurbs. One was from *Sports Illustrated*. One was from a newspaper in Thailand.

But a life is not a blurb. And that is why, on a snowy December night in a western Michigan town that has no stoplights, this sixteen-lane bowling alley was filled with people. They did not come to celebrate the odd circumstance of Doane's death, but the commonness of his life.

And, of course, it was league night.

His widow and son tearfully accepted the honorary "300" rings in front of Lanes 11 and 12. Eleven members of the Muskegon chapter of the United States Bowling Congress wore matching sport coats, shirts and ties.

Among the relatives and friends watching the short ceremony were the eighty members of the Commercial League, which bowls every

Thursday night at 6:30. One of the five-man teams is called Nutt Farms, and it recently had to recruit Doane's replacement.

They set aside their beers and cigarettes and conversations and huddled in silence, just as they did a few Thursdays ago when the volunteer firemen and the paramedics tried to revive Doane.

This was where Doane, sixty-two, bowled the first 300 game of his life. This was where he received the hugs and high-fives. And this was where he turned to shake another hand and collapsed of a heart attack.

"I often wonder if the 300 game caused it, or it would have happened anyway," Frank Coletta, an eighty-year-old with a 166 average, said between frames.

Long ago, Coletta was director of the recreation center, and he knew Doane as a Little League player. But now he remembers shaking Doane's hand and telling him, "Looks like anybody can bowl a 300 game," and Doane, always the likable smart-aleck, responding, "Even a guy your age."

Those might have been Doane's last words. Coletta, like everyone else there that night, remembered Doane falling, the ensuing mayhem, and the eerie silence. Coletta also remembered his wife asking why he was home early. He remembered not being able to respond, then crying.

"The little guy affected me like that," Coletta said.

Doane was about 5 feet 7 inches, with a gambler's guile and a heckler's panache. Golfing buddies like Erv Klein and Doug Henrickson called him Little Feller, the spark plug who always seemed to win, whether in bowling, golf or cards. The 300 game? He had done it again.

A favorite family story involves a traffic officer who tossed coins on the ground and asked Doane to retrieve a quarter, to test his sobriety. Doane picked up two dimes and a nickel. Sober, but given a ride in the squad car.

"That summed him up," his wife, Linda Doane, said.

She met "my husband, my companion, my sparring partner" at

Ravenna Bowl more than forty years ago, when he was already a league regular and she worked the snack stand. He was four years older, just beginning a career as a welder and a machinist. They married in September 1969. She was just out of high school. Their son, Chad, is thirty-six.

Doane had a doo-wopper's swoosh of hair, which went silver years ago, and a persistent golfer's tan. He often told people that he wanted nothing more in life than a hole in one and a 300 game. The ace came in 1999, on the eighth hole at Rogue River Golf Course in Sparta, Michigan. Doane played eighteen holes the morning of his death.

"From a faith point of view, we all hope we can accomplish what God has put before us," said the Reverend Tony De La Rosa at Conklin Reformed Church, where Doane was a deacon. "And that we don't linger, that we get called home. He went out with a bang. What a blessing."

At McNitt Cemetery, a bucket of golf balls sat next to Doane's coffin. One by one, mourners grabbed a ball and tossed it into the grave.

Inside the coffin were two "300" rings, similar to high school class rings. One came from Todd Place, a member of the Nutt Farms team— named for the corn and alfalfa farm owned by the family of Jim Nutt, the bowling alley's owner and a teammate of Doane's since 1963. Place has earned three of the rings. He knew that they took weeks to arrive.

"I wanted him to take a ring with him," Place said.

The other came from Dave Spoelman. He and his wife, Coralee, were best friends with the Doanes. Through the years, they bought boats, snowmobiles and trail bikes, even a cottage on Lake Michigan together. They talked about retiring to a duplex.

Ten years ago, Spoelman rolled his only 300 game. As he described the night, it struck him that it might have happened on Lanes 11 and 12, too. He went silent. Tears backed up in his eyes.

"He gave me a big hug," Spoelman finally said. He stopped again. His wife filled the empty space of the bowling alley restaurant.

"That was Don," she said. "He was always so happy for other people."

Spoelman caught his breath.

"I set my ring down along with him," he said.

Doane was born and raised in Conklin, seven miles from the bowling alley. He lived in a gray house at the corner of the four-way stop. It is a few hundred yards from where he grew up and where his parents still live—his father, Mick, with a broken heart, his mother, Betty, with Alzheimer's disease. She probably does not know that her oldest child is dead.

Mick Doane, eighty-five, helped comfort some of the 1,200 people who came to his son's wake. Many waited in line for more than two hours outside the funeral home.

"Don was on cloud nine" after the perfect game, Mick Doane told well-wishers. "And he liked it so much that he didn't want to come down."

As the story was related on Thursday, Linda Doane turned to him.

"He was halfway to heaven when he hit the floor, wasn't he, Dad?" she said.

The ring ceremony lasted only a couple of minutes, about as long as Doane had to enjoy his perfect game after his twelfth consecutive strike.

It was almost 6:30. Someone, somewhere, pushed a button, and the stoic silence of the bowling alley was interrupted by the sudden rumble and whir of the automatic pin-setting machines.

A moment later, the room filled with bowling's familiar clatter: the thunk of balls hitting hardwood, the hum as they spun down the lanes, the crack of the impact.

Pins were falling. But nobody got them all.

POSTSCRIPT: *This is a rare story where I remember exactly where the idea originated: an editor named Bob Goetz spotted a tiny blurb about Don Doane's unusual death and passed it to me. I called the bowling alley and learned that a memorial was scheduled. So I went.*

5

PERFECTION IN THE HORSESHOE PIT

Defiance, Ohio

From behind a neat, ranch-style house on Melody Lane came the clinking and clanking rhythm of iron striking iron.

Alan Francis stood more than a dozen long-legged strides from an inch-thick stake drilled deep into tacky clay. Perhaps the most dominant athlete in any sport in the country, Francis lifted his right arm, swung it behind him and forward again.

He launched a horseshoe toward the target forty feet away. It weighed a little more than two and a half pounds and spun slowly, sideways. It rose and fell in an arc until its narrow open end, three and a half inches across, caught the stake with percussive perfection.

Clink.

Francis, satisfied but expressionless, pitched another.

Clank.

"Those are the sounds you want," he said, smiling.

Built narrow like a stake, with a mustache and a crew cut, Francis is widely considered the best horseshoe pitcher in history. He has won fifteen world titles, including the past seven. He hopes to extend his streak in early August at the National Horseshoe Pitchers Association world tournament in Cedar Rapids, Iowa.

But the number that most impresses those whom the forty-year-old Francis routinely beats or who gather to watch him pitch is the key statistic in horseshoes: ringer percentage.

Get a ringer 70 percent of the time, and you are in a shrinking class of world-class pitchers. Get one 80 percent of the time, and you are probably in the top two.

Get one 90 percent of the time, and you are Alan Francis.

"Of all the guys that have pitched this game, he's the best," said Gerald Bernard, a veteran of a summer tournament circuit made up almost entirely of people with no hope of beating Francis. "No doubt."

In the championship game of last year's world tournament, which had more than 1,300 participants, Francis fell far behind Vermont's Brian Simmons, a two-time world champion and Francis's only viable rival. Francis pitched ringers on twenty-five of his final twenty-six shoes to win what some call the greatest match in the sport's history.

"When he gets on a roll, you're not going to beat him," Simmons said.

Francis finished the nineteen-game tournament with ringers on 917 of 1,016 pitches, a record 90.26 percent.

In late June, after a five-hour drive, Francis arrived at the Eastern National tournament in Erie, Pennsylvania. For an hour he attracted old friends and a few autograph and picture seekers. When he settled onto one of the courts to warm up, people crowded for the best view.

"He's the man I came to watch," one man said to another.

Clink.

"Jeez," the other said. "He's amazing."

Clank.

"I don't understand why he's practicing," a third onlooker said. "Can't get any better."

Francis began competing when he was nine, and won the first of four consecutive junior (under eighteen) world titles when he was twelve. He won the men's world championship for the first time in 1989, at nineteen. He has won it fourteen of the past seventeen years.

"I've worked hard, honing that skill," Francis said. "At the same time, it's a gift. I think I was given the ability to do it."

Francis was born and raised in Blythedale, Missouri, part of a family of full-time farmers and part-time horseshoe pitchers. His earliest memory is of his father, Larry, pitching shoes in a pasture.

Francis attended his first world tournament in Des Moines in 1978. ("World" is a wishful misnomer in horseshoes, since few competitors come from beyond the United States and Canada.) Walter Ray Williams Jr., who gained greater fame as a professional bowler, won the first of his six world titles.

Also at that tournament was Amy Brown, whose family was equally enamored of horseshoes. Now a three-time world runner-up, she and Francis married in 1996. They have a six-year-old son, Alex, who tosses ringers from short distances.

Women, children and seniors pitch from thirty feet, not forty, and usually flip shoes end over end. But a well-thrown flipped shoe can bounce off the stake, which is why most top men's players spin their horseshoes horizontally. The shoes typically rotate clockwise, one and a quarter or one and three-quarters times, virtually locking themselves onto the stake.

As a boy, Francis heaved horseshoes with a slow counterclockwise rotation. His "three-quarter reverse" remains a trademark.

"I'd say there may be 1 percent or less that throw a three-quarter reverse," Francis said. "But that's the style that works for me, and that's the style I've tried to perfect."

As with baseball pitchers, some windups are compact and quick, others flailing and lurching. Francis has fewer moving parts than anyone—no hitches or stray movements in his arm swing, joints or stride.

He holds the horseshoe sideways in his right hand, the open end pointed left, his thumb on top. Feet nearly together, Francis gently swings his arm, then holds the shoe in front of his face for a beat or two, using it as a frame to stare down the target. His elbow is tight toward his belly button.

Displaying little effort, Francis tosses the shoe as he steps with his left foot. The horseshoe's arc reaches only about eight feet. ("More air, more error," said Simmons, who also has a flat shot.)

Francis's manner is equally consistent. He tosses his two horse-shoes, steps aside to watch his opponent, and strides to the other end to determine the points. Even his wife struggles to read his blank expression.

"I'm not real smart," Francis said with typical self-deprecation. "But I can focus on things that are in front of me."

Francis received $4,000 for winning last year's world title. At that level, players try to reach 40 points under a cancellation method, which means that a ringer by one person (usually worth 3 points) cancels a ringer by the other.

Francis's sole sponsorship deal is with White Distributors, makers of tournament-level horseshoes—including four designs stamped with Francis's name, costing up to $81 a pair. Francis earns up to about $4,000 annually in royalties.

He buys Nike collarless shirts to wear for the dozen or so competitions each year, and tucks them into khaki shorts that are a couple of inches above his knee. Any longer, and his hand or horseshoe might brush against them during the toss.

Francis was the first in his family to go to college, graduating from Northwest Missouri State with an agronomy degree. He struggled to find an agricultural job he liked and surprised everyone, including Amy, by moving from Missouri just months into their romance in 1995.

"When we met, I had the better job," said Amy, the director of financial aid at Defiance College.

Alan Francis is now a purchasing manager for the Hubbard Company, a family-run commercial printing business. He works on the second floor in a wood-paneled office, where the smell of ink from the printing room below hangs in the heavy air.

The office has no mementos of his alter ego—no trophies or plaques or even a lucky horseshoe tacked above the door. Most co-workers have never seen him pitch. ("I've seen him throw on TV," said one, Ken Sanders.)

"Maybe it's the way my parents raised me," Francis said. "I don't brag, and don't try to bring attention to myself if I don't have to."

His horseshoes tell most of the story, and their sound never lies. On warm evenings in Defiance, they can be heard for blocks, emanating from a backyard up on Melody Lane, the percussion of iron striking iron from forty feet.

Clink.

Clank.

It is the backbeat of summer, the sound of perfection.

POSTSCRIPT: *Alan Francis continues to dominate horseshoes, winning every title from 2012 to the publishing of this collection—twenty-four world titles in all. He remains a favorite retort of mine whenever someone suggests that a particular athlete dominates a particular sport like no other. "Have you heard of Alan Francis?" I ask.*

6

WHERE DRIVERS AND DANGER MEET

Indianapolis, Indiana

Figure-eight car racing is like driving full speed through an endless loop of red lights. Luck often expires in a cloudburst of steam and scattered auto parts.

Danger is the timeless allure. Cars snake around two circles, clockwise around one and counterclockwise around the other, crossing paths twice every lap in a lawless intersection called the crossover.

The people who do this, who tenderly build race cars that cost up to $50,000 and then drive them repeatedly into crossing traffic, know that they are wired differently.

"Common sense says you don't take two cars and run them at each other at 70, 80 miles per hour," said Leonard Basham, the 1988 world champion with a central-casting name.

Jack Dossey Jr. may be the best ever at weaving through the chaos. And he could have won his seventh career World Figure 8 Championship at the Indianapolis Speedrome had he made it through the crossover for the 715th time on a recent Saturday night.

He did not. Dossey smashed into the side of Roger Maynor of Bay Shore, New York, and his crumpled car was towed to the off-track pit area. Dossey, a tightly built, tightly wound forty-seven-year-old whose internal thermostat seems set on simmer, marched into his racecar trailer and grabbed a dry-erase board. A dozen or so crew members in matching uniforms stayed quiet and out of the way.

"A Gift From New York. Thanks," Dossey scribbled. He propped the message atop his car's carcass.

Maynor was still inside his mangled machine when the tow truck dropped it next to Dossey's. The right rear panel was obliterated and the hood was shaped like a pup tent.

"Of all the people, it had to be him," said Maynor, a fifty-two-year-old bear of a man with a round, gentle face. His red coveralls were split in the seat, and the knees were worn almost through.

He stepped into his brightly lit trailer, a garage on wheels. On the wall was a picture of his father, Ernie Maynor. Father and son were racing side by side at Islip (New York) Speedway in 1982 when they split around a car in the crossover.

Ernie Maynor, known as The Wrench, clipped the car, lost control, hit the wall and was killed. Roger Maynor, a mechanic like his father, went on to become the most accomplished driver at Long Island's Riverhead Raceway, a regional master of the figure eight.

"My father wasn't a quitter, and he would have been disappointed if I quit," Maynor said. "My mother wasn't crazy about it. Even when I told her I was coming here, she started crying. She gets nervous."

Fate is left to the whims of reflexes, fear and physics. A figure-eight race is a series of wince-inducing near misses interrupted by jarring collisions.

Even the tow trucks, ambulances and pace cars that frequently take to the track to restore order sometimes seem at risk of a broadside.

In the past twelve years, at least three drivers (not including one racing in a school bus) have died in figure-eight crashes in the United States. But there is no governing body for the sport, and it is difficult to surmise how the fatality rate compares with other events. Danger

is mitigated somewhat by lower speeds than other forms of racing, yet insurance for tracks that feature the event is typically higher than for those that do not.

"It's definitely one of the most dangerous types of motor sports there is," said Craig Clarke, whose Florida-based company, Track Rescue, oversees safety for racetracks and movie stunts. "You're crossing the course with itself, and the potential for direct driver impact is imminent."

According to Tim Frost, the publisher of the *National Speedway Directory*, about 60 of the estimated 1,000 oval racetracks in the country—three-quarters of which are not paved—run figure-eight races each year.

Nowhere are they treated with such reverence and panache as at the Indianapolis Speedrome, a small track across town from the far larger, more famous Indianapolis Motor Speedway. The Speedrome opened in 1941 and began holding figure-eight races a few years later on its fifth-of-a-mile oval.

Since 1977, it has held the world championship, a three-hour race of attrition. The car that completes the most laps wins. This year, the winner received $20,035—a huge sum in small-track racing. Most drivers race at their local tracks for $1,000 or less.

"For figure-eight racers, this is our Daytona 500, Indy 500, everything else, rolled into one," said Gordon Brown, a longtime driver and car owner from Florida.

Most cars in the race were custom-built around a high-powered engine (650 horsepower or more), a nimble chassis (center balanced for turns in both directions) and a sturdy roll cage (inspected, along with other required safety features, by Dennis Love, the chief steward for the Speedrome and the Indy Racing League).

Maynor brought his trusty No. 28 (his father drove No. 82), a hefty, old-style stock car with 3,250 pounds of mass around a 550-horsepower engine.

"He brought a knife to a gunfight," Dossey said.

Still, during qualifications the day before the race, Maynor muscled his car through most competitors. But the drive shaft was damaged along the way. Maynor had another in the trailer, but did not have welding equipment powerful enough to make trustworthy repairs.

Dossey came to the rescue. He offered the overnight use of his nearby garage and equipment, and Maynor and his five-man crew rebuilt the guts of the car through the wee hours. By morning, Maynor was at the track wearing a weary smile. He was effusive in his gratitude and reminded his crew to buy beer to repay Dossey.

As darkness fell on a Saturday night, thirty-two cars, lined up in pairs, filled one half of the figure eight to start the race. By the second lap, cars crisscrossed through the intersection.

Once safely through, it takes less than ten seconds to reach the intersection again. The action is relentless.

"It's like you're in a swarm of bees," the driver Jimmy Kirby said.

Halfway around each loop, drivers look over their shoulder across the track to gauge which cars they will meet in the crossover. It is a high-speed game of chicken. Drivers have "a millionth of a second," Basham said, to decide whether to go in front of or behind the other car, and trust that the other driver is thinking the same way.

There are clues. Drivers establish reputations for timidity or temerity. Nose up means the car is accelerating; nose down means the driver is hesitating.

Cars sometimes arrive in packs and seem to magically alternate like shuffling cards. Sometimes, a driver sees no opening and stops, creating a chain reaction of swerves and slammed brakes.

"Sometimes, you tense all up—Woo! I don't know how I did that," said Ben Tunny, the 2009 winner. "You don't know really how it's going to work when you get there, but somehow, it does."

Not always. After a series of mechanical problems from two early-race bumps, Maynor was running steady toward a respectable midpack showing.

Dossey, whose pink No. 20 and fearless driving stand out amid the swirling confusion, was looking to win again. He pitted for fuel and tires with twenty-five minutes left. He returned in third place, slipped into second and headed toward first.

Bam.

Steam blew from Dossey's ruptured radiator. The collision spun Maynor 360 degrees, but he kept going. His race ended minutes later in a six-car pileup.

On pit road, Maynor saw the handwritten sign on Dossey's car. The difference between finishing first (as R. J. Norton of Indianapolis did, with 397 laps) and finishing seventh (as Dossey did, with 357), was $19,006. Dossey said Maynor's hesitation through the crossover was what cost him.

"Roger couldn't make up his mind," Dossey said, still seething, "so I made it up for him."

Several fans thanked Maynor for coming and told him not to worry about the accident. Dossey hit you, they pointed out, not the other way around. It happens.

"I feel terrible," said Maynor, who came in twenty-first, with 171 laps. "The guy helped us. Out of all the people—if it wasn't for him, we wouldn't be here."

Long after midnight, Maynor stood in his trailer, waiting for his check for $1,015—$14 less than Dossey earned. He would like to come back to the world championship, he said, but in a lighter, quicker car. Maybe he could find one to overhaul for next year.

In the meantime, No. 28 needed a lot of repairs, and home was fourteen hours away. Maynor said he planned to race the next weekend back home on Long Island. The photograph of his smiling father hung over his shoulder.

POSTSCRIPT: Roger Maynor continued to race, mostly winning at his home track in New York. Jack Dossey Jr. was inducted into the Indianapolis Speedrome Hall of Fame, but never won another world championship.

7

ENDURING TRADITIONS

Oraibi, Arizona

Above the creased high-desert landscape of northeastern Arizona, the Hopi village Oraibi, continuously inhabited for nearly one thousand years, sits atop a blond mesa crumbling at the edges.

Each fall, during one of the Hopi calendar's dozen or so ceremonial running races, a hundred or more Hopi men gather in a pack on the scrubby plain below, all muted tones of mustard yellows and sage greens. A woman in Hopi dress holds a woven basket in the distance. Onlookers shout, "Nahongvita"—loosely, "stay strong" or "dig deep" in Hopi. A signal is given.

To the Hopi, to run is to pray. And the men run, several miles, past the bean field, beyond the barely marked graves of ancestors, around the decayed façade of a Spanish church and up the precariously steep passages to the top of the mesa, where they are received by a chorus of thanks—"asqwali" from the women, "kwakwai" from the men.

Juwan Nuvayokva, a former all-American cross-country runner at Northern Arizona University, has been the first to the top in dozens of Hopi races. And he would probably win the one scheduled for Saturday in Oraibi, where he was raised, if it did not fall on the day of Arizona's high school cross-country championships, in suburban Phoenix.

Nuvayokva is an assistant coach for the boys' team at Hopi High, vying for its twenty-sixth Arizona state championship in a row. Its streak is the longest in the country for cross-country and the fourth longest active run for any high school sport, boys' or girls', according to the National Federation of State High School Associations.

"Hopi have that running blood in them," Nuvayokva said. "It's up to us to find it and use it."

Hopi High, as modern as any suburban school, has about four hundred students in grades nine through twelve. Before it opened in 1986, many Hopi teenagers, like those from other tribes, went to Indian boarding schools in faraway places.

Among them, more than a century ago, was Lewis Tewanima. Sent to Carlisle Indian Industrial School in Pennsylvania—where he was a classmate and track teammate of Jim Thorpe of the Sac and Fox Nation—Tewanima became a two-time Olympian. He finished ninth in the marathon at the 1908 London Games and won the silver medal in the 10,000 meters in Stockholm in 1912. He remains a Hopi hero, and an annual race is held on the reservation each year in Tewanima's honor.

Rick Baker, fifty-six, grew up in the Hopi village of Tewa, before there was a high school or cross-country team nearby. He ran cross-country eighty miles away at Winslow High and then in college in Oklahoma. He was hired in 1987 as a Hopi High physical education teacher and coach and was asked to start a cross-country program.

"A lot of schools with Hopi kids had won state championships," Baker said. "And I thought if we could get all the Hopis here, we should have a pretty good team."

His first three boys' teams finished in the top ten in one of Arizona's small-school divisions. His fourth, in 1990, won the state title. The team has won every one since.

The championships are a point of pride, but Hopi modesty inhibits boasting. The twenty-five state championship trophies are scattered in a small storage room, five of them on the floor, two on a plastic bin next to a bike tire, one of them broken.

But the pressure to keep the streak intact is palpable. Boys on this year's team admitted to nerves, and Baker uses the streak as motivation—do not be the team that breaks the streak.

"I don't want to be part of the team that doesn't win the twenty-sixth in a row," the freshman Jihad Nodman said.

Darion Fredericks, a senior, said he knew that the team was watched, both by opponents around the state and by Hopi on the reservation.

"They know what we're capable of," he said. "I definitely feel the eyes on me, even in the community. They say, 'Hey, you're the one that runs.'"

Success is built on endurance, not speed. While Hopi High has had its share of individual state champions (Nuvayokva did it twice), winning a team title requires depth. Courses are generally 5,000 meters, or 3.1 miles. Time is less important than order.

The finishing place of each team's top five finishers (out of seven starters) are added together for a team score—1 point for the overall first-place runner, 2 points for the second, 10 points for the 10th, 100 for the 100th, and so on. The team with the lowest score wins. A perfect score is 15, if a team sweeps the first five places. The Hopi did that at state one year.

"A lot of our kids don't have a lot of speed," Baker said. "If you timed them in the 400 meters, they probably wouldn't break 70 seconds. But they have endurance. They can run and run and run."

In early October, a Hopi High bus, painted in the school colors, blue and white, drove five hours to a night meet in Casa Grande, between Phoenix and Tucson. Members of the boys' cross-country team sat in the back half of the bus. The girls' team, the winner of twenty-two state championships in twenty-eight seasons—a seven-year string was broken last year—sat in the front.

The teams sometimes travel together, but they have different coaches and do not practice together. At the Casa Grande meet, they got off the bus and headed in different directions into the cool night.

They were quickly absorbed into an athletic carnival, acres of uniformed teams wandering to and from the course and huddled around team tents. The course crossed soccer fields, a stretch of dirt and a golf course and then snaked back along several fairways to the finish. The air was filled with dust and the sound of generators powering temporary lights.

Baker was nervous. A quiet and poised man, with glasses and spiky black hair lightly freckled with gray, he felt that this year's team was vulnerable. The team was young. It had melted in the heat of a meet in Phoenix the week before.

More broadly, Baker had found it increasingly difficult to find Hopi boys dedicated to running. Fewer committed to the summer running program. There were too many distractions these days. This could be the year that the streak ended.

"People stop me and say, 'How's the team doing?'" Baker said. "They know we didn't start too well. But they say, 'You'll be ready at state.'"

Hopi High ran in the meet's final race, with many of the state's biggest schools. At the start, Baker crowded in with his seven boys, including his son Steven, a sophomore.

"Come on, guys," he shouted. "Be strong! Be a fighter!"

"Nahongvita!" they shouted together.

The starting gun sounded. Baker and Nuvayokva watched a colorful blur of 100 runners fade into the dark of the golf course. Because of the serpentine route, they could jog to a spot on the course to watch and then move to the next switchback to watch the runners pass again, repeating the pattern several times toward the finish.

"Where are they, where are they, where are they?" Baker said to himself, scanning a string of passing runners. "They should be here somewhere."

He and Nuvayokva share an ability both to count runners ("You're in 70th! Move up!" Baker shouted to one of his athletes) and to tally rivals ("That's their fourth! Their fifth!" Nuvayokva shouted as boys from Sedona Red Rock High blurred past).

With each Hopi runner, Baker's calm deportment gave way to full-throated screams and hand gestures. He sometimes ran alongside the runners for a few strides and shouted instructions into their serious faces.

"Two minutes hard! Two minutes hard!" he shouted to one. "Get that guy in the white! Beat him!"

Another Hopi was told in the final mile that his score was going to count.

"You're number five," Baker called, imploring him to sprint and pass as many opposing runners as he could. "Ten guys! You can catch ten guys!"

Individual Hopi runners finished nowhere near the top, and because of a registration glitch, their efforts were not recorded. Still, Baker boarded the bus relaxed and relieved. He saw progress. The bus stopped at Little Caesars to pick up sixteen pizzas and then unloaded the boys and girls at a nearby Holiday Inn Express at about 11 p.m.

"Be glad; be happy you finished," Baker told the boys in the lobby. "But don't be satisfied. Because there's more in you somewhere."

He scheduled a five-mile run for 7 a.m. When the Hopi stayed at the same hotel last year, their morning run took them past a cotton field, and Baker grabbed some to use for a couple of Hopi ceremonies. The field was gone this year, plowed over for a strip mall.

The boys huddled before heading off to bed.

"1-2-3 Hopi!" they shouted.

On the reservation, the low and distant edges of the sky are pierced by spires and plateaus. The twelve villages of the Hopi reservation, surrounded by Navajo land, are connected by the two-lane thread of Highway 264, which winds over and among three large mesas—helpfully named First Mesa, Second Mesa and Third Mesa—about 6,000 feet above sea level.

To the southwest is the snow-tipped summit of Humphreys Peak, the highest point in Arizona, part of a mountain range sacred to the Hopi, who believe it is home to spirits known as kachinas.

Three Fridays after the Casa Grande meet, as the morning sun lit Oraibi, the smell of burning wood and coal came from some of the houses. Like the perch itself, they are built of stone and sit in various states of surrender to time and gravity. Some are patched together with cinder blocks and clay.

The 150 or so residents of Oraibi choose to live with no electricity or running water, and there are thirteen underground kivas used for village ceremonies. Each has a wood ladder poking through a hole in the top.

Nuvayokva, a thirty-six-year-old who smiles his way through nearly everything, wore running shoes and jogged down through the broken edges of the mesa. Parts of the trail were sprinkled with pottery fragments.

"When we were kids, we were told to never pick them up," Nuvayokva said. "Otherwise the people who owned them before will come back and get you."

He ran onto the plain and shrank into a speck, then looped up a trail and returned full-size a few minutes later. As a boy, he often ran to work in his clan's cornfields, one of them sixteen miles away. Last year, training for a marathon, he often ran from the high school, twenty-nine miles away.

Leigh Kuwanwisiwma, director of the Hopi Cultural Preservation Office, said that the tribe's tradition of running flowed from its scouts, men who directed tribal migrations and searches for water. (One of roughly three dozen remaining Hopi clans, the Lizard clan, supposedly got its name from such scouts, who were able to survive in the desert with little water, he said.)

Running was the method of sending messages between Hopi villages. It became part of ceremonies, too, which can last days. Photographs from the early 1900s show Hopi men lined up to run in ceremonial races such as the women's basket dance race, most wearing loincloths and no shoes.

"They are for the blessings of the cloud people, for the rain, for the harvest, so we have a good life, a long life," Kuwanwisiwma said. "That's what these ceremonial runners do. They bring this positiveness to the people."

In some variations, the first to the top receives a gourd of water, which he then carries to his cornfield to bless the crops in all four directions. In other races, winners bury sacred tokens in the ground as offerings.

"It might sound a little funny, but running in cultural races is a lot different than running in high school or college," said Devan Lomayaoma, thirty-three, who won two individual state cross-country titles at Hopi High, ran at Northern Arizona, teaches at a Hopi elementary school and has won many Hopi races. "In cultural races, you never got recognition for it. They have a deeper meaning."

Nuvayokva said the same thing.

"It's different than the Anglo culture, where you run and it's every man for himself," Nuvayokva said. "When I competed in the NCAA, you're trying to beat others. Here, you do it for others."

He had to cut his morning run short because the team had a meet in Holbrook, about ninety minutes south. On a room-temperature day under blue skies and cotton-ball clouds, the Hopi boys finished second among eighteen teams.

Among more than a hundred varsity competitors, the top five Hopi boys finished sixth, twelfth, fifteenth, twenty-first and twenty-third.

The meet was won by Tuba City, a rival school on Navajo land that some Hopi on the western side of the reservation attend. Baker mentioned how much Hopi High had gained on its rivals in the past couple of meets. But Tuba City is a substantially bigger school, in a different classification, so Hopi High will not compete against it head-to-head at the state meet.

"I feel pretty good," Baker said. "Pretty good. We're pretty much on pace for the state meet."

But he also knew that plenty of other schools, including a handful with reasonable hopes of an upset, dreamed of ending the streak.

"We're banquet talk," Baker said. "That's what I tell the boys. At the other teams' banquet, they'll say, 'We beat the Hopi,' or 'You outraced the Hopi kid.'"

As the boys cooled down and put on their white warm-up suits for the awards presentation, a seventy-year-old Hopi man named Lee Grover stood to the side.

He still jogs a few miles in the mornings, to greet and pray to the sun, and hopes that his running motivates the younger generations. The team has helped "put the Hopi back on the map," Grover said, but he worries that even the strongest of traditions can fade.

"We're gifted with this talent of running," Grover said. "It's something we should never let die."

POSTSCRIPT: The Hopi High boys' cross-country team won its twenty-sixth consecutive state title a week later. The streak ended after twenty-seven years, when the team finished second at the state meet.

8

WHERE CREATIVITY
WAGS ITS TAIL

Secaucus, New Jersey

O nce they finished shaving the cats, the glamour event of the dog grooming show began.

For the past two years, Angela Kumpe had won the "creative challenge" event at Intergroom, one of the more prestigious competitions on the calendar. First, she clipped and colored a standard poodle into an ode to Elvis Presley—Elvis on one side, a guitar on the other. Last year, she turned a dog into a peacock. She is one of the best at canine topiary.

This year, Kumpe, a thirty-four-year-old from Little Rock, Arkansas, spent more than six months turning a poodle into a buffalo. It probably would have won Sunday, beating the seahorse, the Lady Gaga and the Mad Hatter.

But Kumpe, who has become the groomer to beat at contests like this, changed her mind about the buffalo after her mother died on February 24. "She was my biggest fan in creative grooming," Kumpe said.

So Kumpe turned a dog into a living memorial.

Intergroom is a three-day trade show for the industry. About 150 exhibitor stalls offered everything from tools (scissors, clippers, combs, brushes), equipment (cages, tubs, dryers), products (shampoos, conditioners, colognes, gels, glitter and coloring) and apparel (mostly smocks for groomers and showier items for the dogs).

Someone offered psychic tarot readings for dogs. Seminars on Sunday included "Clipper Care Clinic," "Pet Facials" and "Blue Terrier Heads."

In the distance, dogs barked. Behind a shield of curtains, people huddled around dogs standing still atop tables. The dogs were sprayed with bright colors (sometimes through a stencil), sculpted with gel, sprinkled in glitter and otherwise primped to Technicolor perfection.

There are few limits in creative grooming. Sometimes, people make dogs look like different animals. There have been lions and ponies and camels that have forced closer examination to verify the species.

"People sometimes say, 'Oh, poor dog,'" the emcee, Teri DiMarino, told the audience that surrounded the show area at the Meadowlands Exposition Center. "But their perception is limited to their front feet. Really. All they know is that people are paying attention to them. They love it."

Contestants generally spend six months or more preparing the dogs. First comes the idea. Then the dog's coat is shaved with clippers, cut with scissors and fine-tuned occasionally. Colors are added in the weeks before the event. Up until competition day, dogs look like nature gone awry, as if they were groomed in the dark with blunt instruments and dipped into a box of melting Crayolas.

"Some people ask, 'Was she born that way?'" said Sami Stanley, busy putting finishing touches on her standard poodle, the dog of choice for its thick, grooming-friendly fur and relatively large size. Stanley's dog, Skye, had a dragon sculpted on one side and a jumping goldfish on the other. Stanley called it Zen Poodle. "If you have a better name than that, let me know," she said with a shrug.

Diane Betelak was the judge. A frequent winner of these increasingly popular contests, Betelak said she looked for whether the clipping was precise and the color vibrant, and whether the design was original, among other things.

"Some ideas have been used over and over, like a carousel horse," Betelak said. "So if you bring me a carousel horse, it better be spectacular."

She awarded third place to the Mad Hatter, which was accompanied by three people fully decked in other *Alice in Wonderland* costumes. The dog "wore" a fur-coat colored brown, had the March Hare on its left rear leg and teacups on its right. Brynn Haynes of Whitehall, Pennsylvania, the groomer and the Red Queen, said she spent twenty-five hours creating it.

Second place went to a dog that, when it stood on its hind legs, was meant to look like a poodle-sized seahorse. It stood before a sea-themed vinyl shower curtain, which hid a man holding a plastic toy that made bubbles drift through the scene.

The winner came as little surprise. After scrapping plans to bring her buffalo-themed poodle—a buffoodle?—Kumpe started from scratch a week ago with a friend's standard poodle that had not been clipped in nearly a year.

A woman's body was sculpted onto one side of the dog, head turned away and hair tied in a bun. "It's a grieving angel for my mom," Kumpe said. Her mother, Linda Smead, was sixty-six when she died less than two months ago. Kumpe was dressed in white and wore white wings. Down the dog's rear leg, and on most of its opposite side, were fragile-looking purple flowers and green leaves, part of the dog's manicured coat and marked with exacting detail. They matched artificial flowers and greenery on the dog's table.

The design drew finger points and picture takers. When DiMarino told the audience that Kumpe's design represented an angel for her mother, a buzz went through the room. Kumpe won the $1,500 first prize.

Her father, Norman Smead, sat in the front row, holding a small dog. The dog's white coat was smeared with faded colors. The father's eyes were filled with tears.

POSTSCRIPT: I have never been to another dog grooming competition, but it remains one of the most memorable days of my career.

9

A LAST HURRAH FOR HOLLYWOOD PARK

Inglewood, California

"And now, ladies and gentlemen, Hollywood Park belongs to you," the race caller, Joe Hernandez, said over the public address system on June 10, 1938. Among the forty thousand people who came for opening day at Southern California's newest racetrack were the era's biggest stars, including Al Jolson, Joan Crawford, Milton Berle, Claudette Colbert, Bob Hope and Barbara Stanwyck.

Most of the track's six hundred original shareholders had a direct connection to Hollywood and the track chairman, Jack Warner. The track itself, built in a bean field, was eleven miles south of Warner Brothers Studios on Sunset Boulevard. About five weeks after opening day, Hollywood Park held its first Gold Cup, which became the biggest annual race on the track's calendar. It was won by a horse named Seabiscuit.

Hollywood Park's last race is scheduled for December 22. Among the relative few likely to witness the track's final moments are those who still remember the serendipitous synchronization of the golden eras of horse racing and Hollywood.

For decades, they have worked at Hollywood Park, up-close observers of the people: the famous and the desperate, the weekend

fun-seekers and the everyday gamblers with names like Frankie Eye-lashes, Fat Eddie and Frank the Hat. They knew little of the horses, less of the hidden rituals in the backstretch stables that have undermined an industry, like the doping of potential champions and the discarding of unwanted thoroughbreds. They just knew what made Hollywood Park different from the rest.

Theirs was the sunny view from the grandstand—a collective memory of history and rumor, of celebrity sightings and mob hustles, of cheats and thrills, of deafening stretch runs and silent decay.

THE BUGLER

Each race starts with thirty-four familiar notes. And for twenty-five years at Hollywood Park, the bugler—officially, the "horn blower"—has been Jay Cohen.

He has played "Call to the Post"—officially, "First Call"—more than 85,000 times, here and elsewhere. He knows this because he keeps track in a notebook.

"No one comes to the track because of the trumpet," Cohen said. "But they all hear it when they're here."

Adding a dose of tradition and formality to the daily proceedings, Cohen wears a "coach guard" uniform. Hollywood Park bought two of them in the 1990s, at $400 each, before the track's attendance descended into its deadly plummet. Cohen's two-tone jacket is deep green with tan accents, and the tan pants are tucked into riding boots. He wears a tan top hat.

Cohen is also a magician, and his coat pockets are filled with novelties for gags and tricks. The right one recently held a miniature horse head, a gadget that makes a squealing sound, and a tiny plastic nun. ("How many do I have in this hand? Nun!" The crowd groans.)

People ask him to play a special song or to come to their birthday party or to appear in their television show or movie. He was the bugler in the 2003 film *Seabiscuit*. About a dozen times a year, he plays a funeral.

Cohen calls each race with the familiar "da-da-da, da-da-da, duh-duh-duh-duh" refrain, followed seamlessly by a second song. Only the first race of the day is always the same: "Call to the Post" followed by "Hooray for Hollywood."

Cohen knows thousands of songs, and he plays to his audience. He honored Veterans Day by playing military marches. When he spots the actress June Lockhart, he will play the theme from *Lassie* or *Lost in Space*.

He has thought hard about Hollywood Park's final song. He considered the Looney Tunes send-off, "That's All, Folks!" But it seemed a bit too glib, even for a man who boards the press box elevator and says to its operator, "Women's lingerie, please!" Conversely, "Taps" would be too bleak. This is a funeral for a place, a time, not a person.

No, the track will close the way each day started: "Hooray for Hollywood."

THE JOCKEY

Everything is expected to go, starting as soon as January. But after Hollywood Park is torn down and 265 acres of horse-racing history are plowed under to make room for retail and office space and three thousand homes, Pincay Drive will remain, cutting east and west between Crenshaw Boulevard and Prairie Avenue.

"If I go to the airport and have a chance to go on my street, I do it, to remind me of the history there," Laffit Pincay Jr. said.

He won 9,530 races, more than any other jockey when he retired in 2003, a mark passed only by Russell Baze since. More of Pincay's victories came at Hollywood Park than anywhere else. It is where Pincay, a debonair Panamanian, became a rival and friend of the legendary Bill Shoemaker, and then surpassed most of his records.

Pincay liked Hollywood Park's large track—one and one-eighth mile of dirt, framing a mile-long turf oval. "If you had any trouble at the beginning, you had time to make it up," he said.

He won the Gold Cup a record nine times. And when Pincay won big races, he found familiarity in the sea of congratulatory faces— Cary Grant, John Wayne and Alfred Hitchcock among them. He found himself at parties, awed by the movie stars and too shy to introduce himself, only to have one of them approach him and say, "Laffit Pincay!"

"Wow," he remembered thinking. "They know who I am."

Now sixty-six, he came to Hollywood Park on a recent Saturday and took a friend to the Directors Room, an exclusive bastion of prestige for track executives and champions high in the grandstand.

"Twenty years ago, it would be packed," Pincay said. "But we were the only people in there. It's really sad."

Pincay circled too many tracks to remember, but Hollywood Park stood out. At least one piece of that history will remain.

"Many years from now, people will drive on Pincay," he said. "And they'll say, 'Who in the world is Pincay?' Well, there used to be a race-track here . . ."

THE MAÎTRE D'

Lawrence Abbott looks a lot like Jack Lemmon.

"Now?" he said, with feigned mortification. Abbott, seventy-six, is a quick wit. Lemmon died in 2001.

Abbott was the maître d' at the Beverly Hills Trader Vic's, the famed tiki bar and Rat Pack hot spot, when the track chairwoman, Marge Everett—a friend of many celebrities—hired him to come to Hollywood Park in 1980 and oversee the members-only Turf Club.

Back then, Abbott said, "Every day was like an event."

Thirty years ago, the club was private and the dress code was formal. Men wore jackets and ties. Women could not wear pants. Now anyone willing to pay ten dollars can get waited on and pretend to be someone from another era. The tables, once a treasured commodity, are rarely filled. Even the menu has shrunk.

"There was an elegance to it," Abbott said. "And that is gone."

But he still wears a tuxedo, and his lectern still overlooks the ter-raced outdoor dining area, shaded by the huge overhang of the grand-stand. Each cloth-covered table offers a perfect view of the track and its manicured grassy infield, sprinkled with ponds and flamingos. It is a green oasis within a crime-ridden neighborhood. The faint sounds of sirens are an intermittent soundtrack, and people like Abbott have stories about dead bodies found here and there—in a pond, hanging from a tree. Every few minutes, a large airplane rumbles overhead and disappears over the soaring grandstand roof as it makes its final approach to Los Angeles International Airport, a few miles straight west.

"As a kid," Abbott said, "I used to ride my bike around here."

THE CELEBRITY

Dick Van Patten began going to tracks in New York—Aqueduct, Belmont, Jamaica—when he was fourteen and already a Broadway actor. He started coming to Hollywood Park in 1970, amid a dizzying stretch of supporting roles in movies and guest appearances on television.

For a long time, he was just one of many celebrities who frequented the racetrack. Now he is the last.

"The name 'Hollywood Park' meant Hollywood," Van Patten said.

At eighty-five, Van Patten comes to the track every day there is racing. He takes the same seat in the front row of Section 31 and has a standing order: the soup of the day, a Coca-Cola and a bucket of ice cubes to suck on.

Van Patten has long owned racehorses, and when he took a role in Mel Brooks's *High Anxiety* in 1977—the same year Van Patten began his role as the father on television's *Eight Is Enough*—he took Brooks to Hollywood Park. Now Brooks, eighty-seven, is a frequent visitor on weekends, sitting alongside Van Patten and Daryl Richard, who had a recurring role on *The Donna Reed Show* as a teenager fifty years ago.

Van Patten exudes calm through his gentle smile. Brooks is more anxious, standing and glancing from the track to the television broadcast, then double-checking the results with his friends.

"I like the idea of catching lightning in a bottle," Brooks said. "I mostly bet on horses that are 30 or 40 to 1, and they rarely win."

Van Patten once said to Brooks that we all had real-life troubles— deaths in the family, illnesses, business losses.

"But for four or five hours, you forget the world," Brooks said. "You just care about number 6 and nothing else, getting into the lead and maybe winning the race. Part of my life is believing in unreality, and it's a wonderful thing to believe in."

As he spoke, Joan Rivers was at a betting window, surrounded by a camera crew and a few onlookers, filming a scene for something.

"It's like the Ambassador Hotel, the Brown Derby," Brooks said. "It's all very sad when happy places like this close down."

THE USHER

Every day at Hollywood Park, people stop to talk to Dick Warren, the usher for Section 211, where the green sign reads: "Reserved Box, Seats Available, $8." If someone had asked him on the day he started his job, sixty-five years ago, whether he thought he would be doing the same thing at eighty-six, he would have laughed.

"I'd say you're nuts," Warren said. "I'm a creature of habit, I guess."

Warren was discharged from the Army in 1947 and returned home to Syracuse, New York. Realizing he no longer appreciated "snow up to my earlobes," he moved to California. He took a job at Hollywood Park and never left.

The old wooden grandstand, a quarter-mile long, burned down in 1949. Warren rushed to the scene to watch. Racing was moved to Santa Anita Park, thirty miles away in Arcadia, and Hollywood Park reopened in 1950, the massive six-story building rebuilt and topped with a metal roof. Warren returned to his post.

"Milton Berle used to ask me for jokes," Warren said. "'You hear anything good today?'"

He was there in 1951 to watch Citation win the Gold Cup and become racing's first million-dollar horse, and Affirmed (ridden by Pincay) become the first $2 million horse by winning the Gold Cup in 1979. He was there in 1965, when the average crowd was 34,516—about ten times what it is these days. He was there when a record 80,348 came for a tote-bag giveaway in 1980, and when the inaugural Breeders' Cup was held at Hollywood Park in 1984.

"I liked it better when there were people here," Warren said.

On a recent Sunday, Hollywood Park honored Warren's service by having him present the trophy to the winner of the day's biggest race. Like a lot of other employees, he plans to continue working at Santa Anita, which will expand its calendar to help absorb the closure of Hollywood Park.

"I'll work until I'm tired," Warren said. "I feel thirty years old. No aches, no pains, no nothing."

The same cannot be said for Hollywood Park.

"I'm so used to seeing it," Warren said. "I can't picture it not being here."

THE CURATOR

On opening day in 1986, his first day employed in the television operation at Hollywood Park, Kip Hannan was asked to shoot celebrity interviews. On his way to the exclusive Gold Cup Room, Michael Jackson and Elizabeth Taylor walked close behind.

"I got his autograph," Hannan said. "And when she smiled, I melted."

In-house television production was a nascent thing then, but it was about to change horse racing—saving it or killing it, depending on the perspective. Within a few years, races at Hollywood Park and elsewhere were widely simulcast to other tracks and betting parlors. The idea was to make it easier for more people to gamble on horse racing. The effect was to give customers a great excuse to stop coming to places like Hollywood Park.

Average attendance dropped nearly 90 percent between 1983 and 2012, from 23,958 in the fall meet to 3,189.

Of the $213.7 million wagered during Hollywood Park's fall meet last year, only $20.3 million was wagered at the track itself. The rest came from off-track betting. Even those who pay $10 to enter Hollywood Park often stand in front of banks of television screens, betting on races at tracks around the globe rather than, or in addition to, the world-class races happening just a few feet away.

"Racing has become a video game, to some extent," Hollywood Park's president, F. Jack Liebau, said.

In 2005, Bay Meadows Land Company bought Hollywood Park from Churchill Downs for $260 million. The track's extinction looked imminent; the same company closed Bay Meadows Racecourse in San Mateo, near San Francisco, in favor of a major mixed-use redevelopment project. Last spring, it was announced that the 2013 fall meet would be the final season at Hollywood Park.

"The land got too expensive, and horse racing was no longer the highest and best use," Liebau said. "The property's just too valuable."

Plans call for leveling the buildings, including the mammoth grandstand and the acres of concrete backstretch stables—the best in horse racing, several trainers said—that contain 1,900 horse stalls and currently house an estimated six hundred workers and their families.

Horse owners and trainers will move their operations to other tracks, and take most of their workers with them. But Hollywood Park has 215 full-time employees, many now looking for other work—people like Hannan, the supervisor of production operations for the television department.

His immediate concern, however, is for Hollywood Park's archives. Much of it is stuffed in what Hannan called his "hoarder's room," a television production room lined with boxes of film and videotape—all the big races, from Seabiscuit to Zenyatta, and priceless footage of Hollywood stars and jammed bleachers. There is even a clip of Hannan, as a boy, handing a program to Jimmy Stewart.

"You walk out there now, and you wonder where it all went," Hannan said.

He has spent years restoring and cataloging the footage. What he does not know is where it all will go once Hollywood Park is gone.

"Sometimes, I feel like I'm the only one who cares," Hannan said. "But I know, come December 22, I can't bring it all to my house."

THE RACE CALLER

Vic Stauffer will have the final word at Hollywood Park. He spends race days alone in a wood-paneled box on the roof of the grandstand, holding binoculars and standing in his socks. His is the voice heard through the public address system. He knows how all the races start—"They're off," in his measured voice—but is tortured by what he will say when the last one ends.

What will be the final words uttered at Hollywood Park?

"I've given a ton of thought to it, and I'm not any closer to knowing what the right thing is," Stauffer said.

Until then, he will stick to routine. Races last about ninety seconds and run every thirty minutes or so. Amid various between-race announcements, Stauffer privately performs a feat of short-term memory. He studies the mostly unfamiliar names of horses in the next race and matches them with the bright hues of racing silks, repeating the names to himself with great enunciation. After the race, he forgets what he has learned and starts over.

"Eight Stitches, Rocky Barboa, Shining Son, Warren's Tyler S," he said as he stared downward through binoculars one afternoon. "Rocky Barboa. Rocky Barboa. Eight Stitches, Shining Son, Warren's Tyler S, Broker Brett, Ranulf. Broker Brett, Eight Stitches . . ."

It took about two minutes. And when the race began, Stauffer, a fifty-four-year-old bear of a man, smoothly called the action, fast-tongued and mistake-free. He stood upright, shuffling his feet like a slow dancer to keep his body aimed at the herd circling the track, his voice rising when one horse made a move and they stormed across the finish line.

A ripple of cheers and moans came from below. The winning jockey steered the winning horse to the winner's circle, and Stauffer introduced the winning owners and trainers. The next post time, Stauffer announced, was in thirty minutes. He flipped a switch that turned the microphone off and pondered a question about what makes Hollywood Park different from other tracks.

"The ghosts are here," Stauffer said. "What's different about walking into Wrigley Field or Fenway Park? There are a couple of racetracks like that. Without a doubt, Hollywood Park is one."

He flipped the switch to announce payouts and a scratch in the next race, then turned the microphone off again.

"It also makes you aware of your own mortality," he said. "If this can die, so can you. It's an inevitability that I don't want to accept."

The only subject that gives him pause is the final race. He has pondered invoking the famed ghosts of the place—trainers, jockeys, horses—as the final group of anonymous horses gallop down the back-stretch. He has considered going silent when they cross the finish line and not uttering another word.

"Part of me would like it to be done like any old race," Stauffer said. "Because it is any old race. It just has the misfortune of being the last one."

POSTSCRIPT: Hollywood Park was razed shortly after it closed. In 2020, SoFi Stadium, home of the NFL's Los Angeles Rams, opened in its place. It is expected to host future Super Bowls and the opening and closing ceremonies of the 2028 Summer Olympics. Fans can enter the parking lots off Pincay Drive.

10

THE LADY JAGUARS

Huntingdon, Tennessee

I. "IT AIN'T ABOUT THE RECORD"

It was early on a Friday morning, and there was an emergency in Carroll Academy's Room 5. A student named Destiny was sitting alone, crying. With cameras in every classroom, she could be seen on the monitor in the security office.

The girls' basketball team at Carroll Academy had lost the night before, 69–9, at home to University School of Jackson, a private college-preparatory school about forty-five minutes away.

Destiny, a seventeen-year-old senior with a crossover dribble, a silky shooting touch and a habit of drug use, was the only one of the nine Carroll Academy players with any previous high school basketball experience. There were games this season when Destiny scored all the team's points. There were times in every game when her passes, delivered at the velocity of someone playing dodgeball, bounced off teammates' hands, leaving Destiny in a quiet fit of grimaces and upturned palms.

On the court the previous night, her street-tough persona boiled toward reckless anger. Defended tightly, often by two opponents, she was all elbows and sneers.

Coach Tonya Lutz did not like what she saw and benched Destiny in the second half. Randy Hatch, the school administrator, did not like what he saw, either.

He had a hunch. And he had a tip. He ordered a drug test for Destiny the next morning.

That was why she was crying in Room 5.

"I'm not going to be able to pass my drug screen," she said when Lutz, Hatch and the school's security director, Patrick Steele, came into the room. And before she was escorted to the restroom to urinate into a cup, she pressed her face into Lutz's shoulder and sobbed.

Carroll Academy is in Huntingdon, about one hundred miles east of Memphis and one hundred miles west of Nashville in West Tennessee. It is a strictly-run day school with about eighty students operated by the Carroll County Juvenile Court, filled with teenagers trying to work their way back to their home schools with the velvet-hammered guidance of parole officers and people like Lutz, Hatch and Steele.

Among the nine girls on the Carroll Academy basketball team, only one lives with both her mother and her father. A seventh grader, she lived with her parents and two younger siblings at a grandmother's house, having been evicted from one trailer and waiting to move into another.

A few of the players moved more than once during the season. A couple have lived for weeks or months in abandoned houses without water, electricity or heat. Few of the parents have steady jobs, and at least one is in jail.

One girl spent time in rehabilitation for alcoholism. At least one regularly smoked marijuana with her mother at one house and her father at another. Two worried aloud about their mothers' regular use of homemade methamphetamine, in a county where the judge signs two or three search warrants each week to break up meth labs. Most of the girls are on medication themselves, for attention-deficit disorder, bipolar disorder or depression. Some say their parents sometimes take the pills instead.

Few had played team sports. Fewer still had played on a basketball team. Most did not know one another, their lives scattered across small, depressed towns and rolling hills in West Tennessee.

The reasons for being ordered to Carroll Academy varied. Three of the girls on the team were kicked out of their home schools for a year, part of a zero-tolerance policy, after taking their parents' prescription pills to school. A few were habitual truants. A few had habits of rage— fighting at school or uncorking violent tempers at home.

For nine girls, ages thirteen to seventeen, basketball is a way to keep their after-school time occupied, to provide them supervision, to give their worlds a bit of structure and to teach them about teamwork and trusting others.

"I want to teach them to be survivors," said Judge Larry Logan of Carroll County Juvenile Court, who helped start the school in 1994 and sends many of the students there as part of their sentence. "If you get knocked down, get back up. It's a good habit to have."

For girls unaccustomed to positive reinforcement, it is reasonable to wonder about the value of losing, game after game after game, by scores this season like 80–8 and 65–7.

"If I looked out and I could see in their eyes that they're depressed about losing, and hated to come out here, it wouldn't be worth it," said Hatch, a fifty-four-year-old lifelong resident of Huntingdon who long served as Carroll Academy's boys and girls basketball coach, as he watched a game from the stands. "But they put it behind them quicker than anybody."

He looked out at the girls, running up and down the court, gamely chasing a team they would never beat.

"But they got experience at it," Hatch said.

Destiny admitted that she had smoked marijuana a couple of nights earlier. A drug bust with several older friends in a Walmart parking lot resulted in Destiny's being sent to juvenile court last year. While she was on probation, she said, threatening text messages to another girl landed her at Carroll Academy.

Destiny bounces between homes. Her father is the youngest of sixteen children in a family that has supplied top athletes to nearby Clarksburg High School for generations. He lives with his parents, works odd jobs and has never seen Destiny play, she said.

Destiny's mother works as a nurse. She recently gave birth to her fourth child from three men she had married, at least one of whom beat Destiny, Destiny's parole officer said.

Yet Destiny does not hold a grudge. Whenever she is told that her mother is outside, waiting to give her a ride home, Destiny's face brightens like a full moon.

Lyda Allen, Destiny's maternal grandmother, was often the only relative of any of the nine girls cheering them from the mostly empty bleachers.

"If this place wasn't here, God knows where she would be," Allen said of Destiny. "I don't know about the others, but the parents are probably the reason why most of these kids are here. But I'm not going to give up on Destiny."

Hatch was not, either. He held Destiny's fate. He could send her to months of drug rehabilitation at a facility far away, which would then release her back to Carroll Academy. But Destiny was a senior. When she turned eighteen in June, she could walk away from school without her diploma. Further trouble after that would probably land her in jail.

Hatch quizzed her. A county parole officer tabbed to run Carroll Academy when it opened eighteen years ago, he used his arsenal of knowledge, instinct and bluffs. He spoke with a serious tone and a gentle expression.

You were out with older kids, weren't you? Yes, she said. You broke curfew, didn't you? Yes, she admitted.

"I knew that, too," Hatch said.

He dismissed Destiny to class, leaving her to worry what her future held.

When the team gathered that night for another game, Lutz felt a strange vibe. She asked the girls to raise their hands if they would fail a drug test. Two did: Summer, a seventeen-year-old senior with a baby, and Alleyah, a tiny fourteen-year-old eighth grader.

They were tested. The others were not.

"There ain't no reason to lie," said Summer, who cried because she feared being separated from her eight-month-old son, DaMarion. "They're going to find out about it anyway."

Summer failed. Alleyah passed. (The theory was that she had either smoked synthetic marijuana, sold over the counter despite concerns about its health dangers, or unsuspectingly smoked some other herb.)

Hatch put them on house arrest for the weekend, meaning they—and their parents—would be in violation of their court orders if the teenagers wandered away. Lutz suspended all three girls for that night's game against Gleason High.

But they would not be kicked out of Carroll Academy.

The suspensions left Lutz with six players. Constance, a soft-spoken, 5-foot-2-inch eighth grader with a penchant for throwing things in anger—most recently her mother's collection of porcelain figurines, leaving craters in the walls—managed a first-quarter free throw.

Leslee, a fast-talking ninth grader who usually started, fouled out in the third quarter. Two other girls were hurt badly enough in collisions to stop the game, but they managed to stay on the floor to the end.

Carroll Academy lost, 44–1.

"It ain't about the record," Hatch said. "You have nine girls. My job, and Tonya's job, and everyone's job, is to go 9–0 with them. If you go 8–1, you've had a losing season."

II. "WE'RE NOT REALLY BAD KIDS"

The Carroll Academy girls' basketball team had just lost by 59 points to Dresden High School, the top team in the conference. Still, Tonya Lutz, Carroll Academy's coach, lauded her team's effort. Randy Hatch, Carroll Academy's day-to-day director and founder of the basketball program, reached into a pocket and slipped $20 to one of the girls, as he usually does after games.

Together, amid giggles, the nine girls on the team bounced to the snack stand in a single-file line. Patrick Steele, the school's straight-faced security director, followed them. Over the years, Steele has overheard taunts, even racial slurs, directed at Carroll Academy students, boys and girls, from opposing fans. He escorts the players wherever they go—from the bus to the gym, to the locker rooms and bathrooms, and back to the bus.

The girls returned to the empty bleachers on the visitors' side of the gym, munching on candy and popcorn. They settled in to watch the boys' teams play, the second half of the usual girls–boys doubleheader.

It might be their favorite time of the day. The pressures of their lives melt away amid gossip and sugar.

But first it was Dresden's Senior Night. One by one, every Dresden senior winter-season athlete was introduced to an admiring crowd. Each carried a bouquet of flowers across the court, handed it to beaming parents and received hugs and kisses.

The Carroll Academy girls watched. Destiny broke the mood by pretending to cry.

"Miss Tonya, can we have parents' night, too?" she asked with a mocking tone. A couple of girls giggled.

"We could do a Senior Night," Hatch whispered. "I could get the sheriff to go round up all their parents."

That morning, sunlight peeked over the trees and mist loitered over the low spots of winter's dormant cotton fields. The fleet of ten white Ford vans, driven by Carroll Academy teachers and staff members, pulled out of the parking lot. They splintered across the countryside, through five counties of rural West Tennessee.

This swath of empty landscape is sprinkled with decaying towns. Some carry incongruent names borrowed from Europe—Paris, Milan, Dresden. Huntingdon, the Carroll County seat, is centered by a stately courthouse in the middle of a picturesque square.

Most of the manufacturing jobs that attracted past generations have dried up. The factory that made Chic jeans and other apparel in nearby Bruceton, employing 2,000 or more for decades, closed more than ten years ago. Hatch's parents worked at a long-gone shirt factory—his mother as a seamstress, his father as a sewing machine mechanic.

Now, double-digit unemployment feels normal. Tennessee's population grew more than 10 percent in the past decade, but it is stagnant in this area. Median household incomes linger in the $30,000 range. About 15 percent of adults have a college degree.

Drug use is rampant, across generations. Tennessee had more methamphetamine-lab seizures in 2010 than any other state, according to the Tennessee Methamphetamine Task Force. Carroll County, with eighteen seizures in a population of about 28,000, had about twice as many per capita as the rest of the state.

Prescription-drug abuse is particularly acute in Tennessee. The state perennially has among the highest number of prescriptions per capita in the country. It has the sixth highest percentage of youth, ages twelve to seventeen, abusing prescription pain medications, according to the Tennessee Department of Health.

It was across this quiet, complex setting that the Carroll Academy vans meandered. They picked up students, some an hour away, and returned past the scrubby trailers along two-lane roads and the tidy brick homes along High Street, to the school's truck-dock entrance.

The school is a single-story wing of a former hospital. The sign outside reads: "Carroll Academy. Home of the Jaguars. A State-Licensed Facility for Grades 6–12 Operated by the Carroll County Juvenile Court."

Most students stay at Carroll Academy for at least six months. Enrollment wavers from about seventy to one hundred, depending on that week's court docket. The vans drop off up to fourteen students at a time. In single-file silence, they slip into a side entrance.

Students are inspected in the school's hallway. There is a dress code: black pants and white button-down shirts. Boys and girls open their mouths to show there is nothing hidden there. They pull their pants pockets inside out, lift their cuffs to show shoes and socks.

Rules are strict. No ballpoint pens, because drugs could be stashed inside. No sagging pants, or else a humiliating belt will be fashioned with duct tape. No piercings, jewelry, hats, makeup, cellphones, food. Short hair for boys, ponytails for girls.

Twenty years ago, Judge Larry Logan of Carroll County Juvenile Court was frustrated that he had only two choices for disciplining teenagers. He could put them on probation and hope that was enough to scare them—and their parents—straight. Or he could place them in state custody, which means foster care or reform school.

"I hate to send kids to reform school," Logan said. "That kind of means I've given up on them."

He helped develop a middle road: Carroll Academy. It was initially financed with a $1.45 million grant from Tennessee's Department of

Children's Services, although its budget has since been carved to about half that.

. About half of the students come through Logan's courtroom in Huntingdon. The rest come from courts in adjoining counties. About 80 percent are boys. All report to probation officers. The goal is to shepherd students through a hierarchy of levels, through good behavior and good grades, and back to their "regular school," as the teenagers call it, in as little as six months.

Carroll Academy students fall into two fairly equal-sized camps: those enrolled because they were "delinquent" and those categorized as "unruly."

The "delinquent" category includes crimes. A recent snapshot showed that fifteen students had taken drugs to school, an offense that gets them kicked out—and often sent to Carroll Academy—for a year. Seven students had committed assault, and six were there for vandalism.

The "unruly" category refers to transgressions specific to minors. Most involve truancy. Seven other students were cited for uncontrollable behavior at home. Three were runaways.

"We're not really bad kids," said Leslee, a bright ninth grader who consumed a handful of her stepmother's Xanax and took the rest to school, a tangled episode that landed her and five others at Carroll Academy. "We're just good kids who made bad decisions."

Hatch, a county probation officer, was chosen to oversee the school when it opened in 1994. He started basketball teams in 1998. A year later, Carroll Academy was admitted as the smallest member of the Tennessee Secondary School Athletic Association and joined a conference that includes the area public high schools.

There are always plenty of Carroll Academy boys to play, and the team wins a few games. The girls are different. There may be only ten or fifteen of them enrolled at any time. Unless they have a compelling reason—a medical issue, for example—the school assigns the girls to the basketball team. Middle school girls play, too, an exception made for Carroll Academy.

The idea is that structure, adult role models and a way to occupy their after-school hours are good for them. Somewhat unwittingly, the players also become ambassadors to a world that usually sneers at troubled youth.

Before Carroll Academy's first basketball game in 1998, the father of an opposing player stepped out of the stands, grabbed Hatch's arm and asked that the Carroll Academy girls not hurt his daughter.

"Sports were the best thing for us," Hatch said. "For four years, people didn't know what we were doing here. Then we got sports, and people said, 'Oh, they're just like our kids.'"

Carroll Academy—the Lady Jaguars—arrived at Dresden and took the court for warm-ups. In their uniforms and sweatsuits, they looked like any other team. They did the three-man weave and layup drills. The starters were introduced, to polite applause, and they shook hands with the Dresden coaches, fist-bumped the officials and high-fived their teammates.

The Lady Jaguars trailed, 28–5, after the first quarter. They trailed by 47–11 at the half.

"Not bad," Lutz said during her halftime talk. "Well, the score's awful."

The girls sat attentively with their hands up, palms out. It's a rule Lutz imposed for all timeouts and while in the locker room to remind the girls to keep their hands up on defense.

She explained a backdoor screen to run. She told Constance to stay in arm's reach of her opponent. She told Summer to get air under her feet when she shoots.

The final score was 75–16. Lutz seemed pleased. Destiny threw up into a garbage can.

"Y'all gave me effort," Lutz said. "You didn't die on me. You didn't quit."

Opponents live in a different world. At Dresden High, summers are filled with basketball camps. Conditioning classes are year-round. Players take basketball as a regularly scheduled class every day, along with math, science and history. It is a system designed for basketball success.

Dresden used to take school buses to away games. But so many parents trailed in their cars that Dresden cut the expense. The girls simply go with their moms and dads.

When it was time to leave, the Carroll Academy girls lined up. None of their parents were there. Steele escorted them out of the gym, past the snack stand and out into the cool night. The youngest players loaded equipment in the back of the school van, and everyone climbed in through the side door.

Lutz turned down a two-lane road, popped in an Usher CD and turned the volume knob clockwise. Through the dark, teenage girls sang and shimmied as the day's last van made its way back to Carroll Academy.

III. "BAD DECISIONS, GOOD INTENTIONS"

Carroll Academy warmed up on one end of the court. Sacred Heart of Jesus, a private Roman Catholic high school in Jackson, Tennessee, warmed up on the other. The thump, thump, thump of basketballs bouncing on the wood floor echoed through the vast emptiness of the Jackson Community College gym.

One side of the gym had a smattering of fans for Sacred Heart. The bleachers set aside for Carroll Academy's Lady Jaguars were virtually empty. Again.

The nine girls on the team usually outnumber their fans in the stands.

"That tells you all you need to know," said Randy Hatch, the day-to-day leader of Carroll Academy, a school in Huntingdon adminis-tered by the juvenile court. "That's why we're here. If their parents had been there all along, maybe we wouldn't be here. Right now, we're the only family they got."

Summer, a seventeen-year-old senior, wore jersey number 14. She held a basketball on her hip and looked downcourt. Though one of her juvenile offenses involved fighting, the white scar over her right eye was a result of an unintentional head butt from an opposing player a month earlier, in early January. Summer had wobbled to the bench, bleeding, and passed out into her coach's arms. An ambulance carried her to the hospital down the street. Carroll Academy lost that game, 62–4.

Summer watched Sacred Heart's warm-up shots carom off the rim. For once, she saw no imposingly tall or overtly talented girls.

"We can win this game, if we try hard," Summer said with the breezy lilt of a songbird.

Summer's bedroom—the one at her grandmother's house in the hills outside of town, with the bed she usually shares with her son and sometimes with her mother—has wood paneling and a bare lightbulb attached to a ceiling fan. The room is stranded between childhood and adulthood.

There are pictures of Summer as a little girl, a sweet grin under freckled cheeks. She used to do ballet, play soccer and softball, and par-ticipate in beauty pageants. There is an "It's a Boy!" banner on the wall and a Pack 'n Play playpen in the corner.

It was a Friday night, and eight-month-old DaMarion was sprawled on the unmade bed. The house smelled of cigarette smoke. The curtains were mostly drawn, and there was a mattress in the dining room.

"Before I got pregnant, I wanted to join the Air Force," Summer said. "After I do that, that would help me go to college."

It was probably a long shot even before she became pregnant. Summer's parents separated when she was in fourth grade. Her mother no longer works. Her father has six children with four women, and a stepdaughter with his live-in girlfriend.

Summer is familiar with soup kitchens and eviction notices. A couple of years ago, with her father and a brother, she lived in the loft of a barn with no heat, electricity or water, she said. They took showers in the owner's nearby house. They moved into a sister's trailer for a while. Eventually, they moved to a trailer in nearby McKenzie. Summer sometimes spent nights with cousins in what some call the projects, a den of poverty.

"I never blame anyone else for the choices I make," Summer said. "But I do think if I was in a better environment, I'd be a better person."

Drinking turned to drug use—marijuana at fourteen, and lots of experimenting with everything from cocaine to hydrocodone, Summer said. She has crushed and snorted Xanax and Adderall. She can list street prices of various drugs and explain where to find them.

Last spring, she got into fights on consecutive days, the second one at school. That got her into the juvenile court system. She was placed on probation and under house arrest.

She was already pregnant, by a longtime boyfriend, a former Carroll Academy student who is now twenty-one. His only job since high school was a short stint at the drive-in restaurant Sonic.

The baby arrived last summer, two months early and weighing 3 pounds, 8 ounces. While the baby was in the neonatal care unit, Summer could be found out drinking with friends, smoking pot and occasionally snorting Xanax, she admitted.

She missed five of the first days of school last fall, just as DaMarion came home. Summer and her father, leaving for work as a welder every morning before dawn, were told that one more absence would land her in trouble as a truant. After a long weekend of parties, while her mother watched the baby, Summer woke up on a Monday afternoon to see the bus dropping friends off after school.

"I thought, oh, no," Summer said. "Carroll Academy."

Deep into the basketball season, Summer had been at Carroll Academy for six months. There were a few hiccups, including two failed drug tests for marijuana, but her grades and behavior at school were good. She was seen as a bit of a leader, especially on the basketball team. To other girls, she had an alluring mix of street credibility and sisterly sweetness.

"Bad decisions, good intentions," Summer said. "That's my saying."

Summer packed a bag for the weekend: clothes for her, diapers and clothes for DaMarion. She buckled the baby into a car seat and arrived at her father's house in McKenzie, where he had just returned from work.

Like most parents of teenagers at Carroll Academy, Summer's father has conflicted feelings about the school. He appreciates that it keeps Summer occupied and creates structure and discipline. He does not like some of the demands on his time, like the requirement that he pick up Summer after basketball practices and games. For people struggling to keep jobs and houses, everything from the time constraints to the gas money can be a burden.

Yet because the students are juveniles, the parents are part of the court orders, too. And school administrators frequently use the threat of jail to get the parents to adhere to their commands. Sometimes it is more than a threat.

But if Summer had stayed in public school?

"She probably would end up in jail, to be honest," her father said. "I hate to say it."

Like Summer, Tonya Lutz, the coach, thought that Carroll Academy might be able to beat Sacred Heart. But a full-court press flustered the Lady Jaguars.

Destiny, the point guard, could not dribble through the traps. Her teammates, including a seventh grader and four others who would not score a point all season, did not have the intuition or experience to get open or otherwise attract the attention of defenders.

Destiny's arms flailed wildly with each stolen ball. Her cheeks filled with exasperation, and her eyes scanned the bench for answers. Carroll Academy trailed, 10–0, after one quarter and by 29–8 at halftime.

Patrick Steele, Carroll Academy's security director, followed the girls into the locker room. He warned Destiny about her attitude.

Lutz closed the door. It did not stop the sound of Sacred Heart's coach screaming at his players in the next room. "You all are playing down to the competition!" he yelled.

The competition, Carroll Academy, heard every insult. A couple of the girls, including Summer, had tears in their eyes.

Lutz simmered, then boiled. "You want to get out there with that coach?" she hollered. "You're ready to cry! You're ready to cry!"

The coaches took turns shouting at their teams, a song-and-answer routine through thin walls. When one paused, the other answered, as if part of an opera.

Lutz, who played point guard on a state championship team in high school, showed Destiny how to step through a defensive trap. She asked a girl to stand up as a prop, then aggressively stepped around her, knocking her into the laps of teammates. She pushed aside another with her backside to demonstrate rebounding technique.

"Use your rear end," she said. "God gave you one. Use it."

Lutz finally dismissed the players. As the team quietly headed back out to the floor, she stopped.

"Real coaches do that," Lutz said of the opposing coach, screaming at his team despite a 21-point halftime lead. "I like that."

Carroll Academy was on its way to losing, 54–15. But early in the third quarter, when the ball went out of bounds under the basket, Lutz ordered an inbounds play that the team had practiced. She reminded Summer to set the screen.

"Yes, ma'am," Summer said.

Summer set the screen. Destiny broke open and received the pass. Her shot swished.

Lutz smiled. Sometimes, it clicks.

IV. "I KNOW WHAT IT FEELS LIKE"

Patrick Steele stood alone near the door to the locker room. It was a Friday night doubleheader, the girls before the boys, and the gym at Big Sandy was as full as any Carroll Academy had seen.

For weeks, there had been whispers of worry about the game at Big Sandy. While blacks make up about 10 percent of the population in Carroll Academy's five-county area, none of Big Sandy's 574 residents were black, according to the latest census.

"Redneck City," one of the girls had said as the van turned on the winding road toward Big Sandy.

"This place is racist," one of the boys on the basketball team said as the Carroll Academy contingent slipped into the brightly lit gym through a side door.

Adults had echoed the perception, but none of the whispers came from Steele, Carroll Academy's omnipresent security director, a man of straight faces and penetrating eyes, the son of a black mother and a mixed-race father.

Always alert to the movements of the players, particularly at road games, he was in his element. He scanned the faces in the crowd. He searched for hints of trouble.

But to him, it was not an issue of race. It was an issue of keeping the students safe. And right now, the girls were behind a closed door, gathered in a circle with their arms locked at the elbows, receiving last-minute instructions from their coach and bowing their heads in prayer.

They were safe.

So Steele, fifty-three, stood near the baseline, outside the locker room minutes before the game, and looked pleased to be there. He let slip a sliver of a smile.

Those girls in the locker room? They were not just basketball players. To Steele, they were something of himself.

———————

The first time Steele saw Alleyah, she was a toddler, all energy and optimism, waving from a front yard. He could never forget that face.

Steele's daily van route to pick up Carroll Academy students has long taken him to the town of McKenzie. For a time, about a decade ago, he dropped off a boy and a girl at a small brick home there.

Last year, Steele had a new girl to pick up. He pulled up in front of that little house, and when the door opened, everything rushed back. The way that little girl melted his heart. The way her smile stretched like taffy. The way it grew whenever he brought her a gift—a toy, a doll, anything for someone who had nothing.

And here she was again, a tiny wisp at fourteen, her wide smile covered in braces, her sweet side cloaked in sassiness and street smarts.

Alleyah.

Every year, around 150 students go through Carroll Academy, a school for troubled teenagers operated by Carroll County Juvenile Court. The school does what it can—picks them up, feeds them, educates them, disciplines them, drops them back home. The idea is to give their worlds some semblance of order and direction, and move them back to their home school wiser and stronger.

You cannot save them all. A few will bounce in and out of Carroll Academy. A few will find their way to college. Some will move from juvenile courts to adult ones, then to prison.

Most, it seems, will go back to living on society's fringes, maybe get a GED or a diploma, then live a life much like the one their parents lead. History repeats.

Of the nine girls on this season's basketball team, Alleyah is the one who worries school officials most. So young. So eager to show the older girls her street-hardened edges. Fighting. Smoking. So deceptively disruptive, like a tornado on a still night.

Yet she remembers Steele—"Mr. Patrick" to the students and everyone else—from years ago, too.

"He brought me a Barbie," she said with an impossibly wide grin.

Alleyah, an eighth grader, came to Carroll Academy because of fighting—hard to believe from someone well under five feet tall and with less than a three-digit weight. When she arrived, she was so angry that a boy she liked chose another girl, Hannah, over her that she set up a fake Facebook page for Hannah and peppered it with cruel comments. Hannah, now a basketball teammate, had no idea why so many people suddenly turned on her. She does not have a computer or a cellphone.

Almost daily, Alleyah is booted from class for talking or passing notes. Almost weekly, she is in detention, where students stand alone in a classroom, holding a clipboard and writing, hundreds of times, that they will not disrupt class or exhibit inappropriate behavior.

In her soft lilt, she tries to explain away the commotion she so casually leaves in her wake. And, far more than most, she finds herself participating in Steele's physical training, or PT, a dreaded form of punishment for most.

It is old-fashioned calisthenics, done in the hallway—push-ups, sit-ups, jumping jacks, deep-knee bends and the like. Under Steele's direction, the students count the repetitions, like soldiers at boot camp. Shirttails come untucked. Faces bead with sweat. Heavier students look ready to pass out, and some throw up.

Not Alleyah. She looks as if she could do a thousand sit-ups, a million jumping jacks.

And when the students are sent back to class, sheepish and sweaty, Steele shakes his head, turns and smiles.

Alleyah.

Students do not often see Steele's soft spot. Some know that he is a Carroll County probation officer and that he runs a karate studio in town. They whisper that he is a black belt, and even the biggest and oldest boys are intimidated by his reputation.

Day to day, it can seem like Steele's school. He directs the security staff—two other full-timers, unarmed—through a walkie-talkie. He directs teachers through the intercom, parents over the phone, students in the security office. When situations get tense—a parent becomes belligerent during a meeting, a student is caught with contraband—Steele gets calmer, as if his heartbeat slows.

Students trust him. In regular school, they say, discipline is doled out without evidence. At Carroll Academy, both sides—student versus student, student versus teacher—receive a full hearing. Steele is the judge and jury. He delivers verdicts face to face, in a near whisper. The quieter the delivery, the greater the gravity.

What most students do not know is how much he has in common with them. Steele grew up in Jackson, Tennessee, a city of about 65,000 about forty-five minutes away. He never knew his father. His mother was an alcoholic. His stepfather beat him, mostly because the boy was too light-skinned for his taste. Steele shoplifted food. He lived in abandoned houses.

When he speaks to Carroll Academy students, he sees a bit of a mirror.

"I know what it feels like because I lived it," Steele said. And he started to cry.

He apologized and regained his stoic composure.

"I know what it feels like to be at school and not have money for lunch," he said. "My mother, she was an alcoholic. All she had to do was go to school and sign the papers for me to get free lunches, but she was too drunk to do that. So I know what it's like when they're here and they have nothing to go home to and look forward to. I know what it feels like to go home with no electricity and no water and no food in the house because that's how I grew up. So I totally understand them. I understand them in a way that the other staff don't.

"It's just that there's still a lot of pain in me from growing up that way. And when I look at these kids, I can see the pain and the hurt in some of them. It just reminds me of me."

It explains why, like most of the adults at Carroll Academy, Steele finds some students grab his heart and do not let go.

"I understand Alleyah," he said.

Soon enough, she was back in the security office, being asked about a raunchy note she traded with another girl. Steele spoke to her sternly and calmly. He sent her back to class and shook his head.

Constance, a quiet eighth grader with a penchant for launching projectiles in anger, drained a three-pointer to give Carroll Academy a quick lead over Big Sandy. It was fleeting. Carroll Academy lost, 45–10.

But it felt like a success. A few parents made the trip. Miranda, a self-deprecating senior from Big Sandy recovering from alcohol problems, corralled a first-half rebound and went to the free-throw line to try for her first points of the season. She missed both shots but beamed when she saw her stepfather, brother and sister cheering.

Leslee, a freshman with the charisma of a future homecoming queen, caught at school with prescription painkillers taken from her father's girlfriend, jammed a finger that left her in tears. But following the game, after a trip to the snack stand with her teammates, she sat with her father and his girlfriend, her fingers taped together like a splint, smiling.

And Alleyah received substantial playing time, too. A bit like a moth, she flitted about on defense, crouched and with her arms up, as she had been taught, long after the nearest opponent had zipped past. On offense, the ball sometimes seemed too heavy for her. She never came close to scoring a point.

Maybe next season. If there is one girl who will return to the team in the fall, it is probably Alleyah. And Steele will be there to pick her up and take her home.

V. "I WON THE BALLGAME"

It was a last chance. The score was close. And Tonya Lutz was not going to let the opportunity slip.

"We can win this ballgame, but y'all have to help me out!" she shouted to her players during a first-half timeout of their district play-off basketball game.

It was a play-in game, of sorts, between ninth-seeded Carroll Academy and eighth-seeded Bruceton High, a school several of her players attended before the juvenile-court system sent them to Carroll Academy.

Lutz hollered instructions about rebounding and defense. "Do you understand that?" she said.

Sweaty, pie-eyed faces nodded back at her.

"This is the end of the trail if y'all don't do that. This is in your court. Y'all have to want it. Y'all understand?"

The girls piled their hands in the middle of the huddle.

"OK," Lutz said. "One, two, three—hustle!"

Destiny, the senior point guard, made a three-pointer. She hit another. Carroll Academy trailed by only three, its smallest second-quarter margin of the season. Murmurs rippled through the crowd at the neutral court in Clarksburg. Bruceton stretched the lead to double digits. Destiny's three-pointer with one second left made the halftime score 24–16.

The couple of dozen Carroll Academy fans in attendance stood and gave the girls their biggest ovation of the season as they disappeared into the locker room.

"Carroll Academy girls have never won a game in the district tournament, ever!" Lutz shouted, talking faster than usual.

The girls looked on, their hands raised and palms out, Lutz's mandated reminder during timeouts and halftimes to always keep their hands up on defense.

"Come on, girls," cried Summer, a seventeen-year-old senior with a baby at home, a recently failed drug test in her file and a history of delinquency on her juvenile record.

Theirs may be a losing team, unappreciated and unloved. But for one coach and nine girls, on a day when they would be together for the last time, there was reason for optimism.

Lutz is a thirty-six-year-old mother of two, with a twangy voice that can pierce the din of a classroom or the roar of a basketball crowd. She is a regular at the biggest church in town and an occasional judge at beauty pageants, where her daughter used to compete.

She desperately wants to be viewed seriously as a coach. "Any good coach, I would challenge to come and do a year or two and see if they can turn a program around," she said. "Because I thought the same thing."

Lutz grew up a few miles away, in Gleason, where she was the point guard on a state championship team nearly twenty years ago. She played basketball at Bethel University in nearby McKenzie and earned a sociology degree. She spent several years doing counseling, then was home for two years after she and her husband had their first child.

When Randy Hatch, the Carroll Academy administrator, hired her to replace him as the girls' coach in 2004, she never looked at the team's record. Even though she had no head coaching experience, she assumed she could overcome the disadvantages—the ever-changing roster, the inexperienced players, the lack of parental support.

"If someone were to look at my record, they'd probably think I can't coach at all," Lutz said.

On the first day of practice in October, Lutz asked her players some basic questions. Where is the free-throw line? What is traveling? How many players are on the court at a time?

Most of the girls replied with blank stares.

"Until Christmas, I was teaching them offense versus defense," Lutz said. "We have a crash course in peewee basketball—dribbling, passing, shooting, defense."

She knows that her record with a team that always loses may preclude her from coaching elsewhere someday. It gnaws at her. But she musters enthusiasm for the job—doggedly challenging referees, for example, or diving for loose balls in practice to set an example.

"I'm going to coach like we're going to win a state championship," Lutz said. "They deserve that."

Players see her as a stable, trustworthy role model, unlike anyone they know. She is fiery, sassy and confident. She gives them pointers on everything from manners to hairstyles.

Typically, she starts games with a pep talk about fundamentals and effort, employs a diatribe at halftime and makes the postgame speech a life lesson about perseverance.

"A lot of people who are in the stands are people who don't see what we're winning at," Lutz said.

And she started to cry.

The district playoff game fell on a Saturday, meaning no at-home pickup for the players. They needed to find a way to school. Hannah, a tall and well-mannered seventh grader, and Alleyah, a smiling tempest of an eighth grader, arrived first. They hung their teammates' uniforms on hooks in the locker room.

One by one, the rest of the players arrived, to the mild surprise of Lutz and Hatch, who presumed that some parents would not provide rides for the girls. They changed into their uniforms in their tiny locker room. They brushed each other's hair and showed each other YouTube videos on the school's computers.

When it was time to go, they loaded gear into one van and slid into the bench seats. The game was at Clarksburg High School, about ten miles south of Huntingdon.

"My dad doesn't want us to win because he's tired of coming to Huntingdon," said Leslee, a ninth grader from a town about twenty miles away. Her mother died when Leslee was seven.

Lutz gathered the girls in a circle in the locker room. They held hands, bowed their heads and recited the Lord's Prayer, which Lutz taught the girls at the beginning of the season.

"Hopefully not our last ballgame, but play your hardest," Lutz said, and the girls headed out for warm-ups.

Four of the girls—a season high—had family members in the stands.

"I'm so glad to have people here," Summer said to Destiny as she nodded toward her father, her infant son, DaMarion, and a few others. "It makes me so happy."

One girl took a charge, something the team had worked on in practices late in the season. Jenna, a stoic junior, grabbed a couple of offensive rebounds. Destiny scored off a designed inbounds play. Constance made a three-pointer.

Maybe, just maybe, this would be the one.

Three nights earlier, Hatch took the boys' and girls' basketball teams to Memphis to see an NBA game between the Grizzlies and the Minnesota Timberwolves. The dress code was loosened. The girls wore tight jeans and makeup and wore their hair down. They flirted with members of the boys' team. Security director Patrick Steele was a bundle of nerves.

For many, it was their first time to Memphis, one-hundred-plus miles away. They were awestruck at the size of the buildings. After walking down Beale Street and entering the 18,000-seat FedEx Forum, they rode an escalator—some for the first time—to the upper level. Some were scared of the height and sat stiffly in their seats. They were dazzled by the scoreboard, the lights and the sounds, much more than the basketball.

But now they were back in the sparsely populated gym in Clarksburg. They trailed by eight points, their smallest halftime deficit of the season.

Lutz turned to Leslee, a rangy freshman.

"I need you to pick it up," Lutz said. Leslee smiled.

Bruceton soon stretched the lead to double digits. Carroll Academy was besieged by its usual inadequacies—rebounding, turnovers, a scoring option besides Destiny. Summer missed two free throws. Miranda just missed a putback, which would have been her first points of the season. Bruceton outscored Carroll Academy, 16–2, in the third quarter, ending with a 10–0 run.

In the huddle, Lutz smiled at Destiny. She knew that, for her only player with previous high school basketball experience, this would be the end of her playing career. "Give it all you have," Lutz said.

Destiny drove and drew fouls. She stopped and shot three-pointers. She finished with a season-high 28 points.

The Lady Jaguars lost, 52–32. It was their biggest output and smallest losing margin of the thirty-two-game season.

"I won the ballgame," Lutz said in the locker room. "I won the ballgame because you gave me effort."

The coach's eyes were dry. But Destiny, Summer and several others cried.

Lutz drove the van ten miles back to Carroll Academy, and a pale, late-day sun drew long shadows on the landscape. The van was practically empty. All but three of the girls found rides home straight from the game. The usual postgame mix of music, whispers and gossip was replaced by quiet melancholy.

Back at the school, Hannah and Miranda carried the water bottles inside. Alleyah carried towels. They dumped the sweaty uniforms in the school's washing machine.

Carroll Academy's lone hallway was dark. The gym, a free-standing building nearby, was empty and locked. The white vans were lined up in the lot, waiting for Monday's deployment to pick up the students.

A cold, late-winter wind blew, and the girls rushed to get into the warmth of awaiting cars, back into a life without a basketball team. In a moment, it seemed, they were scattered like leaves, and it was impossible to know just where they would be blown.

The losing streak, six years running, was dormant, at least until fall. The Lady Jaguars have lost 184 games in a row.

AUTHOR'S NOTE: The first five stories on the Lady Jaguars were published on five consecutive days. The following two stories were published more than a year later, when I returned to Carroll Academy to see what had become of some of my favorite people. The last story was published five years after that.

VI. "THAT'S AS BAD AS IT GETS"

Hannah

Hannah heard her mother's muffled cries for help. They came from the bedroom, a sort of guesthouse that sat behind her grandparents' home off a narrow winding road in the hills of West Tennessee.

Hannah, fourteen, looked in the window and saw her father, his lip bloodied, on top of her mother, choking her.

In the chaos of the next few minutes, after her grandfather unlocked the door with a key and collapsed to the ground, and while her grandmother called the police, Hannah stepped between her parents to prevent them from striking each other. Both her parents went to jail that night.

"My mama was trying to get out of the room and he wouldn't let her," said Hannah, her honeyed voice smoothing edges from her consonants and slowing her vowels. "So he started going towards her to hit her. I got in front of her, stepped in front of her, and told him that he wasn't to hit her. He was counting to three, telling me to get out of the way. And he got to three and I still wouldn't move because I didn't want him hitting her and going to jail or prison forever. But he went to jail anyways."

Wess and Monica did not rebut their daughter's version of events from that Friday night last fall. They were married for eighteen years and had four children, ages five to sixteen. They used to sing in a gospel quintet and take family vacations. Their home was filled with family photographs from a simpler time, not long ago.

"We've just had two bad years," Wess said this past spring. "For some reason."

Hannah saw the worst of it. Her parents admitted that the family

had been tattered by infidelity and addictions to prescription painkillers and antidepressants. They had moved too many times to count, for
a time living without water or electricity. Beyond domestic assaults,
there had been arrests for acts of desperation, like stealing gas and
shoplifting food.

At separate times, each parent spent about a month in jail last fall.
Hannah visited them and cried.

"I didn't like seeing them like that," she said.

The only constant in her life was Carroll Academy, a school run by
the Carroll County Juvenile Court. Hannah has spent parts of the last
three school years there, and played the past two seasons on the girls'
basketball team, the Lady Jaguars, who have now lost 213 games in a row.

For nearly two decades, Carroll Academy, a one-hallway school set
in the one-story wing of a former hospital, has been a catch basin for
teenagers slipping through society's cracks. Through the course of a
typical school year, one hundred or more students from a five-county
area are sent there to try to regain their footing.

Most students come for a few months. Hannah may be there a few years.

"She's one of the top 10 percent of cases here," Randy Hatch, a probation officer who has been the director of Carroll Academy since it opened, said this spring. "It's clearly from lack of parenting, not behavior problems on her behalf. We know there are two active warrants for their arrest. What if they get taken to jail? Where does she go? That's as bad as it gets."

Off a dirt road about thirty miles away, Hannah's parents sat together on a sofa inside the two-bedroom trailer they rented. The family car sat lifelessly outside, its necessary repairs beyond the family budget. Monica, thirty-four, said she could not work because of chronic back pain. Wess, thirty-seven, had unsteady employment at a sawmill.

Hannah would sleep either on the couch or on an air mattress in one of the bedrooms. She and her mother had decorated one bedroom wall with photographs of Hannah playing for the Lady Jaguars, although her parents had never been to Hannah's games.

"She's grown up a whole lot," Monica said, her husband nudged close beside her, all their children gone, staying with other relatives. "Maybe what she's seen, she'll look back and she won't follow it—I hope. She says she won't—which I said, too. I don't know. Stress can do a lot of stuff. It really gets you. But she has. She's growed up a whole lot."

West Tennessee is covered in forests and cotton fields, sprinkled with decaying towns loosely strung together by two-lane roads. From Huntingdon, a shrinking town of about four thousand residents anchored by the stately Carroll County courthouse on a photogenic square, Nashville is about two hours to the east, and Memphis is two hours to the west. Interstate 40, which connects those two cities, is about twenty miles to the south.

It is a rural place, quietly troubled by the hollowing plagues of small-town America—unemployment, drug abuse and teenage pregnancy among them. The problems lurk in the shadows between landscaped brick homes and the bucolic countryside.

West Tennessee may be merely a proxy for anywhere. There might be a thousand Carroll Counties around the country, proud and simple places, fading almost imperceptibly with the slow passing of another time, where old-timers wish for a future more like the past, and the young people have little imagination for anything other than the present.

The area around Huntingdon was once freckled with manufacturing plants, many in the garment industry. For a long time, factory jobs seemed bequeathed from one generation to the next. But over the past couple of decades, coinciding with the lifetimes of today's teenagers, most of the major plants closed. Their shells turned to rust and shrank into the weeds behind leaning fences and locked gates.

In the past year, among other setbacks, a nearby munitions manufacturer and a company that makes farm fences and troughs each cut several hundred jobs. In March, the unemployment rate in Carroll County was 12.3 percent, ranking it ninetieth among ninety-five counties in Tennessee—itself a laggard in employment nationally. The four neighboring counties that make up Carroll Academy's jurisdiction have persistent double-digit unemployment, too.

Drugs are an ever-evolving worry. Carroll County Judge Larry Logan helped create Carroll Academy in 1994 in the midst of what he felt was a crack cocaine epidemic.

"I thought, this is the end of the world," Logan said. "And then meth came along."

He and other judges sign court orders nearly every week granting law enforcement agencies the right to raid suspected methamphetamine labs.

Meth use remains unusual among teenagers, if not their parents, officials said, but marijuana use and prescription-drug abuse are rampant.

"I fear that we have lost two full generations of people to drugs," Logan said.

Those generations are uncommonly condensed. While birthrates among teenagers continue to fall across the country and in Tennessee, the state still has a teenage birthrate about 25 percent higher than the national average. The pregnancy rate in Carroll County, 27.5 per 1,000 female teenagers in 2010, is higher than most. Three of the other four counties served by Carroll Academy are higher than that.

Two of Hannah's teammates from her first season with the Lady Jaguars, among the three who received high school diplomas last year, were single, unemployed and raising babies this spring. A teammate on this season's team had two children from different fathers. A fourteen-year-old boy at the school was absent one day this spring to attend the birth of his child.

It has all combined to create a swath of the population seemingly stuck in a spin cycle of inertia. Many with the ability and drive to leave the area already have. The concern is that many struggling teenagers appear headed toward difficult lives like those of their parents. The cycle repeats.

"I don't know if they realize what's out there," Logan said of many students at Carroll Academy, "because of the way they're living."

A year ago, Hannah was a tall and lanky thirteen-year-old seventh grader. Her cherub face and sweet disposition attracted older boys and made girls jealous. While most of her Lady Jaguars teammates protected themselves with a hard, if fragile, veneer, using bravado to convey worldliness, Hannah wore a cloak of vulnerability.

A year later, Hannah still leaned closer to childhood than adulthood, drawing hearts on her notebooks, absent-mindedly singing to herself, biting her nails and blushing at attention. She had gained a noticeable amount of weight, but kept hidden what she had seen and been through over the past year.

Unlike most of her basketball teammates, she saw Carroll Academy not as a punishment, but as a sanctuary.

The sign in front describes it as a "State-Licensed Facility for Grades 6–12 Operated by the Carroll County Juvenile Court." For most area teenagers, it is a deterrent for bad behavior. Get in trouble, they are warned, and you might end up at Carroll Academy. You might earn your way out with good behavior and grades, but that usually takes at least six months.

Rules are strict. Students must dress in black pants and white button-down shirts. Boys' hair must be cut short; girls must wear theirs short or in a ponytail. Students are brought to school in unmarked white vans, and walk silently in single-file lines to be inspected for contraband, from cellphones and gum to switchblades and drugs.

Transgressions that land teenagers at Carroll Academy generally fall into one of two categories. One is delinquent behavior, the types of things that would get adults arrested: drugs, vandalism, assault. The other is unruly behavior, like truancy and uncontrollable conduct, at home or school. About 80 percent of the students are boys.

Most arrive with a combination of anxiety and fear. Some, like Hannah, quickly realize that it is a cocoon from the world outside—free of bullying, filled with structure, staffed by attentive adults. Students are fed breakfast and lunch; for some, it is all they eat.

Hannah arrived when she was twelve, after she admitted stealing prescription pills from her mother and bringing them to school under orders from girls who had threatened to beat her up. It was Monica, wanting to teach Hannah a lesson, who called the school.

It was only this spring that Hannah acknowledged that it was a lie—a lie conceived by her father, Hannah said, so that he could take the pills and avoid the wrath of his wife.

Yet Hannah wants to graduate from Carroll Academy. She likes the attention and a predictable schedule. She likes playing on the basketball team. She has flitting dreams of becoming a doctor or a veterinarian.

Hannah's parents do not like that she goes to Carroll Academy. Getting her to the van stop in the nearest town is inconvenient, and picking her up after basketball games (when school vans do not run) can cost an hour of time and $20 in gas money, if the car is running at all. But if Hannah does not attend, her parents could end up in jail. The juvenile court views truancy as a parent problem, not a child one.

Ask Hannah what she wants more than anything in her life, and her request is simple. She just wants to go back in time.

"I wish that my mom and dad would stop fighting and everything would be fine," she said. "And we'd go to church."

It was midmorning on a Wednesday in March, and Hannah had missed school for several days. Carroll Academy officials believed her family had moved, but were uncertain where to find them. They feared that they might not see Hannah again.

A car rolled up to the school entrance, tracked by security cameras. Hannah and a man approached the door. They were met by Patrick Steele, the school's no-nonsense security director.

The man, Terry, was a cousin of Wess; their fathers were brothers, and Terry had been a groomsman in Wess and Monica's wedding.

Terry apologized profusely to Steele. He explained that Hannah was staying with him and his wife, Morgan, just as she had for much of last summer, when Terry found the family living without electricity and water, the cupboards bare of food. Terry promised to get Hannah to the van pickup spot on time every morning.

They also discussed why Hannah had not been taking Adderall, long prescribed to treat her diagnosed attention-deficit disorder. The school could tell when Hannah did not take her medication—her work got sloppy and her behavior turned uncharacteristically erratic. The week before, she had failed a math test and spent time in solitary detention for disrupting class.

Her parents did not think she needed Adderall every day, especially on weekends, but relatives believe they wanted the extra pills for themselves, either to consume or sell. Her parents held Hannah's latest prescription, but were unwilling to pass it to relatives or bring the pills to the school.

Legally, Steele needed to deal directly with Hannah's parents, who still had custody of their daughter. Terry dialed a number, asked for Wess, and handed the phone to Steele. He quietly told Wess that he and Monica must arrange a visit to Carroll Academy within the next week.

Hannah held her books to her chest, chewed on her lower lip and listened quietly.

Terry, thirty-two, and Morgan, twenty-three, were raising two children of their own when they decided to take in Hannah and her two younger siblings—a twelve-year-old brother and five-year-old sister.

They lived in a mobile home on a skinny road outside of nearby Camden. Terry had a full-time job as a plant manager for a metal roofing company.

"We're not rich, but we're fed," Terry said.

Terry and Morgan talked about custody of Hannah, at least, but they were leery of the legal wrangling and wading too deep into the convoluted politics of a sprawling family.

"We just want them to eat," Terry said. "Have something to eat, have a place to lay down and go to sleep, where it's warm in the wintertime and cool in the summertime. And for her to get to school and have a fighting chance. If she don't get an education, especially in this part of the country, she's never going to amount to nothing."

Morgan grew up in the area. She got pregnant at fourteen but had a miscarriage, and then had a son at age seventeen. She did not finish high school, and spent time this spring working on her GED, studying some of the same math Hannah was learning at Carroll Academy. Morgan and Terry met a few years ago, married and had a daughter, who was now one.

"I love Hannah to death," Morgan said. "If I could adopt her, I would. For the simple fact that I know what Hannah is going through. I literally know what she's going through."

The couple tried to wrap Hannah in a world more typical of other young teenagers. They got her a cellphone. They took her shopping for a pair of jeans. They treated her to fast food. Morgan took her to have her eyebrows waxed.

Hannah was on birth control pills, but vowed not to have sex until she was married. She had ended relationships with boys who expected otherwise. Morgan told Hannah to wait until she was at least twenty before having children.

"I'm scared she'll end up out of school, no baby's daddy, and won't have nobody—and won't know what to do," Morgan said, speaking from experience. "And around here, that's pretty much to a T what happens to most every girl that doesn't have any parents."

It was twenty minutes before the Lady Jaguars' last regular season game. The band directors at Bethel University, in nearby McKenzie, had not made attendance mandatory, but forty-five of the fifty-five members of the pep band came, wearing T-shirts that read "Carroll Academy Lady Jaguars."

They filled several rows of bleachers. The home cheering section, often almost empty, was larger than that for the visiting side, maybe for the first time since Hatch, the school's director, started the boys' and girls' teams in 1998.

The gym filled with unfamiliar revelry and optimism. The band played the national anthem and a full slate of pep songs during timeouts.

It cheered lustily when a girl named Hayley scored the team's first point midway through the first quarter, closing Camden High's lead to 9–1.

The atmosphere could not prevent Carroll Academy from trailing at halftime, 52–5.

"It was too loud in there," a senior named Caitlyn said in the locker room. "I couldn't concentrate."

Hatch was not pleased with the effort, but his stern words were softened by a face typically on the verge of a smile. He lectured the girls. Hannah bit her nails. Earlier in the season, she scored a team-high 10 points in a game. But her high-arcing three-point shot was not falling today. One overeager effort was blocked by a gym rafter.

"Hold your head up and be proud of who you are," Hatch said.

The final score was 83–10.

Afterward, ten young men from the Bethel band slipped from the bleachers and approached the Lady Jaguars in front of their bench. They sang an a cappella version of the Bruno Mars song "Just the Way You Are," ending on their knees. Each young man handed a girl a stuffed animal to keep. Some girls were in tears.

As the groups huddled together for pictures, Hannah beamed. She was a veteran, one of just two playing for the Lady Jaguars for the second season, but she remained the youngest player.

A few teammates graduated in May, and most of the others will not be back to Carroll Academy in the fall. But Hannah probably will.

"She does not need to leave here," Hatch said. "She should remain here until she's a senior. That way I'll know she gets a diploma."

By the time school got out for the summer, Hannah's world had shuffled again. Her birthday came and went in June without a call from her parents. She no longer lived with Morgan and Terry, who had lost his job. Other cousins had taken her in, wanting to make sure she had a place to sleep, food to eat and a way to get to school when it resumes in August. They, too, talked of requesting long-term custody.

It might be out of necessity. By mid-July, having violated their probations, both of Hannah's parents were in jail.

Tonya

On the first day of practice, last October, there were five girls on Tonya Lutz's basketball team at Carroll Academy. They inherited a 184-game losing streak, probably the longest in the nation, with little chance of ending it.

Lutz had been coaching against hope since 2004.

"Worst hand I've had," Lutz said.

Lutz, thirty-seven, was a former all-district point guard and a high school state champion from a nearby town. Every fall, a new batch of wayward teens appeared on her court. Most had never played organized team sports. Few played much basketball.

One girl, a tenth grader named Kiana, had played a little for the previous season's team. Back then, Kiana was afraid of the ball. Now she was likely to be the team's captain.

Lutz taught the girls what the lines on the court meant. She taught them to dribble, shoot and play defense. She yelled at them, encouraged them and hugged them.

Sometimes the Lady Jaguars lost by nearly 100 points, and sometimes they struggled to score at all. By the end, almost every one of them wished the season could go on forever.

Many wanted to grow into someone like their coach: married, two children, a new brick home outside of town. She seemed to have it all, and more than most could imagine for themselves.

When the girls had big news to report—a good grade, a new job, a college acceptance, a passed drug screen, a pregnancy—Lutz was often the first person they told. They called her Ms. Tonya, the formal salutation paired with the informal first name that is part of the culture of manners in West Tennessee.

And then, two weeks into practice for the Lady Jaguars, two weeks before a season opener, Lutz had something she wanted to tell Kiana: she was thinking of quitting.

"I don't know why I went to her first," Lutz said.

Kiana was raised mostly by a single father and just a hint of a mother. As a ninth grader at a public high school, Kiana hid prescription painkillers that a friend named Leslee had taken from a stepmother. The school's zero-tolerance policy toward drugs landed both girls at Carroll Academy, and onto Lutz's team.

Leslee earned her way back to her former school to start the year. Kiana was still, for now, at Carroll Academy.

Lutz told Kiana that her thirteen-year-old son wanted to play basketball for the middle school. Her nine-year-old daughter was involved in plenty of activities, too. Her husband worked swing shifts at the aluminum plant off the highway. The couple would probably have to hire someone to watch their kids so that Lutz could coach.

That is what gnawed at her, the hypocrisy of it all. To coach girls who needed more role models, she was going to leave her own children with someone else?

Kiana, round-cheeked and soft-spoken, a girl with no mother of her own to count on, told Lutz that her priority should be as a mother.

"She understood," Lutz said, fighting through tears.

She hated the thought of resigning, and the message it would send. For years, Lutz had preached the gospel of never quitting. Not in basketball, no matter the score. Not in life, no matter the odds.

It had not occurred to her that even quitting could be spun into a worthwhile life lesson.

"Hopefully they'll respect me in the end," Lutz said. "Because this is what a mom is supposed to do. A mom is supposed to put her children above anything else."

_____

The idea, fifteen years ago, was simple: use sports to teach lessons that cannot always be taught in a classroom. The students at Carroll Academy might learn teamwork, discipline and trust. If nothing else, basketball provided structure and diversions for children whose lives had little of either.

With enough interest to sometimes require tryouts, the boys' team usually won a few games a year. Not the girls. With a low number of girls enrolled at Carroll Academy, most were required to play on the basketball team. Few had experience. The Lady Jaguars had won six games in their history, and none in the last seven seasons.

Hatch, the school's fifty-four-year-old director, had coached the boys' and girls' teams during their early years. He handed them off nearly a decade ago to spend more time with his family.

Brian McDowell, one of Carroll Academy's security officers, took over the boys' team. Lutz was hired to coach the girls. She taught a life skills class, too, covering topics from creating healthy meals to caring for an infant. But most people thought of her as the basketball coach.

Before she went to work that day last October, she told her husband to pray, because she was not sure she would return with a job at Carroll Academy. Hatch surprised her. He responded to her coaching resignation with a supportive hug.

"You've been here a long time," Lutz said Hatch told her. "These kids love you. You belong in the classroom."

Hatch's first inclination was to cancel the season before it started. It was too late to hire a new coach, and there was no one else on the school's small staff to do it. But when he called the girls together, it was Alleyah who suggested that Hatch just do the job himself.

Hatch sent the text message to his wife at 9:01 a.m. on Monday, October 29.

"Tonya resigned as girls BB coach," it read. "Looks like I'm coming out of retirement."

Those closest to him worried that the stress of coaching would not help his health, including persistent concerns over ulcers and his heart. Hatch used to be temperamental on the sideline, especially when opponents ran up the score on the helpless Jaguars or officials called questionable fouls against a team facing an 80-point deficit. He once pulled his team off the court in protest. He once instructed a player to hand the ball to an opponent several times in a row to embarrass an unbending opposing coach.

"He could really come unglued in his earlier years," Hatch's wife, Vicky, said. "He's a lot more mellow now. He wanted the girls to take it more seriously when he was younger. Now he can see more of the big picture. He wants them to have fun and make memories."

In December, Hatch's Lady Jaguars had a rare halftime lead, 19–16, against Jackson Prep, a private school from another conference. Carroll Academy lost, 40–27. ("Bad coaching," Hatch said.) The game was sandwiched between two losses to area public schools—68–5 and 69–5.

By Christmas, Kiana was gone, having earned her way back to public school. Hatch's roster settled in at nine, including two girls from last season's team: Hannah, an eighth grader, and Alleyah, a ninth grader.

Alleyah scored her only point of the season on a free throw. Hannah, whose ability to make three-pointers was matched only by her willingness to take them, using a two-handed shot from her chest, made three and scored 10 points in a January loss.

The Lady Jaguars finished 0–29. They were outscored, 1,845 to 306, an average defeat of 64–11.

Lutz could not bear to watch. She attended only two games, once to sell admission tickets at the front door and the other to work at the concession stand. Through her peripheral vision, she saw untapped potential.

"It was killing me," she said.

It bothered her seeing how the team took the court. While Hatch's team arrived with unscripted nonchalance, warming up before the games by shooting haphazardly, Lutz had always coached the girls to run onto the floor, circle the court and perform layup drills with hustle.

She thought she could turn Hannah, taller than all her classmates and heavier than a year earlier, into an inside player, one with the shooting form to make her dangerous from outside. She saw other girls, some she had in class, and thought about how they might have reacted to her firebrand style and attention to detail.

"There was a lot of times I was wanting to yell out, because I knew who could drive and who could shoot the three-pointer," Lutz said. "And I had to really bite my tongue. Lot of times I had to back away because I was liable to stand up and start coaching from the sidelines."

There was nothing she could do about it now. The Lady Jaguars were not her team anymore.

On a different court, it was just how Lutz pictured it. The whistle was around her neck, the girls sprinted through drills, and parents cared enough to come to practice.

Finally, she thought. A basketball team I can mold. A team that can win.

There were nine girls, choreographed like a stage production. With a melody of squeaks and thumps, they performed the three-man weave. When Lutz blew the whistle, they rearranged themselves and began a different drill.

The girls wore practice shirts that read Lady Tigers, not Lady Jaguars. They were ages nine, ten and eleven. Lutz waltzed up and down the court, whistle hanging from her mouth, orchestrating their movements. In one practice, she covered the 1-2-1-1 trap, the pivot foot and how to take a charge.

She stepped in to teach the girls the crossover dribble, and the reverse spin dribble to get around a defender. Just a year ago, she was trying to teach Alleyah simply to bring the ball upcourt.

"I'm always like, why can't those girls learn like these girls learn?" Lutz said.

When word spread over the winter that Lutz had stepped down at Carroll Academy, she received a call asking if she wanted to coach younger girls, including her own nine-year-old daughter, Lydia.

Coach? And spend time with her children? Absolutely.

Practices were held at the gleaming Gleason High gym. On the wall at one end of the court were large photographs, eight feet across, of Gleason's state championship teams. One of them was dated 1991–92. On the left end of the front row was a girl with big, curly blond hair. She was number 24, a sophomore point guard named Tonya Parham, who went on to college and married a boy named Chris Lutz.

In the nearby foyer, on the Gleason Wall of Fame, were plaques honoring fifty-two inductees. Tonya Parham was one.

In the first game that Lutz coached for the Lady Tigers, they won. They finished the season 6–4—the same number of victories that Carroll Academy has mustered in fifteen years.

"I hate that I can't bring this over there," Lutz said.

But she just might. And that is because these girls, with their crossover dribbles and well-practiced defensive traps, will soon feed into the area's middle schools and high schools.

And, in a few years, these girls, including Lutz's own daughter, will play the Lady Jaguars from Carroll Academy.

Alleyah

A year earlier, Alleyah was a fourteen-year-old breeze of a girl. She was not quite five feet tall and was close to 100 pounds only if she held a bagful of basketballs. The biggest things about her were a smile as wide as her ears and a fast-talking sassiness refined in the housing projects.

Once, when a Lady Jaguars teammate had the audacity to pass her the ball, Alleyah watched it slip through her fingers. She turned and put a hand on her hip.

"I don't know why y'all are throwing me the damn ball," she said through a mouth full of braces.

But there she was this past January, playing point guard against neighboring Huntingdon High. The Lady Jaguars were without their two best players, girls who could be trusted to bring the ball upcourt and score a few points.

Huntingdon persistently pressured the dribbler, stole the ball and scored on uncontested layups. At halftime, Carroll Academy trailed 57–0. Alleyah cried in the locker room.

"This is hard," she said.

"I'm sorry, honey," Coach Hatch said. "There's no one else."

Alleyah played the whole game. Carroll Academy lost, 91–4.

"I ran out of breath," she said. "I didn't get no breaks. I felt like it was 100 degrees in the gym."

But she did it. The girl who once reprimanded teammates for passing her the ball played every minute at point guard.

"Before it started, I didn't think I could do it," Alleyah said. Her smile, freed from the braces of a year before, stretched wide. "Now, when I accomplished it, I felt proud."

Alleyah, now a fifteen-year-old ninth grader, wanted to get out of Carroll Academy. And it somehow seemed possible.

"I'd like to be a cheerleader," she said in February. "I wanted to be a cheerleader since I was little."

There are no cheerleaders at Carroll Academy, and Alleyah has looked the past couple of years as if she might be a permanent resident there. She got into fights in middle school. Her mother could not control her, and Alleyah was a fixture on the streets of the neighborhood, ripe with dropouts and drug dealers. She was a tiny dynamo of head-shaking self-destruction.

She spent much of last year, when she was not playing for the Lady Jaguars, getting kicked out of class. She talked, she argued and she passed notes. She was a regular in detention. She had been wrung through the various punishments that Carroll Academy doles out, including a grueling string of calisthenics in the hallway that made most misbehaving students nearly collapse from exhaustion.

None of it seemed to faze Alleyah.

The primary incentive for good behavior and good grades is Carroll Academy's system of levels. Students begin at Level 1 and, after sev eral weeks of good grades and a clean disciplinary record, can advance to Level 2. Keep it up for another stretch of weeks, and Level 3 awaits. Perks are slowly added—more talking, an easing of rules about makeup and hair. Get to Level 5, and a return to "regular school," as the students call it, awaits.

A year ago, Alleyah was tethered to Level 1. She failed two drug tests, which set her back again. But this year was different.

"I just want to prove everybody wrong," she said.

Mostly, she wanted to prove it to Steele, the school's security director.

"He says I'm going to be here until I'm eighteen," Alleyah said.

. Steele first noticed her a decade earlier, an effervescent toddler waving to him along his van route. Then, a couple of years ago, Steele had a new stop. It was a seventh grader assigned to Carroll Academy because of unruliness and fighting. He pulled up to the address. Out came a thirteen-year-old Alleyah.

Alleyah has not been back to regular school since.

"I don't want to get a Carroll Academy diploma," she said earlier this spring. "I want to get my high school diploma and I want to go to college and be a cosmetologist. I want to do hair. I used to do the hair on my

Barbie doll. One day, I flat-ironed it, and it melted. I thought it was going to grow back."

Speaking with a confidence unknown a year earlier, a maturity laced with optimism, Alleyah said she had not failed a drug test in more than six months. Only once was she called into the hallway for calisthenics. She generally kept pace with her school work. She had grown to like basketball.

If she could keep it together, she would not have to attend summer school. Her probation officer would send her to regular school in the fall.

The thought was both tantalizing and frightening.

"It would be hard, but I think I could do it," Alleyah said of leaving Carroll Academy. "I just want to be in high school."

Alleyah's bedroom at her father's house was bathed in black light, turning the walls a psychedelic purple. A color wheel on the floor added rotating splashes of color. A lava lamp glowed on the window sill. The room was in perfect order, the bed neatly made, and Alleyah was happy to show it off. She had changed out of her Carroll Academy uniform of black pants, white shirt and a ponytail. Her hair was styled, her face covered in makeup, her wide smile framed in lipstick. She wore jeans, a tight T-shirt and suede boots.

"People say she's a cute girl, and I don't want people taking advantage," said her father, Randall. "It worries me. It worries me. I know how guys are at fifteen. I know what they're thinking. I used to be there. And there are some things little girls aren't going to talk to their daddy about. I know she's smarter than that. We talk about it. Hopefully she just uses her head. A lot of girls don't."

Randall, forty-five, grew up in McKenzie. He had not had full-time employment for several years, since a longtime furniture factory in town closed, eliminating hundreds of jobs. This spring, he had a temporary job, about thirty miles away, making $9.15 an hour on an assembly line building lawn mowers, starting at six each morning.

He usually woke Alleyah at five and dropped her at her mother's house, a few blocks away. After school, the Carroll Academy van usually dropped Alleyah back at her grandmother's house nearby.

"I wonder, did she get off to school OK?" Randall said. "Getting up early and living in this neighborhood, leaving her here, it worries me."

Randall's house was on Walnut Circle, an area of McKenzie that locals call the projects. It is a ring of public housing, simple brick homes set on an open lawn across the railroad tracks from McKenzie's struggling downtown.

In front of her father, Alleyah recited a list of drugs that she could find with little effort a few steps from her door—marijuana, Ecstasy, prescription medications like hydrocodone, Xanax and Adderall. She went through a phase where she smoked synthetic marijuana, available at local convenience stores and now notorious for worrisome side effects.

"I get tempted," Alleyah said. "If I was hanging out here, I'd be smoking. But I try to stay in my little bubble."

She admitted to having smoked marijuana two weeks earlier. In the weeks before that, Randall came home and recognized the smell. He traced it to under Alleyah's bed, not far from the color wheel— an aluminum can, sliced and dented into a makeshift pipe. Alleyah confessed.

"Weed," Randall said. "And alcohol. Those two things worry me. I used to drink heavy, but I haven't done it in eleven years. I know kids that age are going to experiment. They're going to get bored. And she says she does it because she's bored. I tell her to pick up a book. You've got to have books to survive. No education, no cosmetology job."

It was April. Alleyah was at Level 4 at Carroll Academy. An exit was within reach. Her father just wanted her to get to high school and get away from the life he had lived.

"There's nothing to offer her in McKenzie," he said. "I want her to get out. I don't want her to work at McDonald's all her whole life. Or do like Daddy did, and work in a factory and have that factory close and be without a job. I don't want her to take that same path. There's better stuff out there if she can just get away."

Three weeks later, at Carroll Academy, Alleyah was called into the security office. Her probation officer was there. So was Steele.

They had seen her Facebook page. Among the tough-talking posts and below the profile photo of her giving the middle finger were pictures of Alleyah smoking what appeared to be marijuana, including with Summer, a nineteen-year-old former Lady Jaguars teammate who had graduated and was raising a son.

And it showed pictures from the previous weekend of Alleyah drinking and looking intoxicated.

Alleyah was told that she was leaving Carroll Academy. She was assigned to a live-in drug and alcohol rehabilitation center thirty miles away.

"What if I don't go?" she asked Steele. "What if I run away?"

"You can run away," Steele said, "and you'll probably be gone two or three days, maybe a week. And then we'll find you and pick you up. And you'll be put in custody."

The wide smile was long gone. And, from Carroll Academy, so was Alleyah.

VII. "BEYOND THE TREE LINE"

Miranda

Miranda learned she was pregnant on her eighteenth birthday last September. She and her mother soon painted the nursery pink with brown accents, as they had seen in catalogs. Miranda knew it was going to be a girl, and she had a name ready: Akyia Nicole.

By March, the room was in perfect order, as if the baby might arrive in the next moment, not the next month. A mobile dangled over the crib, and the changing table was stocked with diapers and wipes. On top was an album of ultrasound pictures.

"She's got my chin," Miranda said, finding detailed lines in the shadowy shapes.

"You're crazy," her mother, Theresa, said with a laugh.

A rocking chair sat in the corner. The closet was filled with frilly clothes and lots of little shoes, as if every day of Akyia's life would be Sunday.

The bedroom next door was Miranda's room. The door was covered in stickers and drawings with colorful pens, and the walls had posters of Justin Bieber and Lil Wayne. Under a window was a cage with a hamster named Sniffers. At the foot of Miranda's twin bed was a portable playpen, assembled and ready for use.

"I know I'll be a good mom," she said. "But it's kind of scary. I've never raised a baby."

The edge of one bedroom wall held four certificates of which Miranda was especially proud. One was a certificate from Carroll Academy. Another was a high school diploma, granted by the state of Tennessee. The other two were for completing programs at drug and alcohol rehabilitation centers two years ago.

As a child, Miranda was found to have depression and bipolar disorder. She became a heavy drinker in her mid-teens. She was known to explode in anger.

"She put me through some stuff," her mother said. "What kind of trouble was she not getting in? Carroll Academy changed her around. That was the best thing that could have ever happened to her."

At Carroll Academy, after her time in rehabilitation, Miranda played center on the basketball team, but she did not score any points. She missed two free throws during a game at Big Sandy High, her previous school.

"And I always make my free throws," she said. "But I guess I was so nervous doing it in front of Big Sandy, and I missed them. I was so mad, too."

Teammates adored her, because she was earnest and cheerful, never judgmental, with an easily enticed giggle.

"Some kids that go there, when they get out of there, they still do the same stuff they did before," Miranda said. Her round belly pointed toward the ceiling as she sat in the rocking chair where she expected to hold her newborn baby in the coming weeks. "Some people learn from it. Some people don't. But I did. I don't remember when's the last time I've been in some trouble. It's been a long dang time."

Miranda was one of nine girls on Carroll Academy's girls' basketball team the year before, a squad that won none of its thirty-two games and lost many of them by more than fifty points. That loose band of troubled teens, assigned to the school by the county juvenile court system, extended the program's losing streak to 184 games. This season, another winless one, pushed it to 213.

Like all Carroll Academy teams, last year's Lady Jaguars were temporarily tossed together by circumstance and disbanded at season's end. The nine girls splintered in different directions.

Several earned their way back to "regular school," as they called it. A couple stayed at Carroll Academy and played on this past year's team. One moved to Illinois to live with her father.

Three of the girls, however, graduated last year. Miranda, Destiny and Summer were freed from the binds of school, unshackled from the juvenile court system, and set adrift in the broader world of West Tennessee.

They shared one unpredicted sentiment: each wished, in a way, that she could go back to Carroll Academy. They found that life was harder outside the school than inside it.

None of the girls had a job. None went to college or trade school. None had a place of her own. All spent their days in relative isolation, finding structure and routine mostly in the daytime television schedule. Destiny and Summer regularly smoked marijuana and drank alcohol. Miranda was about to join Summer as an unwed teenage mother.

They were caught between two worlds—the one of rules and order that they left behind, and the one filled with responsibilities they did not imagine and hopes they could not reach.

"Our job here is to keep them out of custody and give them the education," said the Carroll Academy director Randy Hatch, who grew up in Huntingdon. "Then we turn them loose into the world. No different than Huntingdon High School, where the locals go. We're putting them out into the world. What's for them to do? What is out there?"

All three girls applied multiple times to the various fast-food restaurants in their towns. Each pondered more education at one of the region's technical schools. But the lack of jobs, and the cost of cars and gas to navigate the stretched-out landscape, made even the first steps into the real world daunting, if not unmanageable.

So they waited, frozen in time and place.

"For someone who's eighteen, you've got one of two choices, that I see," Hatch said. "You're either going to go to college, if you can get in, or you're going to join the military. If you can find a job, it's going to be by the hour. You're not going to find something that's going to help you raise a family. Those jobs are just not here."

Destiny had no car and earned money babysitting for a friend. Summer had a two-year-old and a broken-down car in the front yard. Miranda dreamed of cosmetology school before she became pregnant.

In March, she said her next goal was to move to Paris—Paris, Tennessee, a nearby town of 10,000.

None of the girls wanted to leave. Ambitions rarely extend past the horizon.

"I've said, 'Look, go out and do a 360, and stand around and just look as far as you can see,'" Hatch said. "All you see is trees. I call it the tree line. And I'm telling you, I'm promising you, beyond that tree line, there is a world of opportunity. Not to say there isn't here. But there's a world of opportunity. And you're going to have to reach out and find it. The problem is, how do they get out beyond the tree line, whether it's through education or finding a job or something? It's really difficult."

For most of her pregnancy, Miranda did not want to discuss the baby's father. It was a friend, she said, someone she had hoped to start dating regularly before she became pregnant. But then the two split, and Miranda learned she was pregnant, and she had not talked to him since she told him that the baby was his. She hoped he would come around.

"I want her to have a father in her life," she said in March. "And the child support."

Miranda's reluctance in discussing the baby's father stemmed from the fact that he was black. The 2010 census counted 557 residents of Big Sandy. None were listed as black.

"Black people would be scared to come here," Miranda said. "The only time they would come would be at night, and then they'd still be scared."

Theresa, forty-four, grew up in the area. She said its reputation for being unfriendly to blacks was once deserved, and has been hard to shake. The winding roads to Big Sandy are lined with several homes flying Confederate flags.

"I think it's changed a lot since I was little," Theresa said.

Miranda waited many months before she told her mother about the baby's father.

"I didn't really say nothing," Theresa said. "I just don't believe in blacks and whites together. I ain't got nothing against black people. It's just that I don't believe in it. I don't know. Maybe it's just how I was raised or whatever. But I don't have a problem with them whatsoever."

Miranda planned to stay in her mother's house for at least a few months after the baby was born, but wanted to move to Paris, where blacks make up about 20 percent of the population and mixed-race babies are increasingly common. Theresa agreed that it might be best to have Akyia grow up outside Big Sandy.

On April 12, at a hospital about ninety minutes away in Jackson, Akyia Nicole was born. She was 8 pounds, 5 ounces and deemed perfectly healthy.

Miranda did not try to reach Akyia's father.

"He doesn't know she was born yet," she said, more than a month after the birth. "And I don't feel like telling him. If she wants to know her father, I'll tell her. But until then, no. I don't want her father in and out of her life. I've had two fathers"—a biological one and a stepfather—"and neither of them are in my life. Maybe that's where that comes from."

Into the summer, three generations lived together in the woods outside Big Sandy. Miranda, owner of a driver's license after about a dozen failed attempts on the written test, proudly drove Akyia to see friends from Carroll Academy, like her old basketball coach, Tonya Lutz. She posted photos of Akyia on Facebook almost every day.

The freshly painted and well-equipped nursery went virtually unused. Akyia slept every night with Miranda, in the bedroom with its walls covered in posters of Justin Bieber and certificates from Carroll Academy, and where a small cage under the window was home to a hamster named Sniffers.

Destiny

For the fourth day in a row, Destiny sat on the living room couch, watching a DVD of the movie *Welcome Home Roscoe Jenkins*. She lived rent-free in a brick duplex in the town of Milan, spelled like the northern Italian fashion capital but pronounced MY-lin in West Tennessee. It is not far from Dresden and Paris, other small towns named for grander places.

Destiny, eighteen, knew a twenty-two-year-old woman named Melissa, who saw in Destiny a little bit of herself—a troubled background, a life on the verge, a need for help. Destiny had a high school diploma from Carroll Academy, the same school Melissa had attended for several years. But Destiny had no job, no car, no money and no place to live.

Melissa, with a new job as a home-care provider—helping patients get fed, use the bathroom and keep their homes clean—asked Destiny to come live with her this spring. Melissa had two daughters, ages three and six, and wanted Destiny to walk them to school and to day care, and be there to greet them at the end of the day.

Melissa paid Destiny $40 a week and bought most of her food. She did not charge rent.

"D.J.'s been running from place to place, not having any place to go," Melissa said, using Destiny's nickname. "When the job called me, I knew I had to have somebody help me. It's me versus the world. I've got to make a way for me and my kids. Period. But I knew D.J. was in need, too. She needed a place to stay and a place to call home. She wouldn't have to worry about where she was going to sleep at night."

A year earlier, Destiny was the best player on the Carroll Academy Lady Jaguars, the leading scorer in all but two games. She was a tough, sometimes pugnacious point guard, equally adept at putting her head down and driving toward the basket or lofting rainbow three-pointers. In the final game, she scored 28 points in a 52–32 loss, one of the closer contests of the season.

But she had tenuous, strained relationships with her parents, and often killed time on street corners and in the living rooms of acquaintances, stumbling into her next high. She slept wherever she was invited.

Part of the group that Destiny hung around with included a half-sister of Melissa's. They grew close, and Destiny got a tattoo of the girl's first initial on her left arm. (On her right arm, she had an incomplete cross that she created with a do-it-yourself tattoo kit.) But they went their separate ways this spring, and Melissa reached out to Destiny.

"As long as she stays around people who are going to motivate her, people who are going places and want to do things, she'll be fine," Melissa said.

Destiny said she often woke up, got the children to school and day care, and returned to bed. She spent hours each day watching television. She began playing basketball for the first time since she left Carroll Academy with boys at a nearby playground.

Milan is about twenty miles from Huntingdon and other towns where Destiny knew people. Distractions were few and, with no car, usually out of reach.

"I wanted to get out of Carroll County," Destiny said. "There was too much drama. Here, I don't hardly know nobody, so I can't just walk out and see people, like, 'Hey what's up?' It's very good for me. I like it."

But weekends brought parties, and Destiny found her way to more than a few. Even in the quiet hours at home, she found herself regularly smoking marijuana.

"If I really wanted to stop, I don't have to have it," Destiny said. "But it removes a lot of stress."

Destiny visited Carroll Academy for the first time in nearly a year. She wore jeans and a short-sleeved yellow knit shirt. Hatch, the school director, tossed her a Carroll Academy Lady Jaguars sweatshirt as she folded herself into a large, padded chair.

"I miss Carroll Academy," she said. "I miss it so much. I love it here. I didn't at first, but now I think: Dang, they told me those things for a reason. It's weird. I hated this place with a passion. I did. I tried to do everything I could to get out."

It was across the hall, in the bathroom, where Destiny had taken a urine test for drugs a year before. It immediately came up as positive. She worried that her chance at getting a high school diploma was gone, and that a stint in jail was possible.

But now she wore a smile, one that reflected the comfort she had in these hallways, a shelter from the world outside.

"Everything hits you, all at once," she said. "Smacks you. Like, hey, world. I like being out of school, but I like being in school, too. If you don't have a job, there's nothing to do. I'd rather be sitting here with a pencil in my hand than sitting at home watching TV."

A few nights later, she came to a basketball game with Summer and Constance, two other former Lady Jaguars. She wore a flat-brimmed cap and mostly sneered, interrupting her swagger with occasional bursts of maniacal laughter. From across the floor, the girls on the current Lady Jaguars thought Destiny was trying to show off and rolled their eyes. Those who knew Destiny presumed that she was high on something. Something was not right.

Before the end of the game, Destiny was in a sudden and desperate search for a ride. She had no car, and worried about how she would get to Milan or where she would sleep that night. She left abruptly.

Word of her behavior spread through Carroll Academy the next day. Tonya Lutz, her former coach, called Destiny the next day to see that she was OK.

Weeks later, at the home she shared with Melissa, Destiny was introspective and polite. It was early afternoon, and she had cleaned the house and was watching television. Melissa arrived, between home visits for work, wearing green medical scrubs.

Destiny said that she had applied at all the fast-food places in town, some of them several times. But those jobs were hard to get. She looked online at options for school, maybe down in Jackson or over at the technical trade school in McKenzie, but she did not know what she wanted to do. Besides, she had no car.

"Her biggest thing is that she needs transportation," Melissa said.

Melissa drove a 2001 Buick Century with a broken odometer.

"I might get a car and give her mine," she said. "I feel like she would take care of it. I'm not going to sign her name to it right away—not going to lie—but if I've seen that she's got a job or that she's going to school, I'd sign it over to her. She's just got to show me she's doing something with it."

The two of them stepped onto the front porch to smoke cigarettes. The house sat on a U-shaped street lined with small brick duplexes, public housing for the poor.

Melissa had landed there, a former Carroll Academy student and admitted former drug addict, now a single mother toting two girls from two fathers, with a job she barely tolerated and a twelve-year-old car out front.

She was Destiny's steadying influence.

"A year from now? She'll have a part-time job," Melissa said of Destiny. "Maybe school. She'll be doing something. She doesn't like to be doing nothing. She's not hard to motivate."

Melissa thought for a moment.

"Really," she said, "no one's hard to motivate if they see they're getting something out of it."

Summer

A year ago, after the Lady Jaguars finished their season and before Summer was scheduled to graduate, Summer stopped going to school.

She was a single mother, her son nearly a year old, and she was doing drugs again. Her juvenile probation officer saw Summer walking through a neighborhood in McKenzie. Carroll Academy officials called her, urging her to return. She was only weeks from getting her diploma.

A school employee picked up Summer and brought her in. She sat in the office of Hatch, the school's director.

"Mr. Randy said if I didn't come back to school, he'd have a warrant out for my arrest in every county I could go to," Summer recalled this spring. "And I'd do my homework behind bars. I didn't have a choice."

Hatch smiled at the memory.

"I bluffed her," he said. Carroll Academy and the juvenile court system had no jurisdiction over her, since she had turned eighteen. "But I said, 'If you miss another day, you're going to jail, and we'll bring your books to the jail.'"

Summer finished school. She received her high school diploma. By the end of the school year, she was helping tutor other students.

It was late March this spring, just after her nineteenth birthday, and Summer sat on the couch of the house that her father shared with his girlfriend. Summer watched television, and her twenty-one-month-old son, DaMarion, played on the shag rug at her feet. She wore jeans and a tight T-shirt, exposing a tattoo of her son's name below her left collarbone. On her abdomen was a tattoo of the name of an aunt who was murdered several years ago in Nashville. On the inside of her left wrist was a tattoo of red brass knuckles. Summer's hair was streaked reddish-blond, not the light brown that it was the year before.

The year had not been kind to Summer. The damage, she admitted, was largely self-inflicted.

"A year ago, I probably would have said I'd have a job, have my own place," Summer said in her singsong lilt. "But it's been rough. I'm still learning. Everything didn't go as planned. It's been hell. I've been through lots of stuff."

She bounced from home to home, a string of trailers and old motels with a shifting cast of friends and roommates. She became pregnant again but awoke one morning to stomach pain and soon learned from the doctor that she lost the baby. She got into two fights with other girls, behavior that helped land her at Carroll Academy for her senior year of high school.

Last summer, she said, she smoked marijuana and took several Adderall pills that she said a friend's mother gave them.

"I was up more than twenty-four hours," Summer said. "All of a sudden, I was sitting there, writing a letter, and I started feeling sick. My head hurt and my vision was wigging out. Everything was shifting, all crazy. I was laying there, and it felt like my heart was going to come out of my chest. I was crying and praying. Freaking out. I finally fell asleep. Someone called it speedballing. After that, I kind of slowed down."

Summer said that she still smoked marijuana most days. She drank often, too—cheap vodka, mostly. When someone else watched DaMarion, often her mother, living with her own mother about twenty miles away, Summer and her friends sometimes bought pineapple soda or other flavored soft drinks. They dumped out half of the soda and filled the void with vodka.

"Now we're buying lemonade-flavored vodka," she said.

For part of the year, Summer received $142 a month, and a $15 gas card, she said, from Tennessee's Families First program. It required that she spend a set number of hours looking for a job. She applied mostly at fast-food places and at Walmart. She even talked to a Marine recruiter, Summer said, but she does not want to leave DaMarion behind for military service.

For those unable to find work, the welfare program required community service. Summer worked at a Salvation Army retail store until she argued with a supervisor and walked out. The welfare checks soon stopped.

Summer's father and his girlfriend, a woman in her twenties with two children, were engaged on Valentine's Day. By then, Summer had returned to live with them, in a well-kept ranch-style house on the bend of a country road, a couple of miles off the highway that connects McKenzie and Gleason.

For Summer, it was a blessing and a curse—away from the troublesome distractions that always seemed to pull her in, but uncomfortably distant from friends and the world she knew.

She had no transportation. An old Nissan Maxima could be hers, but it sat broken down in the driveway, its problems too expensive to repair. Her connections were largely through Facebook, her postings mostly stream-of-consciousness doodles of scattered emotions.

DaMarion's father, a former Carroll Academy student, spent part of the past year in jail after being caught by the police with a large stash of marijuana. Summer said she had not seen him for months, until he was out on a work-release program and they bumped into each other at a party.

He worked at McDonald's and spent weekends back in jail, Summer said, which is why he missed her birthday party, where her father barbecued and there was a bonfire in the backyard and people crowded around the television to watch an ultimate fighting bout. But he paid her $300 a month in child support, she said, and with the blessing of Summer's father eventually moved into the house.

"We're saving money to get a place together," Summer said in March. "I'm doing better. Now that I'm back with him, I've got my priorities right. My family—my little family. I'm trying to get a job and get out of here."

A few weeks later, DaMarion's father had moved out.

Summer was a leader of last year's Lady Jaguars, a charismatic, fast-talking senior. During one game, she collided with an opponent and split the corner above her right eye. She wobbled to the bench and passed out. An ambulance carried her to the hospital, where she had several stitches that left a scar. Summer liked it, but it had faded over the past year.

She had been a good athlete as a girl, spending years on travel softball teams. It was when she quit those teams in her mid-teens, her father said, that she stumbled into trouble, filling the vacant hours with drugs and delinquency.

That divide is reflected in a day-to-day life of contradictions. Summer can seem two different people. She picked fights on Facebook and spoke the foul language of ghetto bravado. She finished notes with smiley faces and had insightful conversations with perfect grammar.

SpongeBob SquarePants blared on the television. DaMarion walked around, chewing on snacks and clinging to his mother. When he knocked over a cup of Sprite, Summer quickly and gently dabbed it from the new rug.

"When I went to Carroll Academy, I had someone to talk to," she said. "The students and the teachers, they could understand where you're coming from, because they know what it's like. They're not judgmental."

She checked her phone for messages.

"And then you get out, and you have no one to talk to," she said. "There's no one to support you. I guess that's part of growing up."

Recently, Summer and DaMarion moved out on their own, into a small apartment in Huntingdon. It is not far from Carroll Academy.

VIII. AFTER 312 STRAIGHT LOSSES, JUVENILE COURT'S GIRLS BASKETBALL TEAM PREVAILS

The losing streak had reached 312 games, dating back about a dozen years, when most of the players were toddlers. The girls on the floor for Carroll Academy on Friday night had nothing to do with the start of the streak, or the hundreds of losses since 2005.

But they put an end to it, using two overtimes to get there, in a small gym in Huntingdon, Tennessee. The Lady Jaguars beat Immaculate Conception Cathedral, a small private school in Memphis, 29–27, ending what is presumed to be the longest high-school losing streak in the country.

Carroll Academy and the Lady Jaguars were featured in a five-part series in *The New York Times* in 2012, and again in a series of stories in 2013.

It is a day school operated by the Carroll County Juvenile Court, which sends troubled teens there as a safety net. Some have run afoul of the law, from petty crimes to drug use. Others have a history of truancy or have been kicked out of their home schools for disciplinary reasons. Many are from impoverished, broken homes. All have landed at Carroll Academy as a last chance at completing a high-school education. The school has about a hundred students in a typical year. A large majority of them are boys.

Most girls are encouraged to play on the basketball team, coached most seasons by Randy Hatch, the school's administrator. He was the coach the last time the Lady Jaguars won, and he was on the sideline, co-coaching with his daughter, Hayley, on Friday night.

The Lady Jaguars, sometimes with barely enough girls to compete, and rarely with players experienced in basketball, are routinely on the losing end of laughably lopsided scores. Each season, Hatch sees one or two games on the schedule where he believes, just maybe, the streak could end. One of those games came on Thursday night. Carroll Academy lost, 40–29, one of the closer defeats of the losing streak.

This year's team, however, has one of west Tennessee's top three-point shooters, a senior named Kaitlyn Evans. She scored 22 points on Friday, including a three-pointer at the end of regulation to send the game to overtime.

"Everybody's bawling, and Hayley cried when it went to overtime," Hatch said in a phone interview. "To them, 22–22, that's pretty remarkable."

Hatch told everyone to calm down. The first overtime decided nothing, but Evans put Carroll Academy ahead in the final minute of the second overtime. Immaculate Conception Cathedral could not score again, the buzzer sounded, and Carroll Academy's court filled with girls sharing hugs and tears.

"The girls were bawling and grabbing and holding and hugging," Hatch said. "They were saying, 'Everything's going to be good. This is a sign.' And I said yes. It's a good sign."

For twelve years, Hatch has preached the value of basketball, no matter the score. The girls, he figured, needed structure in their lives. They needed coaches and teammates to depend on, and they needed to know that someone was depending on them.

"It ain't about the record," Hatch told the *Times* in 2012. "If I looked out and I could see in their eyes that they're depressed about losing, and hated to come out here, it wouldn't be worth it. But they put it behind them quicker than anybody."

That season's team, like this one, has nine players. His job, everyone's job, Hatch said, was to go 9–0 with the girls, to get their lives on the right track. "If you go 8–1, you've had a losing season."

Carroll Academy, now 1–2, plays again on Tuesday.

"If the ball goes in, if it doesn't, the work still goes on," he said late Friday night. "But this makes it a little sweeter. We can rest till Tuesday knowing we're on a winning streak."

POSTSCRIPT: The Lady Jaguars have not won a game since ending their losing streak. Randy Hatch, who had a liver transplant and has fought off a variety of serious health issues, planned to retire in 2021. Most of the girls still live in the area.

PART III

HIDING
AND
SEEKING

11

HUNTING SOMETHING
THAT CAN HUNT YOU BACK

Bay Minette, Alabama

When alligator season began last Thursday night in Alabama, those lucky enough to receive one of the state's 260 prized hunting permits wondered if they might do what Mandy Stokes did last year. She and four others captured and killed the largest American alligator on record.

With the sky's last light flickering like dying fire on the Tensaw River, people slipped their boats into the still water, disappeared into the dark maze of creeks and bayous, and went looking for the biggest alligator they could find.

Spotting them is the easy part. Alligators generally hug the shores at night, their reptilian bodies hidden beneath the murky surface, often deathly still. But their eyes, usually just above the waterline, reflect light. A flashlight with a strong beam creates a sparkle from hundreds of yards away, like headlights igniting a reflector far ahead on a lonely road.

The trick is not finding an alligator, but finding one worthy of the time and effort required to capture it. Most want a ten-footer. The one Stokes found, a hundred miles north of here, was fifteen feet long, and it weighed more than 1,000 pounds. Its stomach contained the front and rear halves of an adult white-tailed deer, a pair of squirrel carcasses, the bones of a duck, and teeth believed to be from a young cow.

"Hunting something that can hunt you back—that's kind of cool," said Carlos Garcia, waiting for sunset at the Cliff's Landing boat launch. A departing fisherman rolled to a stop in his truck, whispered that he had spotted a fifteen-footer on Middle River and drove off.

Soon, off the hunters went, disappearing into the moonless night, mostly in fishing boats about the length of the Stokes gator, armed with fishing poles, harpoons and a shotgun, to be used only after the animal has been strapped to the boat.

"It's hunting and fishing in one," Brandon Wailes said before he, Garcia and their crew headed out.

Off went Jake Rosser and two friends in the popular, compact G3, the Honda Accord of fishing boats. A pontoon boat with a multigenerational crew of seven launched at 8:01. A confident trio of burly men arrived late, said that they were veterans of a dozen successful alligator hunts over in Mississippi, and quickly motored upriver.

A retiree named Lou Wallace donned a captain's hat and carried his wife, Shirley, and a friend in his small boat. They towed a homemade wooden platform to carry back their presumed prize. They brought a towel that they had soaked in water and rubbed on their dog.

"They love that dog scent," Wallace said of alligators. Back home, the head of a twelve-foot alligator sat on the hearth.

They and dozens of others, from launches across the southern half of the state, trolled the waters, some as wide as a runway, others as narrow and serpentine as a country road.

The banks were slate silhouettes, a barely perceptible skyline of tall grasses in the south and walls of cypress trees farther north. The water was as still and black as the sky. The running light on the stern of each boat was like a slow-moving shooting star, mirroring the meteor shower above. Spotlights scanned the banks. Alligator eyes shone back like gemstones.

Successful hunters came back in the middle of the night, or when dawn broke, with a dead-eyed and limp alligator, the skin loose in the middle, the jaw shut with tape, a blood-red hole in the top of the skull.

The hunters carried tales of sizing up the alligator, estimating its underwater length by the distance between the eyes and the tip of its nose—an inch of snout equals about a foot of alligator. They cast weighted lines with three-pronged treble hooks, shaped like miniature chandeliers, over the top of the alligator, reeling them back to try to catch its thick skin.

It is where most alligator battles are won or lost. Some hooks caught in the alligator's hide, but most missed or snagged on unseen roots or lilies. Either way, the alligator usually slipped silently underwater, like a submarine, starting an onboard scramble to figure out where it had gone.

Then the wait began: Alligators can hold their breath for an hour or more.

When it finally rose, it shot up, snout first, shattering the surface's calm. More hooks were cast, or a harpoon was jabbed into its side, which usually sent it underwater again, but not for so long. Weakening, the alligator was jabbed again, or its tail or snout was snared in a wire hoop.

Once the alligator was coaxed to the edge of the boat and its size was estimated by everyone on board, the group would agree either to let it go or to shoot it in the back of the head.

You get only one alligator. Make it a good one.

The record alligator has no name, but most people call it the Stokes gator. It is taxidermy now, its insides filled mostly with foam, its thick hide clean and shiny, its mouth forever opened slightly. Somehow, its breath still stinks.

The tail hangs off one end of a sturdy table, almost touching the floor, fifteen feet from the snout. The alligator lies on grass and straw amid small bushes and cattails.

"My husband had the table made in Thomasville," Mandy Stokes said. "And we went to Hobby Lobby to find the closest thing we could figure to swamp vegetation."

Alabama has far fewer alligators than the other Southern states that the animal, part of the order Crocodilia and scientifically named *Alligator mississippiensis*, calls home. To control populations, Florida hands out roughly 5,000 hunting permits each year, each good for up to two alligators, compared with the 260 this year in Alabama that are good for just one.

For now, though, Alabama can boast that it has the biggest. Last Thursday afternoon, Stokes, a thirty-five-year-old mother of two young children, with blond hair and a big voice with a thick drawl, stood inside the Gee's Bend Ferry terminal near Camden, where the Stokes gator was on display for most of the month. It had been caught a few miles north, not far from where Highway 28 crosses Majors Creek.

Every few minutes, people pulled up in their cars and sauntered in. They circled the alligator with curiosity and took photographs. Many of them greeted Stokes, who grew up in Pine Hill, works as an office manager at a veterinary clinic in Camden and is a celebrity in Wilcox County because of what happened a year ago.

Stokes was experienced in the outdoors—fishing, hunting and frog gigging—but had never been alligator hunting. When her name was pulled from a pool of about 5,000 applicants statewide last year, she was granted a permit in the West-Central region, where she lives.

She brought her husband, John; her sister's husband, Kevin Jenkins; and his two teenagers, Savannah and Parker. They borrowed a boat.

"We had heard there was a big one at the dam, over at Mill Creek," Stokes said. Just before the season began, a dog had waded into the water there and did not come out. Big alligator footprints were found on shore.

It was a foggy night. They saw eyes, got closer, and guessed that the alligator was a decent size. It was 10:45 p.m. The crew tossed a hook its way.

The eyes disappeared into shallow water clogged with logs, stumps and water lilies. No one was sure if the line had the alligator or something else. Several lines snapped as they tugged. Others had to be cut and spliced because they were tangled.

After several hours of waiting, trolling, casting and pulling, the alligator playing hide-and-seek, they managed to get three hooks into the alligator and a rope wrapped around a leg. They caught a glimpse of the tail, their first indication of the alligator's size.

With others pulling on the lines, Stokes aimed a 20-gauge shotgun at the back of the alligator's head, just as hunters had been instructed in the state's mandatory training course. But the head was too far underwater, and the shot missed its mark. The alligator surged. It towed the boat about 50 feet before crashing it into a cypress stump, knocking several people into a pile in the boat's bottom.

They managed to get a snare on the tail. The alligator slowly relinquished the fight and came to the surface. Stokes shot it, point-blank. It was nearly 5 a.m.

By the time they wrestled the alligator to shore and arrived at the mandatory inspection site at about 7:30, word had spread through a local radio show. A crowd gathered to see it measured and weighed. A piece of the winch broke. Eventually, the numbers came in: fifteen feet, 1,011.5 pounds. It was estimated to be about twenty-five years old.

It was taken to Ken Owens, a taxidermist in Autaugaville, Alabama. About 150 pounds of alligator meat was pulled out; most of it still sits in Stokes's freezer. Safari Club International measured the skin and detached head at a combined 15 feet 9 inches, declaring it more than a foot longer than the previous record, set in Texas in 2007. The hide was sent to a tannery in New York. In May, the reassembled alligator was unveiled publicly in Montgomery. Researchers in Florida concluded that the Stokes gator, despite myths of larger beasts caught decades ago, was worthy of the size record.

"To our knowledge, this is the largest American alligator yet documented by professional biologists using standardized methods that can be validated with physical evidence," their paper concluded.

Not a day passes without Stokes being asked about the alligator. Not everyone is complimentary. The hunting of large animals is a controversial topic, demonstrated this summer in the killing of a lion in Zimbabwe that caused international outrage. A woman recently left an anonymous voicemail message for Stokes at work.

"I think it's disgusting that somebody who was so cruel to an animal works at a veterinary clinic like that," she said. "I hope to God somebody hunts her down and hunts her children down and lets her know how it feels to be murdered like that."

Stokes and state conservation officials said the animal had been killed legally as part of a tightly managed program.

On a string of leather around Stokes's neck hung a scute, one of the bony ridges that line an alligator's back. She drank from a Florida Gators tumbler. (The rare Alabamian who roots for Florida football, she named her son Tebow.)

She would love to keep the alligator, but it needs a climate-controlled home, and there is no room in her house for that. Someone offered to buy it for $15,000. ("They're way off," she said. It had cost nearly that much to prepare it for presentation.) Maybe it will end up in a museum, which would make Stokes happy, too.

"There are days I don't regret it at all," Stokes said. "And some days I think it's just crazy and I wish I had just put his head on the wall."

People wandered in. Some gaped at the size. Others were less impressed.

"People say, 'I've seen two or three that are bigger,'" Stokes said, which is precisely what an older man had said minutes before she arrived. "My husband's response to that is, 'The problem is getting him in the boat.'"

Through the dark, Chris Nix steered his boat up the Tensaw River, part of a tangled braid of marshy channels that move without urgency toward Mobile Bay.

Most of Alabama's alligator hunting happens in the Mobile–Tensaw River Delta, on six nights over two weekends. Few know the geography better than Nix, a wildlife biologist for Alabama's Department of Conservation and Natural Resources.

He oversees the state's annual alligator hunt. Each year, he does a population survey, spending nights shining lights and counting eyes on the bank of every lake and creek and bayou he can navigate into. Alabama was the first state to protect the alligator, in the 1930s. It was added to the federal list of endangered species in 1967 and removed in 1987. After many ups and downs, the alligator population has been steady for years.

"Do I think there is another alligator out here that big?" Nix said of the Stokes gator. "I don't know. I never thought there was one that big to start with."

Nix, who turns forty on Sunday and has a tight haircut and a calm disposition, was in uniform and carried a pistol on his belt. He approached three men in a boat and flashed his own boat's blue lights to signal that he was an officer. The men had an alligator alongside their boat. A harpoon had caught it in the snout. Black tape held its mouth closed.

"How big is he?" Nix asked. The average of the 147 alligators caught last year in Alabama was 9 feet 2 inches and 235 pounds.

"About eight and a half," one man said. It was always a guess.

They were not sure whether to keep it. After some debate, they wriggled the hooks free, carefully unwound the tape around the alligator's snout and watched it slink into the murk.

"There are a lot more alligators around here," one of the men, Greg Hall, said. "You always want one bigger than you get."

Far to the north, in a shallow cove on snake-shaped Mifflin Lake, the Big Dipper hanging like a string of lanterns just above the cypress trees, Jessie Peacock and his family cornered a promising alligator.

"I ain't seen a nose that big in a long time," Peacock said as he navigated closer.

He and his crew lobbed three hooks toward the alligator. It sank into the black, and the hooks caught nothing but downed logs. The boat circled. Spotlights searched in desperation. The boat paced the cove, searching for movement and glowing eyes.

A seven-foot alligator swam nearby, coming close to the boat, as if taunting the hunters for their greed. After a couple of hours, the Peacock party gave up, passed a dozen or more other alligators lurking near the banks and made plans to return the next weekend.

At the check-in station in Spanish Fort, a crew of wildlife officers and biologists waited for alligators to arrive. There was a report that the first one caught in the West-Central region, about a hundred miles north of where the Stokes gator was found, was a thirteen-footer. The hunter was not Mandy Stokes; she applied for a tag again this year but did not get one.

Now and again, trucks towing a boat pulled into the parking lot and stopped in front of a cinder-block garage. Out of the trucks stepped excited and exhausted hunters. Inside each boat was a limp alligator.

Workers wrapped it in chains and hoisted it with a winch. A digital scale gave the weight. The tails of the biggest ones sagged to the ground and had to be tied up to get an accurate reading. The girth of the belly and tail were measured with a tape.

Smiling hunters posed for pictures before the alligator was lowered to the concrete. Chalk marked the tip of the tail and the tip of the snout, and the distance was measured. A tag was placed into the tip of the tail. A pair of students from the Dauphin Island Sea Lab asked if they could collect tissue samples. If so, they gouged the top of the head and part of a foot and cut off a claw.

Some hunters wanted the meat to eat, the skin for wallets or belts, the claws for jewelry. Some wanted just the head as a trophy. Few planned on stuffing the whole body. Most were not quite sure what to do with a ten-foot dead alligator.

"You ladies want that for research?" one hunter asked the students.

"We'll take it if you don't want it," Caitlin Wessel, a PhD student, replied.

By the first morning, she had four headless alligators wrapped in tarps and ice in the bed of a pickup truck. Twelve other alligators went home with their captors in the back of a boat.

By the end of the weekend, forty-nine alligators were captured in the Mobile–Tensaw River Delta, and a couple dozen more in the three other regions around the state. None of them came particularly close to 15 feet or 1,000 pounds.

For now, the Stokes gator survives, empty of life but still a target, on display for anyone curious to know just how big an alligator can be.

POSTSCRIPT: *State-sanctioned alligator hunts continue in much of the American South, but the Stokes gator still holds the record.*

12

THE MOST PERILOUS PRIZE

Fort Bragg, California

Every year, as steady as the tides, lifeless bodies are pulled from the cold, restless water along the rugged coastline north of San Francisco.

Most of the victims are middle-aged men. They wear black wetsuits, usually hooded. They are often found in small coves framed by crescents of jagged rocks. An abandoned float tube sometimes bobs about nearby. Almost without exception, the victims are found wearing weighted belts that help them sink.

Sometimes the bodies are discovered by friends nearby. If the fog is not too thick, the victims might be spotted from the towering bluffs above, where lifeguards patrol dozens of miles of desolate coast and armed game wardens spy for poachers. Many of the bodies are plucked from the swells by a search-and-rescue helicopter crew accustomed to making daring rope rescues and recoveries several times a year.

The bodies are those of abalone divers.

"There's a lot of death in abalone diving," Nate Buck, a longtime Sonoma County lifeguard, said as he steered a pickup truck south along Highway 1, the Pacific Ocean churning below the cliffs to the right. In fourteen years, he has lost count of how many bodies he has helped retrieve. "Lifeguards know that. Drive around here, and every one of these coves is another reminder."

Abalone is an edible mollusk, a snail-like, single-shell gastropod found in coastal waters around much of the globe. But the red abalone is the biggest and the most prized, found only on the west coast of North America. In California, with a litany of restrictions to protect its fragile population, the hunt for wild red abalone is permitted only north of San Francisco, and only for sport.

Part of the enduring allure is how easy it is to take part. No experience and little equipment are necessary. Air tanks are illegal. Abalone divers simply slip into the murky water and hold their breath, in search of a hidden prize.

The red abalone's thick, domed single shell grows to more than 12 inches in diameter. Brick red on the outside and pearly silver on the inside, they are trophies, framed for the wall, mounted above a mantel or set along walkways as yard decorations. The meat inside, sometimes several pounds' worth, is a delicacy, with a taste and texture not unlike calamari.

"It really is an iconic species for California," said Laura Rogers-Bennett of the University of California at Davis Bodega Marine Laboratory and a senior biologist for the California Department of Fish and Wildlife. "It is a species that is part of our fishing heritage. And because of the size of red abalone, the biggest in the world, it's not unlike the redwood or the sequoia."

During the seven-month diving season—April through November, with a hiatus in July—thousands arrive each weekend to the wild edges of Sonoma and Mendocino counties, mostly, in serpentine parades from the south and the east. Divers are rooted in tradition and thrive on camaraderie, like those who hunt deer or pheasant elsewhere. They pour from cars and trucks and vans, dress themselves in rubber suits, burden themselves with as much equipment as they can carry and trudge down treacherous rocks to the ocean's edge.

Those brave enough to dive deep below the water's surface for abalone or pick through the shoreline rocks during low tides are allowed to take no more than three in a day and eighteen for the year. Each abalone has to be at least 7 inches in diameter, meaning it is probably at least ten years old. Each shell must be tagged and recorded immediately. It cannot be resold.

But temptations are real, and the black market for poached red abalone is active, because a full-size one can fetch $100 or more.

With roughly 250,000 red abalone legally captured for sport in California annually, and estimates that at least as many are taken illegally each year, the California Department of Fish and Wildlife, including its undercover Special Operations Unit, spends as much time and resources protecting abalone as any other creature in California.

Abalone, in other words, is a big deal in Northern California.

"It's like the last warrior-hunter thing to do," said Sydney Smith-Tallman, whose family owns a dive shop in Fort Bragg that caters mostly to abalone hunters. "There's danger, thrill, beauty."

And, though no one tracks the numbers specifically, up to a dozen people die doing it every year.

The holy grail for divers is an abalone with a 10-inch shell. No one has caught more than Dwayne Dinucci, a retired high school technical arts teacher who lives on a cul-de-sac in Union City, California, near Oakland. The license plate of his truck reads, "POPNAB"—"pop an ab," the widely used expression for plucking abalone, or abs, from their suctioned underwater homes on the rocks.

"Ten inches is a landmark, the dream of a diver," he said. "To this day, forty-five years later, when I find a 10-inch abalone, I am thrilled."

Dinucci had captured 343 abalone before the start of this season, including twenty that were more than 11 inches. The biggest he has caught is $11^{29}/_{32}$ inches, just shy of the world record of $12^{5}/_{16}$ inches, found in 1993 by John Pepper, a former student of Dinucci's.

Dinucci has four of the top ten largest abalone caught on record in California, according to the California Department of Fish and Wildlife.

"The lure is finding the world's largest abalone," Dinucci said. "And on my gravestone it'll say, 'Never found it, but sure as hell tried.'"

The walls and rafters of his two-car garage are covered in hundreds of abalone shells, like hubcaps. They are perfectly aligned on hooks and labeled: size, date, time, location. The locations are intentionally vague, because a good abalone diver does not reveal such secrets.

Dinucci, with a rim of gray hair and a salt-and-pepper mustache, usually dives with a group of like-minded, trophy-hunting friends. While some coves can be jammed with dozens of divers and pickers, Dinucci and his crew look for open water about 12 feet deep, disguising rocky shoals. From an inflatable boat, they drop into the water, one held breath at a time.

Dinucci has a customized boogie board—most use a float tube, which Dinucci finds too cumbersome—fitted with straps so he can hike up and down cliffs with it on his back. The board has hooks to connect to his necessary tools, such as fins, goggles, a waterproof flashlight and an abalone iron, like a small crowbar, used to pry abalone from rocks. Divers are required to carry gauges that measure 7 inches, the legal size, but Dinucci's is 10, because he wants nothing smaller than that.

He has no special ability for holding his breath—a minute at best—but has patience to dive and resurface dozens of times in pursuit of a single abalone. With tight limits on the catch, Dinucci does not want to pluck one that he will regret if he happens upon something larger.

The water, besides being cold and rough, can be as murky as soup. Dinucci prowls the underwater rock formations, feeling with his hands, shining a light into dark holes. Some of his best catches have required him to squirm through narrow passageways. Others have necessitated great patience and reach, inserting the bar into a nook and under the abalone, hoping the slow-moving animal will slide and attach itself firmly enough to let Dinucci carry it to the surface like a Popsicle.

"I've gone into holes and all of a sudden a swell will come over and suck you into the hole, even farther than you wanted to come in," he said. "I wouldn't say I've come close to losing my life. But I've had some scares. Which is good."

Dinucci said he had been thrown into rocks by sudden swells and so-called sneaker waves, known to pull unsuspecting beachgoers off the shore. In many places, the shoreline can be inaccessible because of cliffs.

"Why do a lot of these people die?" he asked. "Mostly inexperience. We get a lot of Southern California divers, but the North Coast is different. It's rough. And it can get rough"—Dinucci snapped his fingers—"like that. The key is to know where you're coming out. Getting in is easy. Coming out is the hard part."

The man on the phone wanted forty-five abalone. The seller agreed to deliver them to him in San Francisco for $2,500, a reasonable black-market bulk price.

A few days later, a car approached an auto repair shop on the west side of San Francisco, far from the tourist sites. It was met by an employee in coveralls and ushered into a service bay. Three coolers were removed and placed in the back of a Toyota Prius. Cash changed hands.

"Our guy's leaving," a voice on a walkie-talkie radio said. Unbeknown to the buyer, the seller worked for the Special Operations Unit of the state Fish and Wildlife Department. The shop was surrounded by agents in eight cars, parked on surrounding streets, connected by radios and cellphones.

The ten-member unit is a type of SWAT team, charged with protecting California's wildlife resources from poachers and the black market. Among its chief concerns are sturgeon eggs, part of the high-dollar caviar market, and black bears, prized for body parts such as paws and gall bladders.

Abalone, though, is the top priority. It was first harvested with regularity in California by Chinese immigrants in the mid-1800s, who mostly dried and exported it. The Japanese created many of the state's hundreds of commercial operations in the early twentieth century. With the advent of scuba, divers could eventually collect two thousand or more abalone a day.

Concern grew as the red abalone population plummeted through the 1970s and 1980s. California took serious action in the 1990s, banning all commercial operations and declaring that sport diving (unassisted by air tanks, with no reselling allowed) could take place only north of the Golden Gate Bridge. (There remains a legal, niche business for small, farm-raised abalone steaks, sold to restaurants and consumers for roughly $125 per pound.)

These days, about 98 percent of the legal abalone diving in California occurs off the remote coasts of Sonoma and Mendocino counties. Even so, if biologists' estimates are correct, at least a quarter-million abalone are illegally poached each year off the coast of California, and the street value could be $25 million.

"It's not endangered, but it's scarce," said Captain Robert Farrell, head of the special operations unit. "But with lots of money from the black market, it could be endangered quickly."

Last August, using armed wardens from across the state, Farrell's team led simultaneous early-morning raids on fourteen homes in Sacramento, Oakland and several Bay Area suburbs. It was dubbed Operation Oakland Abalone Syndicate. Thirteen men, most of them Vietnamese, were charged with illegal possession of abalone, believed to be part of a black-market network.

"We've seen him to date take fifty-seven abalone," Lieutenant Patrick Foy said outside one Oakland house, noting that the annual limit in 2013 was twenty-four. (It was reduced to eighteen in 2014.) "We believe it's for commercial sale."

Abalone remains a delicacy in many Asian cultures, treasured not only for taste but also for medicinal qualities, including as an aphrodisiac. In drugstores in San Francisco's Chinatown, in glass apothecary jars kept on high shelves behind the counter, dried abalone can sell for $2,000 or more per pound. Frozen abalone, too, is commonly found in Asian restaurants and seafood markets, but often out of its original packaging and without proper paperwork. One Chinatown market recently offered it for $55 per pound in plain bags.

Not all abalone is illegal—there are dozens of varieties, and many can be imported from other countries. For investigators, though, paperwork trails get lost in translation, and promising leads disappear in mistaken identities. Leads have led to massage parlors, nail salons and other businesses viewed skeptically as fronts for seafood poaching, among other illicit activities.

The belief is that California abalone not only finances criminal activity, but makes its way across the ocean. In other countries, such as Australia and South Africa (where, this month, investigators found 36,340 abalone hidden inside a house), the authorities have connected abalone poaching directly to drug and arms cartels.

California officials have been unable to draw as many straight lines. But they have made a string of large-scale abalone busts over the past two decades. In 2004, Warden Dennis McKiver boarded a commercial sea urchin boat in Mendocino County and found it jammed with 458 abalone—a load, presumably not the first, probably worth $40,000 on the black market.

The two men aboard were arrested, barred from fishing for life, fined a combined $60,000 and sent to jail for two years. They remain oft-cited examples of the type of temptations facing divers of all kinds.

"Sea urchins are nickels," McKiver said. "But next to those nickels are $100 gold pieces. And it's very tempting for those guys to grab a couple. And then it grows from there."

Along the coast, wardens sometimes dress in camouflage and hide on bluffs and in trees, spying on abalone divers through binoculars, recording what they see and citing offenders as they return to their cars.

On a couple of busy weekends each season, they erect abalone checkpoints along the meandering two-lane highways leading to and from the coast. Hundreds of cars returning inland from abalone diving are diverted, their drivers and passengers politely questioned by uniformed wardens.

Often, as cars approach the backup, abalone can be seen being flung out windows in desperate attempts to avoid detection. Confiscated abalone is donated to area fund-raisers and local soup kitchens. Wardens mostly find improperly completed log sheets and an extra abalone or two. Even those can be costly violations.

At the Mendocino County courthouse in Fort Bragg, about a four-hour drive north of San Francisco, the docket is filled with abalone cases. A majority involve Asian defendants from the Bay Area, often requiring Vietnamese, Mandarin or Cantonese interpreters.

Most want to avoid the headache of repeated trips to the court-house and are circumspect about their chances of winning a trial. They accept a plea bargain, usually losing their fishing license for a year and paying more than $1,000 in fines and fees.

Investigators, of course, want meaningful arrests. After unsus-pectingly buying the forty-five abalone from an informant in May, the suspect at the auto repair shop in San Francisco continued his shift, unaware that he was surrounded by a constellation of law enforcement agents. They had their dealer. They wanted to see what he intended to do with his stash.

Two older men arrived in a pickup truck and went inside.

"Product one out of the box, into white plastic bags," an agent reported through the radio. "Product two out of the box, into a plas-tic bag."

It appeared that four or five abalone changed hands. The men left. Agents had already run checks on their car, and had at least one name and address. They would find the men later. They stayed with the abalone.

A couple of hours and many legitimate car repair customers later, another man left with four or five abalone. A woman accompanying him carried one in a bag. They left, also unfollowed.

At closing time, the suspect left and unwittingly led a parade of cars, mostly SUVs, through the streets of San Francisco. He pulled into an auto body shop in Daly City. Agents parked nearby and watched. An hour later, the suspect left in his car and drove to a home in South San

Francisco. A woman came out. The man carried two of three coolers into the garage and closed it. She got in the car and they left. Several agents followed. Others stayed within sight of the house. And, taking turns, they staked it out, unnoticed, for four more days as the supply of abalone in the coolers dwindled.

The man, a first-time offender, had no single buyer, just a lot of small ones. Some paid about $100 per abalone, investigators said, and others may have been given the abalone as a gift or a returned favor. The man was charged with unlawful purchase and sale of sport-caught fish/ abalone. His web of connections was noted.

"It's a hard community for us to infiltrate," Lieutenant Adrian Foss, who led the sting operation, said during the stakeout. "But as they become more desperate for product, they have to reach beyond their own circle in search of it."

It is just another kind of risk taken in the search for abalone.

Not all abalone-related deaths are by drowning. In June, a fifty-five-year-old man fell to his death immediately after diving while climbing a 100-foot cliff near Mendocino.

Most out-of-water victims, however, are struck by heart attacks. They may drive hours to get to the coast and are eager to return with abalone, a quiet desperation that causes them to overlook ominous clues that the surf, tides and weather conditions silently provide to experienced divers. Water temperatures usually range from 47 to 56 degrees. The ability to see the rubber fins dangling from your toes counts as clarity.

Divers wear constricting wetsuits and weight belts, up to 30 pounds, designed to help offset their buoyancy. They sometimes panic when swept into riptides or swamped by sudden swells. Other dangers lurk in the depths, ranging from tangled forests of kelp to great white sharks.

"All these things are layers upon layers of stress," said Buck, the

Sonoma County lifeguard. "And all that, unfortunately, is too much for people sometimes."

Twelve years ago, when Buck was twenty-one, he was diving off the rocks of Salt Point State Park with a fifty-two-year-old uncle, an experienced diver from Southern California and an "ocean mentor" to Buck. The man climbed out of the water and had a heart attack on the rocks. Help was slow to come, as it is along this part of the coast, where traffic is light and cellphone reception is spotty.

"The hardest part was calling my mother and telling her that her brother died," Buck said. "Hearing her anguish on the other end of the line is a sound I'll never forget."

Like Buck, most lifeguards in Sonoma County gained experience much farther south, where beaches are sandy and dotted with *Baywatch*-style lifeguard stations. In Sonoma County, lifeguards work out of pickup trucks. They go where instinct, experience and unfamiliar parked cars tell them to look. The air temperature can be cold (often in the 50s in the summer) and so foggy that the high-pitched wail of young harbor seals is sometimes confused with that of a person in distress.

"I was a lifeguard in Southern California," said Tim Murphy, one of two uniformed state park peace officers who double as lifeguards on the Sonoma County coast. "I never had a rescue where I worried about getting the person back to shore, nevertheless myself. Up here, it really is a mixed bag. You're in the water sometimes thinking, 'I hope my backup is here soon, because I'm not sure I can pull this off myself.'"

Lifeguards learn to scan a cove of bobbing divers and instantly detect discomfort or inexperience by the way they hold their heads above the water or cling to their float tubes. They urge some out of the water with polite coaxing. If there are no imminent signs of trouble, they hike on to the next cove, or drive farther up the highway.

"You are not expected to have drownings in Southern California," Buck said as he stood on rocks near where another lifeguard nearly lost his life a few years ago in an ill-considered, unsuccessful rescue attempt in churning water. "Here, it's sort of the norm."

Abalone season opens each year on April 1. By early May last year, four men had died while searching for abalone—three of them on the same weekend, the other a week later.

On the last weekend of last season, during still weather in late November, a sixty-seven-year-old man from San Francisco was found in the same cove where Buck's uncle had died more than a decade before. A day later, divers noticed an unattended float a few miles south, near Fort Ross State Park. Buck rushed to the scene, where he found a fifty-seven-year-old man from Oakland on the floor of the ocean with his weight belt on. He was the seventh and final casualty of the season.

"It's not a matter of if some will die," Murphy said in late May this year. "But when."

Within two weeks, two abalone divers were dead near Mendocino. And on June 29, a forty-four-year-old man became the season's third victim. He was sucked into an underwater cave. It took two days to recover the body because of high tides and strong swells.

Most abalone divers, of course, do not see their hobby as a risk, but a reward—a chance for companionship, to enjoy the ocean and, if all goes well, capture an abalone that others envy. Abalone diving in Northern California is celebrated, not feared.

The World Championship Abalone Cook-Off began at a dive shop in the late 1980s, but it now finds a home each fall at Noyo Harbor in Fort Bragg. On a sunbaked day last October, there were twenty booths, offering abalone wontons, abalone salsa, abalone ceviche (two kinds), abalone sausage, even abalone wrapped with dates, goat cheese and bacon, all of it deep fried.

It is the pursuit of abalone, more than anything, that fills the campgrounds, motor lodges and bed-and-breakfasts up and down the coast in both directions. Fort Bragg used to have thriving lumber mills and commercial fishing operations. They have dried up.

"What we depend on now is tourism," said Charlie Lorenz, the self-proclaimed Abalone Hunter, who interviewed people at the cook-off for MendocinoTV.com. "And what brings people here? Abalone."

The festive air belied an undercurrent of concern about the state of abalone diving. The total legal catch in Northern California has dropped more than half in the past twenty-five years, and restrictions tightened further in 2014. Longtime abalone divers worry about the trend and see a day when diving is banned completely. Some say it would be catastrophic to the area's economy and culture, and suggest it might make abalone more susceptible to poaching, not less, as if it were an illegal drug.

The only certainty is that the coves that scallop the coastline would be emptier. And the lifeguards who patrol the bluffs and rough waters would have it easier, if they had a job at all.

"Abalone divers make up the bulk of our rescues," Buck said. "They're the reason we're here."

POSTSCRIPT: *Legal abalone hunting on California's northern coast has been suspended since 2018 because of dwindling numbers of red abalone. Warming ocean waters and decreasing kelp forests are among the issues plaguing the population.*

13

THE ULTIMATE PURSUIT

Rocky Boy's Reservation, Montana

For the herd of bighorn sheep, the rocky cliffs were a safe place, with 360-degree views and plenty of nooks to blend into the gray rocks. The ground was sprinkled with scat, and the air carried a scent like a barnyard. Thousands of feet below, the landscape unfurled into a smooth checkerboard of ranch land that stretched to the horizon. The only threat up here would be to newborn lambs, susceptible to being plucked away by eagles.

Crouched behind a stand of rocks last spring, Brendan Burns, a thirty-eight-year-old with a growing reputation as a sheep hunter and guide, peered over the edge, careful not to be seen or heard. Wild sheep have acute senses, and when they spook, they bolt as one, like a flock of birds. But the sheep were not home. Amid the panorama below, Burns spotted a constellation of tiny dots in a faraway meadow. The horns gave them away.

"There aren't a lot of circles in the wild," Burns whispered. "When you see something curved—and they kind of shine, they have this kind of glow to them—you learn to pick them up. You just train your eye to it."

He pulled a high-powered Swarovski scope from his pack and

aimed it downhill. Eight years before, there were no sheep here. Then twenty-one ewes and five juvenile rams were transplanted to the Rocky Boy's Reservation of the Chippewa Cree, which straddles part of the Bears Paw Mountains, an island-like rise on the plains.

The herd quickly grew to one hundred, and forty were relocated to South Dakota. It has again grown to over one hundred, and another forty are likely to be transplanted this spring, part of broad attempts to replant sheep populations that are a fraction of what they once were in the West.

"There's obviously no coyotes around, for them to be that low and feel comfortable," Burns whispered. "This is a nice day to be a sheep."

There were more sheep on a closer ridge, but in this group, Burns counted thirty-eight, including eleven rams.

"That gray one in the middle is the oldest one," he said. "We'll probably come back and hunt him in the fall."

A man from Michigan had paid $100,000 for the year's only chance to hunt one sheep in the herd on the Rocky Boy's Reservation. Burns brought him there in October, and the men traipsed through the steep and rocky terrain for days before getting themselves in position for a clean shot. The ram was ten years old, with a scar on its forehead, a cloudy eye and several missing teeth.

Its massive horns and about eighty pounds of meat were hauled back to Michigan. In exchange, the Chippewa Cree tribe at Rocky Boy's received the $100,000, which was used to fund two tribal game wardens overseeing wildlife on the reservation.

It is a paradox of hunting, rarely so conspicuous as with wild sheep: the hunters are often the primary conservationists. In 2013, a permit in Montana sold for $480,000, still a record. Burns assisted on that hunt, too, over eighteen days in the Upper Missouri River Breaks. The result was a large ram, and hundreds of thousands of dollars that went into the budget of Montana Fish, Wildlife and Parks.

"As far as sheep-hunting being a rich man's sport, that's absolutely true," said Vance Corrigan, eighty-four, who lives along the Yellowstone River in Livingston, Montana, and is one of the most accomplished big-game hunters in the world. "But if it weren't for the·rich man, those sheep wouldn't be there."

Non-hunters often presume that the biggest prize in North America is something large and fierce—some kind of bear, perhaps, or an elk, a moose or a mountain lion. But the widespread belief among serious hunters is that rams are the ultimate pursuit.

That is for two reasons. One, opportunities to hunt sheep are scarce, and often prohibitively expensive. Two, the hunts are among the most difficult, often lasting weeks in some of the most remote regions on Earth.

"For a hundred years, it's been somewhat at the pinnacle of big-game hunting, especially in the United States," said Bob Anderson, a hunter and author of books on sheep-hunting. "But there weren't a lot of people or sheep on the mountains. Now it's become a cocktail party of sorts. Some well-to-do people have gotten into it, and they've driven the market up."

At the Wild Sheep Foundation's convention each January, single hunting permits from various states, provinces and Indian reservations are auctioned off to the highest bidders. Most go for well over $100,000.

"People who pay $300,000 for a tag, they just paid to recover thirty sheep to places that haven't had sheep in a hundred years," Corrigan said. "Lewis and Clark saw sheep on every ridge. Those people buying tags are helping put sheep back where they were before we arrived."

Globally, there are dozens of species and subspecies of wild sheep, many in Central Asia. The Wild Sheep Foundation, based in Bozeman, Montana, considers there to be four primary wild sheep species in North America: the Rocky Mountain bighorn, the desert bighorn (in the American Southwest and Mexico), Dall's sheep (commonly called Dall sheep, in Alaska, British Columbia, the Northwest Territories and the Yukon) and Stone's sheep (or Stone sheep, in British Columbia and the Yukon).

Dall's and Stone's sheep are considered thinhorns, in contrast to bighorns. A subspecies, the Sierra Nevada bighorn, is federally protected, with population figures in the hundreds.

Some have estimated that there were millions of wild sheep in North America two hundred years ago. But by the 1950s, squeezed out by people and livestock and decimated by diseases (especially carried by domestic sheep), the wild sheep population dwindled into the tens of thousands.

Conservation efforts saved the sheep and have expanded their territory again, often by transplanting herds and greatly limiting hunting opportunities. It is estimated that there are now nearly 200,000 wild sheep in North America.

The privilege of killing one (or "harvesting" one, in a hunting euphemism) remains limited to the very few. It requires a lot of money or a lot of luck.

The United States Fish and Wildlife Service estimates that there are more than 10 million big-game hunters in the United States. But only about 2,500 wild sheep are hunted each year across North America, a fraction compared with nearly every other animal.

"They're like the collector's edition Ferrari," said Lance Kronberger, who owns Freelance Outdoor Adventures in Alaska and guides big-game hunts of all kinds. "There's two hundred of them made, and you have to get lucky to get one."

Generally, there are two ways to hunt wild sheep. One is hunting's version of the lottery—pay a few dollars and apply for one of the limited number of licenses that are restricted to certain territories and raffled off. Odds of winning can be infinitesimal. In Montana, 19,439 applications were submitted by state residents in 2015; licenses went to 111, a success rate of about 1 in 200. Nonresidents have a tougher time.

"I've been putting in for a sheep tag since I was twelve years old and never gotten one, and I'm sixty-seven," said George Dieruf, whose father opened Powder Horn Outfitters in downtown Bozeman in 1946. It is now part of Schnee's, another outdoors institution, and Dieruf oversees the hunting department. Its high walls are crowded with taxidermy animals the family has collected from all over the world.

"I've had moose tags," Dieruf said. "But I'd trade all four for one sheep."

The second way to secure a chance at a wild sheep is to spend a lot of money. While residents of Alaska and those in Canada generally can hunt sheep within their own state, province or territory, nonresidents are required to hire a registered outfitter. The laws of supply and demand push the price of hunting a Dall's sheep up to about $25,000 and a Stone's sheep to about $50,000. Hunts in Mexico, through outfitters or private landowners, can reach $100,000.

A wealthy few go beyond that. They bid on exclusive permits that are auctioned off annually to raise money for states, provinces and Indian reservations, seeing their lavish spending as a charitable donation, a tax write-off and a chance to capture one of hunting's premier trophies.

"Some rich people are into yachts or floor tickets to the Lakers," Burns said. "Some sheep-hunt."

What they are not buying is an easy trophy. Sheep live in steep and treeless terrain, above the timberline in the mountains or in the rugged hills of the desert. Sheep hunts can take hunters into places few humans have gone, and can include weeks of trekking and stalking.

"For the true hunter, you can't buy them behind the fence," Kronberger said. "You have to climb the mountain. The fat rich guy is going to have a much harder time. Anybody can kill a bear if they sit on the beach or along the stream long enough. I could take a guy in a wheelchair and get him a bear. You can go and get your deer, get your elk. You can't do that with sheep. You have to go and get it."

All that can be hard for non-hunters to understand. Those who have trophy rooms filled with a wide selection of mounts, like Corrigan and Kronberger, said that guests are rarely attracted to the sheep at first, instead taken by the more glamorous and fearsome animals. It is like a litmus test for hunting credibility.

"If I brought a thousand people into my trophy room, almost all of them would go to the bears and say, 'Wow, look at the bears,'" Kronberger said. "Only a few know to go to the sheep—the other sheep hunters. Half the time, people call the sheep a goat."

Brendan Burns sat in a padded stackable chair in the Tuscany Ballroom of the Peppermill Resort Spa Casino in Reno, Nevada. It was a Friday night in January, and there were about 1,000 people sitting at a hundred round tables, having just eaten the one entree offered: steak. A convention of hunters was no place for a vegetarian option.

On stage was an auctioneer. The next item for bid, number 15, was the California Desert Bighorn Sheep Permit. The year before, it went for $165,000, a state record.

Burns, a former wrestler at Ohio State, grew up in Montana. He is lean, as if still making weight, and keeps his hair to little more than the stubble of a three-day beard. Away from the hunt, he often wears crisp, untucked oxfords, and when he stands, he stuffs his hands into the front pockets of his jeans and rocks on his sneakers.

He wears few signs that he is a world-class hunter or an executive for KUIU, a fast-growing gear and apparel company. Named for an island in southeastern Alaska and pronounced KOO-yoo, it has, in just a few years, positioned itself as a Patagonia or The North Face of the camouflage set.

Burns held his phone to his ear. The voice on the other side belonged to Jason Hairston, KUIU's forty-five-year-old founder. A former linebacker at the University of California at Davis, Hairston long ago saw a business opportunity for high-end gear marketed specifically to hunters. In 2005, he and a partner launched Sitka. It grew exponentially and was sold, leaving Hairston in 2011 to start KUIU, a direct-to-consumer maker of expedition-ready gear designed to handle the worst elements a hunter might face—something like a sheep hunt.

The first person Hairston hired at KUIU was Burns, whose title is guide and outfitters program director.

Among Hairston's friends is Donald Trump Jr., a son of the president and an avid big-game hunter.

It was why Hairston missed the sheep convention for the first time in years. He was in Washington, as a guest of the Trumps. The night of the auction for the California permit was the day of the presidential inauguration.

Hairston wanted the California permit. He saw it as a way to pay back his home state and an appropriate place to finish his "grand slam," the term applied to those who have killed all four types of the North American wild sheep. (Grand Slam/Ovis officially tracks grand slams— it has documented more than 1,500 legally taken grand slams—and claims rights to the phrase among hunters.) A year earlier, he was the last one to drop out of the bidding.

Hairston was in a tuxedo at an inaugural ball at the Trump International Hotel. He handed the phone to his wife, Kirstyn, who wore a white strapless gown. Afraid that her husband might drop out and be left disappointed again, she wanted to do the bidding through Burns. She took the phone to a quiet corner and left Hairston alone to wait for the result.

Donald Trump Jr. approached Hairston moments later and asked where Kristyn was. Told that she was bidding on the California tag, Trump waited, too, curious to know how it turned out.

The auctioneer opened the bidding at $100,000. Patrolling the floor, wearing cowboy hats, were a dozen bid spotters. One parked himself in front of Burns, who had his phone to his ear and no expression on his face.

Four other bidders quickly took the tag to $135,000. Burns whispered into the phone, then nodded to the spotter. Hundred-and-fifty,

Burns mouthed, and the spotter shouted it back to the auctioneer and the crowd let out a cheer. Burns hoped it would end there.

But the price nudged up, $5,000 at a time, until it was Burns and one other bidder somewhere in the back of the huge ballroom. Eyes forward, face in poker mode, the price already a record, Burns nodded to $180,000, then to $190,000. The person in back kept delaying, testing the auctioneer's voice and patience, before ratcheting the price farther.

At $195,000, Burns turned to see if he could see whom he was bidding against. He could not. He put up two fingers for $200,000. "Ladies and gentlemen, $200,000!" the auctioneer shouted. "Let's keep it going!"

The pace of his opponent slowed. Burns was decisive. After he nodded to $235,000, there was no response from the back. The tag, going once, going twice, was sold. The crowd applauded. Burns ended the call and people shook his hand.

"That was more than she wanted to pay, but she never hesitated," Burns said.

In Washington, Hairston hugged his wife and high-fived Trump, who asked if he could come along on the hunt.

"There's a particular sheep that we know about, and that the outfitter working with the other bidder knows about, and it could be a state record," Hairston said a few days later. "That drove the price up. But he's old. He's eleven or twelve. The question is whether he'll still be alive, if he'll make it through this winter. And then the question is whether we can find him."

Sheep hunters sometimes stalk their future prey for years. That familiarity, rare in hunting, leads to enough of a connection that hunters often name rams that they hope to someday hunt. Hairston called this particular one Goliath.

"There are no guarantees," Hairston said. "The hunt starts November 1. That's about when the rut starts, and during the rut he sometimes moves out of the area where you can hunt. That's been the challenge with this sheep in the past."

Whether he gets a ram or not, the California Department of Fish and Wildlife receives 95 percent of the auction price—in this case, a record $223,250. That is fed into a general big-game budget of about $10 million, according to Regina Abella, California's desert bighorn sheep coordinator. The money pays for sheep-specific employees and conservation efforts, like helicopter surveys and captures to test the animals for disease and collar them to track their health and movements. (Another major funding mechanism for American wildlife conservation comes through the Pittman–Robertson Act, which taxes hunting goods, like rifles and bows.)

No other game tags come close to creating the kind of revenues that the sheep tag does, Abella said. The elk tag might attract $30,000.

"The sheep tag, it's a whole other level," Abella said.

The thirty or so tags auctioned annually at the convention tend to draw bids from a small circle of wealthy hunters, perhaps twenty-five of them. Many have someone else do the bidding for them, even if they are in the ballroom, too.

Such anonymity helps keep other potential bidders from knowing whom they are competing against for a coveted tag. More important, perhaps, it helps avoid the publicity that can fuel hunting's critics.

"Some of the big donors are CEOs and presidents of large companies," Hairston said. "I don't think anybody, as a hunter, has a fear of saying that they're a hunter. But in their role professionally, the concern is how it potentially affects their business."

Jimmy John Liautaud, founder of the sandwich chain that bears his name, is a frequent bidder for sheep tags, including the one for British

Columbia that he bought this year, by phone, for $210,000. Liautaud found himself in the sights of anti-hunters in 2015 when pictures from five years earlier surfaced showing him with dead elephants, a rhinoceros and a leopard shot in Africa. He has since said that he no longer hunts big game in Africa, but he does make frequent trips for sheep and other animals in Asia.

He has successfully bid on the Montana Governor's Permit four times since 2009, for a total of more than $1 million. In 2013, he lost out to Douglas Leech, a former bank executive from West Virginia, who paid $480,000 for the tag, still a record.

Like Liautaud, Leech declined to be interviewed.

Combined, the auction of about thirty permits over three nights in Reno raises about $3 million annually. The Wild Sheep Foundation adds money to that total and, last year, gave about $4.7 million to conservation efforts, mostly through state and provincial game departments or directly to Indian reservations.

Donations come in other forms, too. Liautaud recently spent about $3 million for a three-mile fence near the Taos Pueblo reservation in New Mexico, according to reservation officials, along a stretch where sheep from a growing herd were getting hit on a highway.

But the conservation efforts have created a catch-22. Sheep numbers are on the rise, leading some states to raise the number of permits available through the lotteries, to cull old rams and help keep populations down in specific areas. In turn, more hunters can increase competition for top rams, which can lower the price the wealthy are willing to pay for an auction tag, thus hurting the budgets of those involved in conservation.

It's a concern for those, like Bob Anderson, the historian of hunting, who have witnessed all the positive changes over recent decades.

"There's some fear," Anderson said, "that sheep hunting will strangle on its success."

Ray Alt, a slight seventy-six-year-old with his shirt tucked into his Wranglers, opened the door to his stone house in Livingston, Montana, where he was born and raised. The heads and horns of three sheep were mounted high on the living room wall. Around a corner and down some stairs was a trophy room, which used to be the garage, its walls filled with animals that Alt shot, with a bow or rifle, over a lifetime of hunting. The first animal he got as a boy, with a bow, was a porcupine. His favorites, though, are the sheep. He has eight of them.

"It's sheep fever," Alt said. "I don't know how to explain it. It's the love of the curly horns, I guess."

Despite his fascination, it took Alt forty-six years to get one of each kind in North America, the last a desert bighorn in 2014. The first ram he got was in 1968, snowshoeing through the nearby Beartooth Mountains, a vast and wickedly rugged landscape just north of Yellowstone National Park. The Beartooth Mountains are the only place where hunters in the lower forty-eight states can buy a permit over the counter, for $125, and try their luck at sheep hunting. But it's a daunting exercise, one of the toughest hunts possible. The area is nearly a million acres, with perhaps just ten rams of legal age and size.

But in 1968, Alt shot one with a bow, a ram so big that it held up as the record for twelve years. It hung unblinking in his trophy room. The fat horns were ringed, one for each year, which is how hunters determine a ram's age, and the tips were battle-worn and ragged, or "broomed" in hunting parlance.

"When you get to an older, broomed ram, they are special animals," Alt said. "As they grow, they are closer to a full curl and bust off the ends of the horns. An older broomed ram, he's like a monarch."

———

Burns grew up in Livingston and considers Alt a mentor. Like Alt and other guides, Burns has assisted on many hunts but could not afford to buy a tag at auction. For years, he applied for tags through the lottery system, to no avail. He said he spent about $4,500 a year to enter drawings.

In 2012, a friend sent Burns a photograph of a magnificent ram he had seen during a deer hunt in the Bob Marshall Wilderness, more than a million acres of forest and granite straddling the Continental Divide south of Glacier National Park. Burns made the photo his screen saver and the ram his quest. He repeatedly applied for one of that area's two annual tags, and had about a 1-in-30 chance of getting it.

His name was drawn in 2015.

"The big question was if he was still alive," Burns said.

That fall, Burns spent twenty-two days wandering the Bob, as it is called, carrying a bow and searching for his sheep. He figures he walked about 150 miles.

"I equate finding a big ram with walking into a big gravel pit looking for a diamond," Burns said.

He found thirty-six rams in his first eighteen days, but not the one he was looking for. He made mental notes, thinking which one would be his second choice or his third. But the three-year-old photo he carried also showed two younger rams in the frame. To Burns and other sheep hunters, each ram looks different than others, the way identical twins are easily distinguished by family and friends. He had not seen any of those in the photo.

"I was missing one band of rams," he said. "I figured my ram was in it."

He found them on day twenty-three, after he heard the clash of butting heads over a ridge. He saw the ram he wanted. Using a satellite phone, he called the friend who first spotted the ram three years before and asked him to come. The friend hiked ten hours overnight to be there for the kill.

That morning, Burns silently slipped himself into position, looking for the right angle. "With rifle hunting, they say that when you're two hundred yards away, it's game over," Burns said. "With a bow, the game's just starting."

He managed to get closer, but the herd smelled him before he could get an open shot. The sheep shuffled away and settled again. Burns positioned himself within about 80 yards. Back home, Burns practices from that distance daily with his bow, shooting into a life-size Dall's sheep made of foam. The arrow travels about 300 feet a second, and Burns rarely misses.

"I literally told myself, I shoot this shot every day," Burns said. "I got it."

The arrow pierced the ram behind the front shoulder. It ran about a hundred yards, dropped and died. Burns and his friend skinned and cleaned the animal. They packed out nearly one hundred pounds of meat, fifty pounds of the skull and horns, and the sheep's full cape. They left behind just bones and guts, sure to be cleaned quickly to nothing but a white skeleton by wolves or coyotes.

The ram was thirteen years old, the oldest of the more than one hundred rams killed in Montana in 2015. Its horns, measured with a formula that combines length and mass, scored 189⅝, believed to be the biggest ram killed by a bow in North America that year. At the Wild Sheep Foundation's show in Reno, Burns won the award for "top archery bighorn," proclaimed on a big belt buckle presented in a wooden case.

A few months after the hunt, several pounds of the ram's meat sizzled on the backyard barbecue, and the skull and massive horns sat on a garage workbench. The skull was still red and unbleached. Burns figured he would someday get it mounted, but said that the prize was the memory, not the trophy.

"It was the greatest hunt of my life," he said. "Every time I see him, I smile."

POSTSCRIPT: *Jason Hairston used the $235,000 tag he bought at auction to complete his Grand Slam, capturing "Goliath" that November. A little over a year later, Hairston shot and killed himself at his home. An examination of his brain found chronic-traumatic encephalopathy, the degenerative neurological disease associated with repeated blows to the head; Hairston had been a star linebacker in college. Donald Trump Jr. was among those at the funeral.*

14

"YOU'RE EITHER THE HUNTER OR THE HUNTED"

Stinson Beach, California

The toughest part of the Dipsea, said to be the country's oldest trail-running race, might not be the first mile, which contains nearly 700 stairs rising through the forests above Mill Valley.

It is not the jiggly-legged drop into Muir Woods, or the steep rise up Dynamite, so named because your churning legs might feel ready to explode. And it is not even the next big hill, called Cardiac. (If your legs have not burst, maybe your heart will.)

It is not the treacherous plunge toward the ocean, the crooked depths and broken steps of Steep Ravine, even the poison oak that crowds the skinny trails and tickles the legs before blooming into a postrace rash. And it's not the course's maze of permissible shortcuts, like the one named Suicide, that give locals an advantage as long as they stay upright and do not get lost.

No, unexpectedly, the toughest part of the 7.5-mile Dipsea, a topographically schizophrenic romp that was first run in 1905, could be mental.

It is knowing that the slowest runners are given head starts and the fastest ones begin at the back. It is like unloading a zoo's worth of animals in reverse order of mobility and releasing the cheetahs at the end.

The race is handicapped in an unusually calculated attempt to get the top runners in every age group to the finish line at the same time. The youngest children and the oldest adults are stacked at the front. The fittest, fastest men are at the back, released twenty-five minutes later. Everyone else starts in waves in between, distributed by a complex algorithm of gender and age. A different wave is released from the starting line every minute, each one (theoretically) moving faster than the one before it.

"It's a very different dynamic," said Alex Varner, a thirty-two-year-old who, before this year's race last Sunday, had the fastest Dipsea time seven times—but had never won, not quite able to sprint and maneuver past every one of the 600 to 700 competitors who started in front of him. "You're either the hunter or the hunted."

That is how the winners over the past decade include an eight-year-old girl (barely beating a sixty-eight-year-old woman) and a seventy-two-year-old man.

And that is how I started Sunday's race five minutes behind the defending champion, a forty-seven-year-old woman named Chris Lundy.

Dipsea organizers placed me, comically, in the "invitational" section for accomplished runners, rather than the broader "runner" section behind it. Starting in the thick of the competitive pack would provide a better perspective of the race. At my age, fifty, with a six-minute head start in front of the "scratch" runners—those in the last group, men aged nineteen to thirty—most of the invitational section would start in front of me, including all the women.

I live not far from where the race takes place, and I jog the hills a few times a week, five or six miles at a time. Barry Spitz, author of *Dipsea: The Greatest Race* and the longtime finish-line announcer, asked me over coffee last month what other races I regularly run. Well, none, really, I said.

He silently and skeptically scanned me from head to toe and back again.

"I don't mean to be negative, but you probably won't pass anyone," he said.

Seeking an outsider's perspective, and a more optimistic one, I called Amby Burfoot, the longtime editor of *Runner's World* and the 1968 Boston Marathon champion. The Dipsea was on his must-do list for decades, he said. He finally did it last year, at age seventy.

Burfoot thought, with his 21-minute head start, he might finish in the top 100. He finished 541st, with the 1,063rd-fastest time (1 hour 37 minutes 31 seconds).

"Never in my life have I been passed by so many people," he said.

This month, he said, he was headed on vacation, not to the Dipsea.

"It's a fabulous race," Burfoot said, "but I don't have an urge to do it again."

In 1904, as Spitz tells it, more than thirty years before Marin County was connected to San Francisco by a bridge across the Golden Gate, someone had the idea of racing between the Mill Valley train depot and the Dipsea Inn, on the sand of what later became Stinson Beach.

There was no course, just wild terrain and a few scattered trails up and around the shoulders of 2,571-foot Mount Tamalpais. A man named Charles Boas apparently beat another named Alfons Coney and, deemed a success, the two-man event was renewed into an annual race beginning in 1905. It is considered the second-oldest major running race in the country, behind the Boston Marathon, which started in 1897.

Organizers made two monumental decisions at the outset. One was not setting a precise route; runners could create their own path, deciding if a shorter but steeper incline, for example, was better than a longer way around.

That notion persists, far more limited these days because of environmental concerns surrounding an otherwise established "consensus" course. But there are still places where even the top runners pass someone, only to see that person ahead of them again later in the race.

"Shortcuts are kind of like the family jewels," said Roy Rivers, a former winner. "If you have one, you don't talk about it."

The second, more notable decision was the use of head starts.

"Sometimes it's the right thing to do to give other people a better chance to win," said James Weil, an MIT-educated engineer who has been the Dipsea's handicapper for about forty years.

Weil uses historical race data to conclude, for instance, that sixty-year-old men should be placed in the same starting group as twelve-year-old girls and women aged forty-five to forty-eight, all leaving the starting line 12 minutes before the scratch runners.

Theoretically, if you are the best among your age and gender, you could finish first.

"I want the winner to win by less than a minute," Weil said. "I want the top ten finishers to have started in different groups. And I want a representation of women in the top five. The fourth criteria, which is really difficult, I would like a scratch runner in the top ten. I don't think I've done all four. I've done the first three."

Handicapping, and the headache of starting at the rear, is one reason most world-class runners do not bother with the Dipsea. Besides, there is no prize money. A scratch runner has not won the race since 1966.

"There's no incentive for them," Spitz said. "There's no money. It's dangerous. It's in June, in peak racing season. They have bigger fish to fry."

Typical contenders are locals who know the course intimately. They are often strong Dipsea veterans in their forties, fifties and sixties— those who turn a year older and gain another minute of a head start, but whose actual running time does not increase a minute.

As Spitz said during Sunday's award ceremony, if you want to win, or at least get one of the treasured black shirts given to the top thirty-five finishers, "get faster and get older."

The actor Robin Williams ran it a couple of times. ("Besides the hills, the stairs and the downhill, it wasn't bad," he said after finishing a respectable 232nd in 1984.) So did a young Robert S. Mueller III, long before his pursuits included the current president. Elmo Shropshire, known for singing "Grandma Got Run Over by a Reindeer," has run it seventeen times. Now eighty-one, and still running competitively, he stopped doing the Dipsea a few years ago.

"When you're seventy-five, you max out the head-start minutes you get," Shropshire said last week. "I was falling back in the pack, and it felt like it was getting a little dangerous."

The local flavor makes the Dipsea feel like a throwback in an era of gimmicky races. The starting area in Mill Valley on every second Sunday in June has the mellow air of a farmer's market, not a major sporting event. The race has no costumes, no man-made obstacles, no music. Sponsor names are not strewn about the course or on the backs of T-shirts. ("We like the shirt to look like a race shirt, not a billboard," said Edda Stickle, the race director.) There is no encampment of sponsor tents and giveaways at the beachside finish.

The Dipsea is routinely approached by big-name sponsors, including one recently, offering lots of money and outfits for the army of volunteers.

"It'd be the so-and-so Dipsea Race," Stickle said dismissively. "We said thank you, but this will be nothing but the Dipsea race."

I never saw Varner go past. But less than a mile into the race, climbing staircases so long that the top cannot be seen from the bottom, I was aware that dozens were passing me. They were getting younger by the minute.

Beyond the race's midpoint, heading downhill, the field thinned. I was alone when I ducked under a fallen tree to take a well-used shortcut called "the swoop," a thin, tangled thread of a trail dropping fast through thorny thickets and trees. Relieved to hear no footsteps behind me, I tripped over a hidden root and fell into a bush, bruising only my ego.

I later passed the feet of a person on a stretcher sticking out of the bushes, surrounded by three paramedics who smiled and told me everything was fine. I learned later that a teenage girl somewhere else collapsed and was helicoptered to a hospital. (She was released later in the day.)

The week before the race, I interviewed eighty-year-old Russ Kiernan, a three-time winner who won thirty black shirts in forty-nine career starts. On Sunday, he got dizzy at Cardiac and was taken away by stretcher. (He, too, was home that night.)

More people caught me. It is the downhill dashes where the top runners make up the most time, bounding down steps and rocks and daringly passing the competition on narrow and tight corners like short-track speed-skaters.

There is a lot of touching, hands on sweaty backs and shoulders, to keep in control. (The late Jack Kirk, who finished the Dipsea sixty-seven times in a row, the last when he was ninety-five, took to wearing a shirt that read "Do Not Touch Me" on the back.) Only occasionally does the convivial civility turn to trail rage. One man shoved another at the finish line, sending him tumbling into the timing equipment.

I was not there yet. Darting down a meandering trail overgrown with bushes, I heard footsteps behind me. "On your left!" a voice shouted over my shoulder. It was followed by an "oops!" and a "sorry!" as the man bounced past me on the right and disappeared into the bramble.

Nobody gobbled up more runners than Varner, who began with a one-minute head start on the scratch runners. He ran at Davidson College and finished twenty-sixth at the 2013 Boston Marathon. He lives in Marin County, does a few trail races a year, and seems pleasantly unbothered by his inability to win the Dipsea.

By the last mile, he had only one more person to catch: Lundy, a local veterinarian and an accomplished national trail runner. In 2017, she had an 11-minute head start on Varner and beat him to the finish by 20 seconds. This time, she had a 10-minute head start.

She, too, had passed hundreds by the time she topped out at Cardiac, where the Pacific Ocean comes into view. When she slid past sixty-year-old Diana Fitzpatrick, a former champion, on the spiraling steps into Steep Ravine, about six miles in, she figured she must be in the lead.

"But I knew Alex was closing in," she said later.

Varner ran out of time and space again. Despite one of his fastest times ever, 48:51, and the race's overall fastest time for the eighth time, he finished in second, again, this time 15 seconds behind Lundy.

"I was closer than I was last year, but she's such a strong runner," Varner said. "I ran what I hoped to run. No complaints."

Nine of the top eleven came from different start groups. Winners of the thirty-five black shirts included three teenagers and seven runners in their sixties. Their median age was fifty-three. The top scratch runner finished thirtieth.

"I've resigned myself to the fact that I might have to wait ten, twenty years before I win," Varner said. "It's the way the race is designed. They did it because they want to give everybody a shot, and if you look at the results, it works out remarkably well. It's hard to argue with."

I finished 580th. By my calculations, analyzing the final results, I was passed by 247 people.

The good news is that I passed 39. And in another two years, if I get the urge to do the Dipsea again, I will gain another minute of a head start.

POSTSCRIPT: I have not had the urge to do the Dipsea again.

15

DELIVERANCE FROM 27,000 FEET

Mount Everest

Five Sherpas surrounded the frozen corpse. They swung axes at the body's edges, trying to pry it from its icy tomb. They knocked chunks of snow from the body, and the shattered pieces skittered down the mountain. When they finally freed a leg and lifted it, the entire stiff and contorted body shifted, down to its fingertips.

The sun was shining, but the air was dangerously cold and thin at 27,300 feet above sea level. A plume of snow clouded the ridge toward the summit of Mount Everest, so close above. When the Sherpas arrived—masks on their faces, oxygen tanks on their backs—the only movement on the steep face came from the dead man's frayed jacket pockets. They were inside out and flapping in the whipping wind.

More than a year of exposure to the world's wickedest elements had blackened and shriveled the man's bare face and hands. His hydrant-yellow summit suit had dulled to the hue of a fallen leaf. The bottom of his boots pointed uphill. His frozen arms were bent at the elbows and splayed downhill over his head. It was as if the man sat down for a rest, fell backward and froze that way.

The Sherpas picked at the body and used gestures and muffled words to decide how best to move it off the mountain. The ghoulish face and bone-white teeth scared them, so they covered the head with the jacket's hood.

There was no time to linger. That altitude is called the "death zone" for good reason. The Sherpas knew from experience how difficult it was to scale the world's highest mountain. The only thing more daunting might be to haul a dead body back down.

The man's name was Goutam Ghosh, and the last time anyone saw him alive was on the evening of May 21, 2016, when it was obvious that he would become another fatality statistic, soon frozen and as inanimate as the boulders around him.

Ghosh was a fifty-year-old police officer from Kolkata, part of a doomed eight-person expedition—four climbers from the Indian state of West Bengal and four Sherpa guides from Nepal—that ran out of time and oxygen near the top of Everest. The four Bengali climbers were eventually abandoned by their guides and left to die. Three did; only one, a forty-two-year-old woman named Sunita Hazra, survived, as did the guides.

At the time of the tragedy, the climbing season for Everest was almost over. On their way to the summit over the next two nights, the last two dozen of the year's climbers had come upon Ghosh's rigid corpse on a steep section of rock and ice.

To get around him, climbers and their guides, sucking oxygen through masks and double-clipped to a rope for safety, stripped off their puffy mittens. They untethered the clips one at a time, stepped over and reached around Ghosh's body, and clipped themselves to the rope above him.

Some numbly treated the body as an obstacle. Others paused to make sense of what they saw—a twisted man still affixed to the rope, reclined on the slope as if he might continue climbing after waking from his awkward slumber.

Apparently abandoned at his time of greatest need, he was a mute

embodiment of their worst fears. One climber stepped on the dead man and apologized profusely. Another saw the body and nearly turned around, spooked by the thought of his own worried family back home. Another paused on his descent to hold a one-sided conversation with the corpse stretched across the route.

Who are you? Who left you here? And is anyone coming to take you home?

THE ULTIMATE CONQUEST

Mount Everest occupies a rare spot in the collective imagination—a misty mix of wonder, reverence and trepidation. Hundreds of people successfully and safely reach the summit most years and return home with inspirational tales of conquest and perseverance. Other stories detail the occasional tragedies that leave a few people dead in a typical year. Those disaster stories are now their own genre in books and film.

Where most of those stories end is where this one begins, long after hope is gone—the quiet, desperate and dangerous pursuit, usually at the insistence of a distraught family far away, to bring the dead home. The only search is for some semblance of closure.

That was why the Sherpas with their oxygen masks and ice axes had come this far, this high, more than a year later.

The four Indian climbers, from a vibrant climbing culture in West Bengal, were like so many others attempting Everest. They saw the mountain as the ultimate conquest, a bucket-list item that would bring personal satisfaction and prestige. They dreamed of it for years and made it the focus of their training. As motivation, they surrounded themselves with photographs of the mountain, from their Facebook pages to the walls of their homes.

In other ways, however, they were different. Climbing Everest is an expensive endeavor, something to be both bought and earned. Many climbers are middle-aged Westerners—doctors, lawyers and other professionals—with the kind of wealth that the group from India could not fathom. Some spend $100,000 to ensure the best guides, service and safety.

These four climbers measured monthly salaries in the hundreds of dollars. They borrowed money and sold off possessions simply for a chance. They cut costs and corners, because otherwise Everest was completely out of reach.

Ghosh shared an apartment with eight members of his extended family. Paresh Nath, fifty-eight, was a one-handed tailor who barely scraped by with his wife and young son. Subhas Paul, forty-four, drove a small-goods truck and used his father's pension to pay for his Everest attempt. Hazra was a nurse, married and raising a son.

They knew one another from the climbing circles of West Bengal, connected more by their common mission than strong friendships.

About 5,000 people have reached the 29,029-foot (8,848-meter) summit of Everest at least once since Tenzing Norgay and Edmund Hillary first did it in 1953. Nearly 300 people have died on the mountain in that period, according to the Himalayan Database, which tracks such things.

Nepal officials estimate that about 200 bodies remain scattered across Everest. A few are so familiar, so well preserved by the subfreezing temperatures, that they serve as macabre mileposts for the living, including one corpse commonly called Green Boots. Other bodies remaining on Everest include those of George Mallory, dating to his fatal attempt in 1924, and the guide Scott Fischer, part of the 1996 disaster depicted in *Into Thin Air*.

Most of the bodies are far out of sight. Some have been moved, dumped over cliffs or into crevasses at the behest of families bothered that their loved ones were someone else's landmark or at the direction of Nepali officials who worry that the sight of dead bodies hinders the country's tourist trade.

More and more, however, families and friends of those who die on Everest and the world's other highest peaks want and expect the bodies to be brought home. For them and those tasked with recovering the bodies—an exercise that can be more dangerous and far more costly than the expedition that killed the climber in the first place—the drama begins with death.

When someone dies, those left behind, from climbing partners on the scene to family and friends half a world away, are immediately faced with enormously daunting decisions and tasks. The rituals, customs and logistics of what happens next are always different.

There are practical considerations, including whether to search for the bodies of those presumed missing or dead, if that is even feasible, and whether to recover the body or let it rest eternally where it is. There are emotional considerations, maybe cultural and religious ones, often in the name of closure, which can mean different things to different people. There are the wishes of the deceased, if those were ever communicated. There are logistical concerns, including danger and cost, local customs and international laws. Sometimes, in some places, recovery of a body is not just wanted, it is needed, to prove a death so that benefits can be provided to a family in desperate need of financial support.

All these things came into play after the bodies of three men from India were scattered high on Everest in 2016. The dim hopes for rescue kindled into demands for recovery, led by the West Bengal government.

Within a few days, in the short window between the last of the season's summit attempts and the start of the summer monsoon that racks the Himalayas and shuts down the climbing season until the following year, a recovery team of six hired Sherpas tried to find the deceased and carry them down. They had neither the manpower nor the time.

The first they found was Paul, the delivery driver and a part-time guitar instructor who lived with his sprawling family, including his wife and ten-year-old daughter, in the small town of Bankura. He was steps from the well-worn route below Camp 4, roughly 26,000 feet above sea level. He was face-up, but only the toes of his boots stuck out of the fresh snow. It took four hours to chip and pry him from his icy grave and another twelve to drag him to Camp 2, where a helicopter carried the body to Base Camp.

A few days later, thousands crowded Bankura's rough and narrow streets for a miles-long procession of Paul's body, which was carried on the open bed of Paul's small truck. The procession led to the banks of the Dwarakeswar River, where the body was cremated and the soul set free, according to Hindu tradition. There was heartache, but also closure.

Back on Everest, above where Paul's body was extricated, two of the Sherpas moved up to Camp 4. At roughly 26,000 feet, higher than all but about fifteen of Earth's peaks, it sits at the edge of the oxygen-depleted death zone and is the last rest stop for climbers before their final push to the summit. The Sherpas searched the abandoned tents, some shredded to ribbons by wind, until they found the body of another of the missing Indian climbers. They knew it was Nath, the tailor, because he had only one hand; the other had been lost in a child-hood firecracker accident.

Raging winds kept them from climbing any higher in search of Ghosh, and the men were called back. The summer monsoon was on the way, ending the climbing season. Everyone rushed to pack up camp and get off the mountain. Ghosh and Nath, left dead in the death zone, would remain on Everest for at least a year, and maybe forever.

The thought of Ghosh somewhere up there—alone and frozen, or maybe wandering around the Himalayas lost and crying into the wind for help—haunted his wife, his brothers, his mother and all those who lived in the cramped home off Old Calcutta Road, hundreds of miles away. Kolkata lies on the improbably flat and vast plain of the Hooghly River, a slow and wide offshoot of the Ganges in eastern India. There is nothing, not even a hill, to poke the horizon, and the thought of a mountain like Everest feels as far away as another planet.

And so his wife, Chandana, kept the vermilion sindoor in the part of her hair, and the red and white bangles on her right wrist, to indicate that she was a married woman. She would not remove them until she was certain she was a widow. She left the calendar on the wall of the bedroom turned to May 2016. In her mind, that was when time stopped.

"I still believe he is alive," she said in her home in February. "I am not a widow. I am the married wife to Goutam Ghosh. Not a widow. Unless I see him, and we cremate him, I will not change."

In the steel town of Durgapur, a hundred miles northwest of Kolk-ata, Nath's wife, Sabita, tried to move on. She and Nath were poor, even by Indian standards, and she had no money to bring the body home. She and her husband never spoke about what to do if he died, but now she convinced herself that he would want to be left on the mountain. He dreamed about Everest so much that a photo of the mountain was one of the few things that decorated the chipped concrete walls of their bedroom.

The two of them sat side by side through countless nights sewing backpacks and jackets to sell to support his quest. People in town marveled at his ability to cut and sew with just one hand, just as climbers wondered how he could navigate the ropes and harnesses used in mountaineering.

Sabita let herself imagine that she might awake and find him sitting behind his sewing machine. The couple's nine-year-old son silently pretended that nothing had happened, that his father was simply on a long trip.

That's what happens when the body is left on the mountain. Death feels like hearsay. Only the body coming through the door at home could make it something more than a haunting phantom in the imagination. Its return could bring honor and closure. It might not answer all the questions, but it could end the nightmares.

But even if it could happen, even if the bodies of Ghosh and Nath were found where they were last seen, and even if impossibly huge sums could be raised to pay to recover them, and even if there were people willing to risk their own lives on Everest to honor the dead and appease the living, nothing could happen right now. It would have to wait a year.

THE SUMMIT WITHIN REACH

On the afternoon of May 20, 2016, Ghosh, Nath, Paul and Hazra anxiously rested inside a tent at Camp 4. They wore oxygen masks and bright, bulky snowsuits filled with down. They sipped tea and munched crackers. There was little chatter.

They did not know one another well, but formed a ragtag group of modestly accomplished climbers, joined by their individual desires to summit Everest and their common need for a low-budget expedition.

All had spent ten years or more saving, borrowing and raising money for an Everest expedition. They found a company popular with West Bengali climbers that charged them each about $30,000, cheaper than other outfitters but still a daunting sum, far more than any of them dreamed of making in a year.

Adding to their desperation was that it was their third attempt in three years. Their 2014 quest was scuttled by an avalanche that killed sixteen Sherpas, ending the season just as it was about to start. The 2015 season was canceled after an earthquake rocked Nepal in late April, killing nearly 9,000 people. It caused an avalanche that roared into Everest Base Camp, killing eighteen.

Now, finally, after weeks at Base Camp and on the lower slopes of Everest, they were within reach of the summit. If all went well, they would be back at Camp 4 within twenty-four hours, on their way home to India, where Everest summiters are revered as conquering heroes. "Everesters," they are called.

In the early evening, after dark and later than they had planned, they emerged from the tent, each with a guide. (Guides in the Himalayas are often called Sherpas, though not all are part of the ethnic group of Sherpa, from which many take their surname.) The sky was clear and the moon was full. A line of headlamps slinked up the face of the mountain above them.

The summit of Everest cannot be seen from Camp 4, but much of the route can. It leads up a series of ropes, used by every Everest climber, that are tied to anchors drilled into the rock and ice and set by Sherpas at the start of the season.

The route leads across a barren ice field, sliced with deep crevasses, and shoots up a steep and rocky slope until it reaches a small flat spot, a burr on the side of the mountain. The landing is known as the Balcony, and from there it is two hours or more along the exposed, knife-edged Southeast Ridge to the South Summit—at 28,700 feet, it would be the world's second-highest peak, if it were considered separate from Everest. From the South Summit, the top of Everest finally emerges in full view, tantalizingly close up a serrated ridge.

The round-trip journey from Camp 4 takes some people less than twelve hours, and experienced guides and climbers know that it should take no more than about eighteen—twelve hours up, six hours back. Most follow a rule that at a predetermined time—rarely later than noon—all climbers still moving up should retreat. Prolonged exposure is dangerous, and sometimes deadly, because of the unpredictability of afternoon weather, the limited number of oxygen bottles that can be carried and the toll caused by extreme elevation and temperatures.

A woman and two guides were the first of seventy-four people to reach the summit that day, at 3:36 a.m., according to the Himalayan Database. The last recorded time for climbers reaching the summit was 11 a.m.

The West Bengal expedition stood at the Balcony well after dawn, resting and taking in the majestic views of snow-covered peaks and cloud-shrouded valleys. There were four clients and only three guides because Nath's guide appeared to stay behind at Camp 4, for reasons never understood. Other climbers were already coming down, having reached the summit hours before.

The Base Camp manager for the Indian expedition received a radio call from Bishnu Gurung, the only one of the group's guides with experience reaching the summit of Everest. He said he recommended to the clients that they turn back, but they refused.

"I told them, 'If we are still on the Balcony at ten in the morning, how can we reach the top?'" Gurung said.

Ghosh cried at the prospect of giving up, Gurung later said. Paul began ascending on his own.

"I stopped there just to check if he will return back if I didn't continue," Lakpa Sherpa, Paul's guide, said. "I thought he would listen to me.

Sherpas can't use force or hit him in that situation. They are our guest. All we could do is convince. As he wasn't convinced, I followed him."

Only Nath was persuaded to turn back to Camp 4. The three other Indian climbers persisted. The three guides joined them, carrying a dwindling amount of oxygen and a growing sense of dread.

"I thought that I won't return back," Lakpa Sherpa recalled.

"IT'S LATE"

Throughout the late morning and early afternoon, dozens who had reached the summit descended past the Indian climbers. Paul Pottinger, a Seattle doctor, reached the summit at 7:48 that morning. He wore a camera on his head to record much of his daylight descent on the rope, a one-way lane used by both those going up and coming down. Negotiating past oncoming climbers can be a slow, clumsy and dangerous exercise.

Pottinger passed Paul and his guide, Lakpa Sherpa, well below the South Summit. Lakpa Sherpa asked for the time. Pottinger lifted the sleeve of his jacket to expose his watch, visible to the camera. It was 10:23. He repeatedly told the guide that it was 10:20. He later speculated that the guide wanted Paul, his client, to hear how late it was.

"Who climbs Everest without a watch?" Pottinger said months later. "Now I wonder if he had a watch. And I wonder if he was really saying, 'Please tell my guy to stop because I can't.'"

Minutes later, Pottinger passed Pasang Sherpa, Hazra's guide, climbing alone. At 10:45, on a particularly steep pitch at an anchor tangled in a knot of ropes, Pottinger passed a group of three: Ghosh, Gurung and Hazra.

"The timing could scarcely have been worse for all of us, jammed together at the steepest section of the day," Pottinger wrote in an online diary of his expedition. "But they made it by and continued up. How many more people will be headed up at this time of day? Damn it's late. But, as before, I said nothing to them about this. And, as before, it haunts me to this day."

Paul and Lakpa Sherpa reached the summit at 1:45 p.m., according to the camera later recovered from Paul's body. There were thirty-one photographs taken at the summit over sixteen minutes.

The others in their group—Ghosh, Hazra, Nath and their guides—were somewhere below.

The last photograph of Ghosh taken with his camera appeared to be at the South Summit at 1:57 p.m. He wore an oxygen mask. He held flags and banners that he had carried in his backpack. A video recorder dangled around his neck. Ghosh turned it on.

Wind whipped through the camera's microphone, but not enough to obscure the sound of Ghosh's quick-paced breathing. It was as if Ghosh were checking himself in a mirror. With a bare hand, he lifted his sunglasses to his forehead. His eyes were bloodshot. He pulled his oxygen mask to his chin, briefly showing his teeth and his gray-speckled mustache.

"Goutam," a voice said, and Ghosh glanced in its direction, put his mask on and reached to turn off the camera. It was the last record of him alive.

Yet Gurung, Ghosh's guide, apparently kept going, alone. About forty minutes later, he photographed himself twenty-one times with Ghosh's camera at what appeared to be the summit. There was no sign of Ghosh.

(Hazra, the lone survivor, said that she reached the summit at about 3 p.m. There is no evidence that she got there. She has petitioned for a summit certificate from Nepal's Department of Tourism, the arbiter of such matters, without success.)

STOP OR CONTINUE?

In the area above 8,000 meters (over 26,000 feet), from Camp 4 to the summit, a dearth of oxygen and brutal weather kill those who dare stay exposed too long. As altitude increases, atmospheric pressure decreases, and with the thin air comes less oxygen for the lungs and the bloodstream.

The body tries to overcome it by sending more blood to the brain, which can cause swelling, leading to symptoms like headaches, nausea and exhaustion. At extreme heights, a condition known as high-altitude cerebral edema can also cause a lack of muscle coordination, impaired speech, confusion and hallucinations. As the body continues to fight for equilibrium, it sends blood to the lungs. High-altitude pulmonary edema results in coughing and major breathing problems.

The sun's strong rays at high altitudes can burn the skin and eyes, causing snow blindness. The subfreezing temperatures, exacerbated by perpetually strong winds, cause frostbite, killing the skin and the underlying tissue, especially in the extremities.

Confused and numb, climbers sometimes react to the onset of hypothermia by shedding their clothes, believing they are burning up, not freezing to death. It is why those who die in extreme conditions, like the ones on the slopes of Everest, are often discovered in a state of undress.

Back in West Bengal, vague and inaccurate news reports spread quickly on May 21: the climbers had reached the summit. The houses of the climbers filled with friends offering congratulations and customary sweets.

By nightfall, however, the festive mood faded. Updated reports from Everest arrived. The West Bengali climbers were lost on their way down.

That evening, down at Camp 4, the first group to leave for a summit attempt included an experienced American climber and photographer, Thom Pollard, and his Nepali guide.

They first passed a Sherpa, then another, both cold, scared and without oxygen. Then they came across climbers below the Balcony. One was a woman. One was a man in a yellow snowsuit, lying sideways across the hill, still attached to the rope. His hands were uncovered. He appeared close to death.

Options for would-be rescuers are few at such extreme altitudes. There is no realistic way to carry someone off the mountain. Even giving aid can be difficult or risky. Climbers carry finite amounts of oxygen, just enough for their own expected need, because of the weight of the canisters. They worry about their own survival, knowing that extra time exposed to the elements can prove fatal. They are often in a depleted state, physically and mentally. Even if they have all their faculties, they have paid tens of thousands of dollars, perhaps devoted many years of their lives, to this one day, and might be reluctant to abort it all for a faceless stranger whose needs cannot be assessed easily and who, most likely, speaks a different language.

Pollard and his guide stopped, discussed the situation and continued past. Dozens of others came and went, too.

"I've wrestled with this for a year," Pollard said from his home in New Hampshire.

Pollard and his guide were the first to summit on the morning of May 22, at 2:40 a.m. On their descent, still in the dark, they were relieved to see Hazra was gone. There were marks in the snow where she had either scooted downhill or been dragged away.

But Ghosh was still there, splayed on the slope and now alone.

"He was dead," said Pollard's guide, Lhakpa Gyaljen Sherpa. "I shouted, 'Hello, hello!' There was no response. Looking at his face, he was dead. That's why the others must have left him."

Sunita Hazra's memories of that night are spotty, but she remembered leaving Ghosh, her closest friend on the expedition.

"I told Goutam, 'You must come,'" she said in the living room of her home near Kolkata. "I thought if I started moving downward, he would follow me. I had neither the strength to help him or to even look behind me to make sure he was coming."

She believes she would have died, too, if not for Leslie Binns, a British climber who was ascending above Camp 4 when he found her with her mittens off and her jacket unzipped. He gave her a shot of oxygen, which lifted her energy, but soon realized she would not make it to Camp 4 on her own. He aborted his own summit attempt to drag, encourage and cajole her downhill.

They soon discovered Subhas Paul, in a dazed and hypothermic state of his own. Binns slowly coaxed the two Indian climbers down, sharing hits of oxygen and trying to lift them when they collapsed. They lost track of the roped route. Paul fell into a shallow crevasse and flailed his arms.

Binns eventually made a decision to try to save one or the other. Figuring Paul had energy to expend, he chose Hazra and escorted her to a tent.

"When I got to Camp 4, Subhas was not behind me," Hazra said. "I thought he was there. I thought Goutam and Nath were somewhere safe."

Some in Camp 4 later awoke in the night to someone shouting, rhythmically but incoherently, over and over. They presumed it came from within the camp, part of another expedition. No one ventured into the dark to explore.

When climbers emerged from their tents in the first rays of sunlight, they realized the shouting was from Paul, about 100 yards uphill from camp. He had been out in the elements for at least thirty-two hours.

Paul was helped down to the camp. Hazra and Paul were reunited with their three guides in the tent. They did not know where Ghosh and Nath were.

By midafternoon, persuaded by doctors from other expeditions to get to lower altitude immediately, the group was on its way downhill again, without Ghosh and Nath, carrying the last bits of oxygen it had stashed at Camp 4. Paul soon collapsed.

"Subhas started getting very weak," Lakpa Sherpa said. "He wasn't getting better even after supplying oxygen. His hands froze. We tried very hard to rescue him from there."

Two guides stayed with Paul. The third led Hazra downward, but soon left her behind, feeling he was in worse condition than she was, suffering from frostbite on his hands and feet. Darkness came, bringing snow and wind.

Alone, Hazra fell and broke her wrist. She had frostbite on her hands. Eventually, the other two guides caught up to her.

"I understood from the Sherpas that Subhas sat down to rest," Hazra said at her home earlier this year. She began to cry. "And they left him," she said.

Hazra and the guides made their way to the icy landing spot above Camp 2, where a helicopter winched Hazra to Base Camp. Ferried to Kathmandu, she was hospitalized for her injuries. A few days later, she received a hero's welcome at the airport in Kolkata.

She knew little of what happened behind her, up the mountain. At about the time that Paul, Hazra and the three guides left Camp 4 to descend toward Camp 3, another Indian expedition returning from the summit spotted Nath off the trail in afternoon light. He was upright and alive, mindlessly digging into the ice with his one hand.

Nath was carried to Camp 4. His eyes were swollen shut with snow blindness.

By the next morning, the last day that anyone would summit Everest for the season, Nath was too weak to hold a bowl of soup. He died in a tent at Camp 4.

Goutam Ghosh was still somewhere higher on the mountain. At least twenty-seven people stepped over him on their way to the summit and again on their way down before the season ended and the mountain emptied for most of a year.

A NEW SEASON

Every spring, as hopeful climbers from around the world trek to Everest Base Camp in Nepal, at an elevation of about 17,500 feet, to begin acclimating for a summit push in May, a team of local Sherpas is hired to create the season's route up the mountain. They establish the course up more than two vertical miles that hundreds of others will follow.

First, the "icefall doctors" set ropes, ladders and makeshift bridges through the notoriously dangerous, ever-shifting Khumbu Icefall immediately above Base Camp. Others keep moving upward, setting anchors and stringing ropes until they reach the summit. The process can take weeks, and is often delayed by bad weather.

Only when the ropes are fixed to the top does the Everest climbing season open. It usually lasts only a few weeks, squeezed between the route opening in early May and the projected start of the monsoon at the end of the month.

Everest is rarely climbed at any other time of the year. That meant the rope-fixing Sherpas were likely to be the first to see Ghosh and Nath, if their bodies were still there from the year before. The forces of wind, snow, ice and gravity could have moved them or hidden them.

Nath was last seen in a tent at Camp 4, at more than 26,000 feet, which gets battered into something unrecognizable from one year to the next. Ghosh was last seen higher on the mountain, clipped to a rope on a steep section called the Triangular Face, just below the perch called the Balcony. If that rope from last year's route was damaged—perhaps by a falling piece of ice—Ghosh's body could have fallen and disappeared for good.

There were three major reasons the Ghosh family desperately wanted Goutam's body returned. The first was emotional. The idea that he lay near the summit of Everest, alone, exposed to the elements, left to serve as a tragic tourist marker for future climbers, was nearly too much to bear. And they wanted answers about what had happened. Maybe his body could provide those answers. Maybe that video camera around his neck, if it was still there and still worked, held clues. Maybe there were memory cards from his camera in his pockets or backpack. Maybe a message for the family. Something.

The second was religious. Hindus believe the body is merely a temporary vessel for the soul. Once the soul is severed from the body through cremation, it is reincarnated in another body. Like most in West Bengal and across India, the Ghoshes were devoutly Hindu. To them, closure required a cremation and all the ceremonies that came with it.

The third reason, as important as the others, was financial. Legally, in India, Ghosh was considered a missing person. Only when a body was produced, or seven years had passed, would the Indian government issue a death certificate, which the Ghosh family needed to gain access to his modest bank accounts and to receive financial death benefits like life insurance and the pension he had earned as a police officer.

Ghosh was a police sub-inspector, the second in command at the local precinct of the Kolkata police. It was a good job that paid about $500 a month. Ghosh was a talented player of tabla, the Indian bongo-like drums, and sometimes performed with his wife, Chandana. He took army courses to become an adept equestrian and was known in the neighborhood as a good soccer player. He had been mountaineering and rock climbing for most of his life.

It might seem a strange hobby in Kolkata, hundreds of miles from the Himalayan foothills, but West Bengal is a surprising hive of mountaineering. There are hundreds of mountaineering clubs, in just about every small town and every neighborhood of the cities. Kolkata has dozens of them. The state government heavily promotes the activity through the West Bengal Mountaineering and Adventure Sports Foundation, where a 60-foot climbing wall rises outside its offices.

The foundation gives grants to those who apply with realistic ambitions of scaling the biggest peaks. In the case of Ghosh, Paul, Nath and Hazra, it granted each 500,000 rupees, or about $7,500, toward their quest to climb Everest.

Ghosh was the most experienced of the mountaineers—not a well-known climber in West Bengal, but a respected one. He was an instructor at summer camps held at a climbing center on Susunia Hill, a 1,450-foot hiccup on the plain a couple of hours' drive northwest of Kolkata. He had successfully climbed a number of 7,000-meter peaks in the Himalayas. In the bedroom he shared with Chandana was a poster of Everest. It hung there for twenty years.

"We try to go through our routines," Chandana Ghosh said in February. "The peace is not there. We try to eat and we try to sleep. But all the time we are thinking about the beloved man of this family, lying up there all alone."

Goutam Ghosh was the youngest of three brothers, all in their fifties. They lived with their parents, wives and children in a dim, two-story apartment in the concrete jumble of Barrackpore, a district of northern Kolkata. Their father had recently died. The door from the street led to an outside hallway, open to a sky obscured by rambling apartments, one on top of another, squeezed tight. The bathroom was to the left, a hole behind a half wall and a pitcher of water next to a hose.

Debasish Ghosh, fifty-three, unlike his younger brother, was not a mountaineer. A small man with a bushy mustache and a bit of a paunch, he ran a fast-food stall, serving chow mein and mutton rolls, not far from the family's home near the Barrackpore train station. He made a vow: if the body could be found, he would bring Goutam home.

Debasish Ghosh hoped that the West Bengal government would coordinate and finance a retrieval attempt a year later. For months, he requested meetings with officials, slowly climbing the government's chain of command, until he and Chandana met with Mamata Banerjee, the chief minister of West Bengal.

She expressed concern for the cost, Debasish Ghosh said, and asked who would venture up Everest to bring back the bodies. She wondered about the state's responsibility if members of a recovery team were hurt or killed.

Without a commitment from the state government, the Ghosh family sent a letter to Prime Minister Narendra Modi of India. His office forwarded it to the state government, with a note that said "for action as appropriate." Secretly, the state government approved money for the operation, but it did not share its plans with the Ghosh and Nath families.

"They were saying that only if the body is located will they take up the decision," Debasish Ghosh said. "But who will inform us that the body is there? It has to be the Sherpas, because otherwise nobody is obligated to find the body."

So the family hired an experienced guide who was known among West Bengali climbers and who had been to the Everest summit five times. He told Debasish Ghosh that he would recover his brother's body

for 26.3 lakh rupees, or roughly $40,000—more than the cost of Gou-
tam Ghosh's original expedition.

The family agreed to pay 2.5 lakh rupees (about $4,000) upfront, to
organize and buy oxygen for those who would make the initial search,
following closely behind the rope-fixing teams. The rest would be paid
at intervals along the way—when photographs were produced, for
example, and when the body reached Kathmandu.

The Ghosh family did not have the money, but agreed to sell a small
lot in Kolkata that Goutam owned, where he hoped to someday build
a house. They sold jewelry, including a gold necklace that Chandana
wore at her wedding. Family members and mountaineering club members scrounged the small bits of savings that they had. By early May, as
the rope-fixing team was doing its work, it was still not enough.

"We have arranged about 20 lakh so far," Debasish Ghosh said
in Kolkata.

A day later, too anxious to wait helplessly any longer, he packed a small
yellow daypack with a few changes of clothes, plastic containers of homemade chicken and roti, and a folder of paperwork, protected in plastic
sleeves. The sleeves held copies of Goutam Ghosh's identification card, his
police service card, his permit for climbing Everest—all things that would
help identify a body and cut through the logistics of bringing it home.

He knelt at his mother's bed and touched his mother's feet, a sign
of respect. He prayed with her as she cried. He stepped into the hot sun
and through a huddle of well-wishers. Accompanied by one of Goutam
Ghosh's friends, he waved and disappeared around a corner, swallowed
by a street filled with cars, rickshaws, scooters, bicycles, walkers and
cows, and walked to the train station.

"I cannot keep my mind cool staying at home," Debasish said. "I
want to be closer."

After two trains, two buses and forty hours, the two men were in
Kathmandu. They found a $5-a-night room to share, and waited.

"LET HIM BE"

The rope-fixing team reached Camp 4 on April 23, but weather stopped the Sherpas from going higher. The team descended to refresh at lower altitude in anticipation of its next push, carrying rumors that a body was seen amid the tatters and rubble at Camp 4—the body of Paresh Nath, presumably.

His wife, Sabita Nath, had little communication with the government for nearly a year. No one reached out to the family to discuss what might happen if the body was found. No one, in fact, had asked her if she even wanted her husband's body back.

Sabita Nath did not share her tiny home with a large, extended family. With her husband gone, it was just her and their nine-year-old son, Adrishikar, living behind a storefront where her husband sold his handmade backpacks and jackets.

"After a while, I began to think there is no reason to bring him here," she said at her home one day, sitting near the sewing machines where they used to work side by side. "He loved the mountains like God. If he is there, let him be. His soul must be happy somewhere."

She and Paresh were not deeply religious. Some of Nath's relatives performed rituals after it was clear that he had died in 2016, but Sabita did not attend. She allowed herself the traditional ten days of mourning, then removed all the signs of being a wedded woman—the circular red bindi from her forehead, the vermilion sindoor along the part of her hair and the red and white bangles on her wrist. She was a widow.

Money was an issue. Paresh Nath once had a life insurance policy, his wife said, but the premiums were not paid and it was worthless. Sabita got busy at her sewing machine, making simple nylon shopping bags she sold to a nearby grocery market for about 1,500 rupees (about $23) per month. Climbers and friends provided donations of about 2,500 rupees per month ($39) to keep her financially afloat.

For most of a year, Adrishikar did not ask if his father was dead, and his mother did not have the heart to tell him.

"I tell him that papa has built a room on Everest that he is living in," Sabita Nath said in February. "I can't tell him the real fact, that he is gone."

Like many Indians, the Naths ate without utensils, and Adrishikar carefully washed his father's one hand after meals. Paresh Nath drove the boy to school on a scooter even though he had no license because of his disability. Theirs was a special bond, Sabita Nath said, and her focus was on the boy's well-being, not her husband's body.

"Even if the government brings the body, what's the use to me?" she said. "It is just a mortal body. To me, the more urgent thing is a job, so I can raise our son. To bring a body from Everest is a huge cost. And I cannot spend that money."

If the government wanted to help financially, she said, the money would be better spent on her son's education than on her husband's dead body. She reiterated her stance in May, just before photographs of Nath's body appeared on social media. He was identified by his boots and the snowsuit he had sewn himself.

Nath's family and friends were stunned by the photographs. Sabita experienced chest pains and went to the doctor.

"I felt sick," she said afterward at her home in Durgapur. "Until that day, I was trying to console myself by thinking that maybe he was still alive and only lost."

THE RED TAPE

The route to the summit of Everest changes slightly each year, depending on variable conditions, like the snowpack or snow slides. In 2017, it opened on May 15, later than usual. The new route was strung near previous ones, and the worn, faded ropes of past seasons could be seen threaded among the rocks and through the snow.

The rope-fixing team returned down the mountain and reported seeing a body most of the way up the Triangular Face, below the Balcony—just where Goutam Ghosh's body was last seen, about 360 days before.

"I think that was the body of the Indian climber," Chime Chundub Gurung, one member of the team, said at the airport in Kathmandu a few days later. "The body was upside down with legs up. It was very close to the new rope. I didn't touch it, and I didn't see the face. I only saw boots, and he was wearing mountaineering clothes."

The hundreds of climbers below, eager for the route to open and seeing a forecast for good weather, began to stream toward the summit. Within days, dozens reached the summit and came back again. Few of them saw Paresh Nath's body, stashed away on a far side of Camp 4. But every one of them climbed within feet of Ghosh's body.

The first photographs arrived on Tuesday, May 16. Debasish Ghosh received one on his phone at 6:17 that evening while sitting at his hotel. Numbly, he stared at it, tugging the edges with his fingertips to zoom in for a better look. He sent the message to his son and to Chandana at home in Kolkata. He also sent it to Sunita Hazra, the only survivor among the four Indians in the expedition the year before.

The photo showed a body in a faded yellow snowsuit bent like a horseshoe and half-buried in snow. It looked like something archaeologists were midway through excavating. There was no face visible, but the boots and the gear matched what Ghosh was wearing a year before. The pattern of the yellow-and-black snowsuit matched what Sunita had in her closet at home, the one she had bought alongside Ghosh at a little shop in Kathmandu.

Everyone agreed: It was Ghosh's body.

Three men from the West Bengal government rushed to Kathmandu, taking the ninety-minute commercial flight that Debasish Ghosh could not afford. They quickly struck a deal with Mingma Sherpa, the owner of Seven Summit Treks, a major Himalayan expedition company based in Kathmandu. The sides agreed on a price that the government would pay for the two bodies to be recovered: $90,000, roughly the amount the government quietly set aside weeks earlier. The government announced it would pay for the retrievals.

Sabita Nath and Chandana Ghosh received calls from a government official asking them to sign a "no objection" certificate to allow for the attempted recoveries. They agreed.

Nepal's Department of Tourism, which oversees the country's mountaineering trade, placed only one major provision on the operation: it did not want the bodies coming down at the same time that hundreds of climbers were going up.

"We just want to ensure that other mountaineers who planned to go up this season will not be hampered," Director General Dinesh Bhattarai said. "I have talked to them, and they will try to bring them down at nighttime, and when there are less climbers moving up."

The issue, he admitted, was one of optics as much as congestion.

"The climbers, they know pretty well that it is dangerous, and they are ready to encounter these kinds of incidents," Bhattarai said. "They are mentally prepared for that. It's more about not hampering the existing climber. But at the same time, we are also concerned about what they see."

It was also a matter of practicality. Digging out and dragging a body off the mountain typically requires at least six Sherpas. This effort needed about a dozen people. And most of the Sherpa guides were either still on the mountain with clients, or just returning, too exhausted to turn right back around and go up.

The days of waiting piled up.

THE RETRIEVALS BEGIN

It was late May, the tail end of the Everest climbing season, when five hired Sherpas quietly left Camp 2 at 1 a.m. Into the dark they carried ropes and oxygen canisters, but no food, only a little bit of water and a plastic half-liter bottle of Coke. The Coke froze quickly in the bitter temperatures, even inside their packs. When they wanted a sip, they used a small stove to melt ice and put the bottle in the warm water to turn it back to liquid.

They turned their oxygen on low at what they called the "crampon point," an hour above Camp 2, where the trail becomes predominantly ice and climbers attach crampons, with fang-like spikes, to the soles of their boots.

Sherpas typically use oxygen only in the death zone, at Camp 4 and above, but they wanted to move quickly. Oxygen was fuel, feeding the lungs and the blood, and it allowed them to keep a brisker pace than usual. Each man had two bottles, enough to last about twenty-four hours, they figured.

The leader was Dawa Finjhok Sherpa, a twenty-nine-year-old guide who had been to the summit of Everest five times. He had received a call a couple of weeks before from Mingma Sherpa, the owner of Seven Summits. The company needed an experienced guide to lead an expedition to retrieve a pair of bodies, he was told.

Guides often did two, even three, major expeditions in the Himalayas each spring. By late May, many were either already home or exhausted. Mingma Sherpa dangled a $3,000 payout for a few days of work and scrounged up about a dozen men. He promised beer if they were successful.

Like most Sherpas, Dawa Finjhok Sherpa did not love working as a guide, carrying heavy loads and the hopes and demands of foreigners— and sometimes the foreigners themselves—up and down the world's highest peaks. But it paid better than anything else.

Many of the guides came from remote villages, and there was little work there. Some, like Dawa Finjhok Sherpa, were from Kathmandu. They knew that more conventional jobs, in construction or retail or finance or anything else, wouldn't give them the same money for the same amount of work. But it did not mean they liked it.

"I've almost quit this job," Dawa Finjhok Sherpa said over a beer in Kathmandu one evening, "because there are so many ways to die."

About 11 a.m., the retrieval Sherpas reached Camp 4, a ghost town of abandoned tents and gear so late in the season. They heated their Coke and sipped from the plastic bottles, but did not dawdle. Once rested, the five men stood in the midday light, put on their packs, secured their oxygen masks and kept moving, up the Triangular Face toward the Balcony of Everest, looking for a frozen man who had waited a long time for someone to take him home.

A few hours behind them, following the same route, six more Sherpas left Camp 2 and headed to Camp 4. Their mission was to recover Paresh Nath.

The danger increased with every foot of altitude toward the summit, where the air grew thinner and the chances of rescue, should anything go wrong, grew slimmer. The same threats faced by climbers from around the world were faced by Sherpas from Nepal. But Mingma Sherpa, an experienced climber himself, said no mission to recover bodies was off limits, if the price was right.

"Above the South Summit, from the South Summit to the summit, we might have to think about it," Mingma Sherpa said. "But below the Balcony, the only question is weather. I cannot fight the weather. The technical part, we can handle. The weather can kill us."

If it all went right, then, the bodies of the Indian climbers would return from Everest. They would be among the highest-altitude recoveries ever made.

At 1:39 local time on a Wednesday afternoon, the recovery team searching for Goutam Ghosh got to his body, a pale-yellow crescent on a steep black-and-white backdrop, icebound between jagged rocks the color of coal.

The head was downhill, the face turned slightly to the outside. The arms were splayed overhead, the back was arched and the feet were curled to the right. His once-bright clothes were bleached by the elements. So was the rope that was still attached to the rigging around his waist. It was red when all the Everest summiters of the year before climbed it, but was now faded to a dusky pink.

There were no signs of his depleted oxygen bottles, probably scavenged and sold in Kathmandu for a hundred dollars. There were no signs of his mittens, likely pulled off by Ghosh in his final desperate, hypoxic moments. The snowsuit was unzipped to the waist, a sign that hypothermia had tricked Ghosh into thinking he was overheating.

A skull cap that Ghosh wore the day of the summit attempt was still on, but the yellow down-filled hood attached to his snowsuit was loose and filled with snow. It was still knotted where Ghosh had cinched it at the chin. His hands were bare, black and leathery, like his face. His white teeth, like the silver crampons still attached to his boots, gleamed in the sunshine.

The men were able to pry Ghosh's hood loose and pull it over his face. They tied the hood with rope so they would not have to see the face.

"At first when we saw him, we were a little bit afraid," Dawa Finjhok Sherpa said. "If we don't see the skin, it's easier."

The Sherpas connected Ghosh to a new rope, anchored in a rock about thirty feet uphill, and used ice axes to dig and pry the body from the snow. When the body moved, it moved as one piece, without torque, all the limbs, muscles and joints frozen solid. Pulling on a wrist turned the body all the way to the toes. Once the body was freed from the mountain's grip, the men hammered blocks of ice from it. Dawa Finjhok Sherpa estimated the load weighed more than 300 pounds, double

Ghosh's weight when he was alive. Two men could not lift the body. Three struggled to maneuver it.

They tied ropes through Ghosh's carabiner. They lowered him by rigging a pulley-type system through the same anchors used for climbers attempting the summit. They used Ghosh's jumar, a ratcheting device used in climbing, to help belay the load, sliding it downhill one stretch of rope at a time.

They had the mountain to themselves above Camp 4, which they could see far below in the saddle between Everest and Lhotse.

"It was easier because there was a lot of snow this year, so the rocks were covered in snow and we could slide him," Dawa Finjhok Sherpa said. "But the snowy, flat areas were hard. He was heavy."

Not far from where they found Ghosh's body that morning was another body that Dawa Finjhok Sherpa estimated had been there for five or six years. And somewhere nearby, they knew, was the body of a doctor from Alabama who had died a few days before. There was no plan to bring it down.

It took an hour to drag Ghosh's body to Camp 4, where Dawa Finjhok Sherpa opened Ghosh's backpack. Inside he found a video camera and a pair of gloves. There were banners and printouts of the India and West Bengal flags, and for the Kolkata police department and Ghosh's climbing club.

Dawa Finjhok Sherpa put the gloves on Ghosh's hands and put the video camera in his own backpack. He left Ghosh's backpack at Camp 4, with the wind-torn remains of the 2017 climbing season.

The recovery team had a rolled-up plastic toboggan that it intended to use as a stretcher, but Ghosh's body was too stiff and contorted to fit on it properly. So the men found an abandoned blue plastic tarp, wrapped it around Ghosh's lower body and lashed it tight with mismatched pieces of rope. They found a thin, gray foam sleeping pad and did the same thing for his upper body.

The men tried to keep the body on its back, but it slid better face-down. Soon the snowsuit was ripped open at the elbows, spilling down feathers.

By nightfall, the team was pulling, lifting and sliding Ghosh down the mountain, past where Subhas Paul had died the year before. It came across the group assigned to retrieve Paresh Nath, which was on its way up. There were few other climbers. The mountain was practically empty so late in the season, and those who remained traveled different parts of the slopes at different times. Like drivers familiar with a city's traffic patterns, the recovery Sherpas knew the rhythms of the route.

They rested in the middle of the night at Camp 3, which is carved into the precipitous ice of the Lhotse Face. A Seven Summits cook had hiked up from Camp 2 to meet them, and fed them noodles and juice. The Sherpas trudged downhill from there.

"I started to make a system to belay the body below Camp 3," Dawa Finjhok Sherpa said. "My partner was holding the rope, but he fell asleep. He let the rope slip just as I was hooking up our system. Three of us held on as tight as we could and we screamed. We all got rope burns. If we wouldn't have held on, the body would have slipped down the mountain."

At dawn, Ghosh's body arrived at the crampon point. The Sherpas assigned to get his body had been working nearly twenty-eight hours, but Ghosh's journey was held up, awaiting Nath and the helicopter that would carry them off the mountain.

Clouds shrouded Everest. Ghosh's recovery team sought shelter down at Camp 2, leaving Ghosh alone on the mountain again. The body was soon covered in snow.

LEAVING EVEREST

The body of Paresh Nath, still in the red-and-black snowsuit that he sewed for himself, reached the crampon point at about 2 p.m. on Thursday, May 25. He was wrapped in a malleable plastic stretcher, with a tangle of ropes laced through grommets at its edges.

Nath's right hand, his one hand, was bare and appeared to grip a rope across his chest. His other arm was tucked along his side. It was the position he died in a year before. His body was hard as stone.

Their toughest work done, the sun shining again, the Sherpas assigned to Nath's recovery shed their outer layers. They huddled on the snow and were presented with noodles and juice.

The Ghosh team came up the short distance from Camp 2, and, having strapped the contorted Ghosh into a plastic stretcher of his own, his arms sticking over the edges, coaxed both men downhill on their makeshift sleds. It was not an easy journey, the trail pocked by crags and crevasses. In an hour, they got to the helicopter landing spot, nothing but a relatively flat space covered in snow and ice near the tents at Camp 2. At more than 21,000 feet, it is the highest spot on the mountain that most helicopters can reasonably reach.

When the Sherpas called to Base Camp, they were told the helicopter would not come that day. It would come tomorrow, the 26th. The next day, reports were the same. The helicopter would come the 27th.

The excuse was weather; it was raining in Kathmandu, and clouds were thick between there and Everest. What the Sherpas did not know, and what the families of Ghosh and Nath did not know, was that they were also waiting for the body of another Indian climber, one who had died just days before.

A third team of Sherpas hired by Seven Summits had rappelled into a crevasse near the Balcony and pulled him out. The team followed the teams of Ghosh and Nath back down the mountain, and arrived at Camp 2 late on May 26, well after dark.

The biggest expense for most recovery operations is helicopters. Seven Summits wanted to minimize the cost by ferrying three bodies down at once, rather than performing multiple missions over several days.

Finally, on May 28, the bodies were in place and the sky was clear and blue. A helicopter curled around the valley and touched down, just for a moment, in a cloud of blowing snow. Its skids briefly tickled the slope, and the helicopter spun sideways. Its tail nearly wiped away the man trying to direct it.

The pilot brought it around for another try, flying about ten feet above the ground as he approached. The helicopter landed and slid twenty or thirty feet before it stopped. The pilot kept the rotors on to hold the copter on the icy shelf. Three men pulled Ghosh's body to the vessel, and a fourth helped them lift it into the small space behind the pilot, who breathed oxygen from a tank through a tube to his nose.

The helicopter, already at its altitude limit, unable to take more than one body at a time because of the thin air, lifted off the snow only slightly and followed the throat of the snow-filled valley downhill, into some low clouds and over the steep, chunky landscape of the Khumbu Icefall.

A year before, the climb between Base Camp and Camp 2 took Ghosh and his colleagues about twenty hours, divided by a night's sleep at Camp 1. The ride down took two minutes.

The icefall gave way to a barren strip of gray moraine dotted with yellow and orange tents, the remnants of the season's Base Camp. The helicopter landed in front of about two dozen people, some pointing cameras and others shielding their faces from the dust.

Two men pulled Ghosh's body out of the copter, letting it drop to the rocks, and another four carried it by the ropes. Soon the helicopter was gone again, to get Paresh Nath.

Over a couple of hours that morning, the bodies, along with guides and supplies coming off the mountain for the season, were ferried to a green plain at about 14,000 feet. At noon, the bodies of Ghosh, Nath and the other Indian climber were piled on top in the small cargo space behind the pilot's seat. Several guides climbed on top of the bodies, happy to have a ride downhill.

They flew down a cloud-covered river bed, thick with spring run-off. Seven minutes later, the helicopter landed at Lukla in a cold, light rain. Men muscled the bodies to the ground.

Among the men waiting who converged on the cargo was one of the three West Bengal government officials and several police officers from Lukla. Soon, more officers arrived, in uniform. Part of their job was to identify and investigate dead bodies coming out of the mountains above.

"The police tried to take the bodies inside, but we didn't have the manpower to move them," Dawa Finjhok Sherpa said. "They asked us to remove the clothes and the wraps, but they were all frozen. So they said, OK, just unwrap their faces. They took pictures of their faces."

The formal investigation took a couple of hours. Down in Kathmandu, Debasish Ghosh stood among about three dozen people waiting at a hospital helipad in the late-afternoon light. The helicopter soon appeared as a silent dot over the city's skyline. It grew larger and louder until it touched down in a swirl of wind and dust.

"I cannot stop thinking about the money spent to retrieve his body," Debasish Ghosh said. "If we had spent the money earlier, if we had helped Goutam when he was alive, so that he could find a better agency, or buy more oxygen or make better preparations, could he have survived? Would he be home now, alive? Did we contribute to his death because we didn't help him until now?"

No one paid Debasish much attention. Not the government officials from West Bengal, quick to reach the helicopter the moment it landed. Not Loben Sherpa, who had organized the fateful expedition the year before, or Mingma Sherpa, the owner of Seven Summits, who was paid to recover the bodies. Not the few journalists who had gathered, nor the neighborhood children who rushed to see what the excitement was about.

Debasish stood back, without expression, his hands folded behind him. His brother's body was the first out, laid stiffly on the concrete. People surged forward to get closer. Debasish crossed his arms.

Within a couple of minutes, the helicopter was emptied of its cargo and gone again. People and their cameras followed its skyward arc, but Debasish stared intently at his brother's corpse. No one spoke to him. No one asked if he wanted to get closer to the body. No one comforted him. No one offered to have him meet Dawa Finjhok Sherpa, who led the recovery effort and accompanied the body every step from its year-long home near the Balcony of Everest to the helipad in Kathmandu.

The bodies were lifted into the back of a waiting, unmarked sport utility vehicle and driven around the vast compound of Tribhuvan University Teaching Hospital, to the service entrance at the Department of Forensic Medicine. Government officials arrived quickly by car. Nobody offered Debasish a ride. He walked the ten minutes, alone.

On the ground floor was a warm, dimly lit hallway where a dead body lay uncovered on a table. The lights and air-conditioning in the building had been on sporadically because of power failures, a persistent problem. A service entrance from the dock was on one end. A table was at the other, where a police representative kept guard.

Two silver, dented doors opened into what was called the Forensic Demonstration Room. There were three stainless steel tables, each framed with edges to keep things from spilling off. The tables had drains that fed into tubes under the table, and the tile floors had drains, too. Above each table was an electrical outlet to plug in power tools.

The three bodies were unloaded from the car and carried into the service entrance. Ghosh's and Nath's were placed on the floor of the hallway, to one side. Their names were written in marker on the tattered coverings that had wrapped them all the way from near the summit of Everest.

Debasish Ghosh was escorted inside. He told someone that his brother's name was misspelled.

The bodies were not unwrapped, and Debasish did not see his brother's face. He touched the body only through the layers of clothes and wrappings, and tried to give it a squeeze. It needed to thaw for a couple of days before it could be examined.

CAUSE OF DEATH

At 11 a.m. on May 31, a team of forensic doctors huddled over the body of Goutam Ghosh.

The bodies had been placed on their own examination tables the day before. A pipe ran warm water over them to help them thaw. For the first time, Debasish Ghosh was taken to look at his brother's face. He was struck not by overwhelming emotion, but by how black his brother's face was. He was in the room for less than a minute.

Bodies found at such high elevations, where the temperatures remain below freezing, are well preserved. The outside of the body appears intact, if shrunken and mummified. There is little decomposition internally. Threats found in other remote locations, such as heat, soggy conditions or animal scavengers, are not an issue at such high elevations.

The university's forensics department, led by Dr. Pramod Kumar Shrestha, performs six to eight post-mortems on a typical day. Maybe fifteen examinations a year are for people who died high in the Himalayas, some of them climbers, some of them villagers.

"After one year, it may be difficult to determine the cause of death," Shrestha said. "But we eliminate the possibilities one by one, until we are left with plausible explanations."

Many climbers who succumb to the elements are said to have died of high-altitude illness, a vague diagnosis. It was presumed to be what happened to Ghosh and Nath.

"The head-regulating mechanics stop functioning when you're in extreme cold temperatures," Shrestha said. "With a lack of oxygen, the brain stops functioning. It is not able to coordinate various functions of the body. It's the brain that coordinates the regulation of your body."

Sometimes there are several possible explanations.

"They may have some injuries from falling or something," Shrestha said. "They may have broken bones, internal injuries, a skull fracture, bruises. It depends on the conditions of their death. A lack of oxygen, an exposure to cold, starves the brain. The lungs get a froth in the respiratory passages. But it could be accompanied by a disease. Maybe they died there, but they had heart disease. We check all the internal organs for signs of pre-existing conditions."

With Ghosh, the doctors began with external observations, something often done by a police investigator looking for clues to a violent death. "The face appears partially mummified. Both the feet are soddened," the doctors wrote in the final report for Ghosh. The eyes were "shrunken and collapsed," they reported. They found lacerations on his right hand, perhaps stemming from rough handling during the recovery. There were no broken bones.

A saw was used to cut into the head to retrieve the brain and to split the rib cage to inspect internal organs. The saw cut from behind one ear to the other, over the top of the head. The skin was pulled back, front to back, the skull opened and the brain removed. It was weighed and examined. No abnormalities were found. The brain was replaced, the skull fitted together and the skin sewn.

"We try to keep the body as presentable as possible," Shrestha said.

There was an abnormal amount of fluid in the lungs. The chambers of the heart contained only "post-mortem clot." The kidneys "appear congested," the report said. But the heart and Ghosh's other organs, most of them removed and weighed, were determined to be normal for a fifty-year-old man.

The abdomen and the chest were sewn back together, leaving a crude, thick laceration. The exam lasted about forty-five minutes. In the final report, the doctors listed the cause of death as "undetermined."

A similar examination for Nath, noting his missing left hand and some abrasions, ended with the same conclusion.

The bodies of Ghosh and Nath were carted to a nearby room, in the Department of Anatomy, for embalming. A mix of formaldehyde, glycerin and rectified spirits was injected into their cavities and soft tissue. The bodies were shrouded in plastic wrapping and placed inside wood coffins, along with white cotton cloths.

On one coffin was a photocopy of Ghosh's passport. On the other was a copy of Nath's. They were attached to the lids of the coffins with clear packing tape.

Before the coffins were sealed, though, Debasish Ghosh, wearing a surgical mask, entered and took another look at his brother. He asked for his brother's boots as a memento. And he asked for the boots of Nath, to give to his family.

LAST RESPECTS

Preparations were complete at the Ghosh house when the sun came up in Kolkata on June 2, the temperature on its way past 100 degrees. The family's sitting room, really an unused storefront with yellow walls, was cleared of furniture and the roll-up door raised. Ghosh's faded climbing boots sat in a corner near his photograph.

"I must see him again," his wife, Chandana, said in the room the day before. "Most times, the bodies are left on Everest. No one can see the body again. No one can touch the body again. At least I will see him once more. I will touch him one more time."

The hearse crept into the crowd, and was immediately surrounded

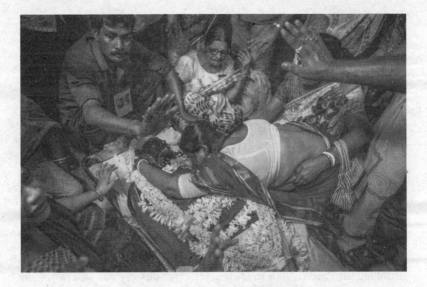

by mourners. Some hung on to the vehicle and cried. Many aimed their cameras inside, where Ghosh's body was out of the coffin, draped in white cloths, his feet and face exposed for all to see. A yellow cap, like the one he wore when he died, was on his head. It covered the scar from the autopsy on his skull.

The women of the family rushed inside the house, and the body was carried through the throng and placed on the floor. A human chain formed to keep people back amid pushing and shouting. The room, about ten feet by twenty feet, was stuffed with fifty people. It was swelteringly hot. Women knelt at Ghosh's side and cried.

Chandana broke down near her husband's left hip and flung herself on top of his corpse. She sat up again, inconsolable, her face and hair wet with tears and sweat. Her nephew lifted a cup of water to her lips and wiped her face with a wet cloth.

Ghosh's mother, her face anguished, wailed and fell atop her dead son.

After twenty minutes, the body was carried across the street, onto a platform in the shade. A line formed to pay respects, starting down the block and curling around Ghosh's body, soon piled with flowers.

After an hour in the midday heat, the body was lifted back into the hearse. A group with a banner led the procession onto Old Calcutta Road, followed by mourners in two single-file lines. The hearse followed, and then family members and close friends, some dropping puffed rice and splashing water to the ground, followed by police and military officers. Debasish's teenage son had downloaded the music of his uncle's favorite singer into his phone, and Kishore Kumar's voice warbled from the hearse's speakers en route to the crematory.

At the same time, a hundred miles to the northwest, a similar ritual unfolded for Paresh Nath in Durgapur. His body arrived in a hearse to the courtyard of his home, where a huge crowd awaited. The lid of the coffin was pried off, and the plastic wrap that encased his body was torn open at the head. A flag of the Durgapur Mountaineers Association was draped on top of him. The body was soon smothered in garlands and petals.

Sabita Nath sobbed, and held tight to her son, Adrishikar, now ten, who came face to face with the corpse of his father after a year of denying his death. The body was taken to the mountaineering club, where another crowd gathered, and then to the Birbhanpur cremation ground along the Damodar River.

Adrishikar, as Nath's son, was responsible for the cremation rituals. He was shown all the ritualistic steps and performed them—the touching of rice and water and fire to the lips, the chanting, the circling. The young boy who had washed his father's hand after meals when his father was alive was there when his father's body was slid into the incinerator, and there to take the ashes to the river, and to break the urn, and to dunk himself in the water. And when it was over, he returned home and held his mother again.

Thirteen men carried Ghosh's body up some steps inside the dim, dusty crematory in Kolkata. In the room upstairs, fluorescent bulbs overhead did not provide enough light, and a ceiling fan did not provide enough breeze. One side of the room had an iron gate that opened to an incinerator.

The group lifted Ghosh's body onto a bamboo stretcher. The white linen sheet that covered him was pulled back to reveal a red-and-black track suit. The jacket was opened, exposing a thick, zipperlike scar from the autopsy.

Several sticks of incense were lit. In a bowl, rice, banana and ghee were mashed together. A nephew fed it to his uncle's lips. He poured sacred Ganges water into his hand and sprinkled it on Ghosh's blackened face, then over the rest of his body. The group chanted prayers and mantras. Debasish Ghosh stood in the corner, expressionless.

The body was carried and placed head-first on rails that disappeared under the metal door of a 10-foot-tall oven. Several times, a man called, "Balo Hari." The group answered, "Hari Bol," a plea to Lord

Krishna to take Ghosh from Earth to heaven. The door opened slightly to reveal an orange glow. Someone pulled a lever, and the body slid into the opening. The door closed behind it.

Back at the Ghosh house, Ghosh's widow, Chandana, had changed clothes. Gone was the colorful sari, replaced by a white one with small, subtle flowers. She had no sindoor tilak, the vermilion smear along the hairline that signaled marriage, and no red bindi dot on her forehead.

The red and white bangles on her wrist were gone, too. While her husband's body was cremated, she broke them. A year after her husband died on Everest, she was finally a widow.

The calendar on the bedroom wall still showed May 2016.

POSTSCRIPT: After eleven deaths and an outcry over crowding on Mount Everest in 2019, Nepal's government vowed to require more experience among climbers seeking permits. The 2020 season was called off because of the coronavirus pandemic. The Ghosh family, seeking to hold someone responsible, continues pushing the Indian government to investigate the circumstances of Goutam Ghosh's death.

PART IV

DYING
AND
LIVING

16

SEEING THE WORLD BEYOND THE COURT

Oakland, California

The last time Steve Kerr was in Beirut, his birthplace, with the bombs pounding the runway and the assassination of his father six months away, he left by car.

The airport was closed. There was talk of taking a cruise ship to Cyprus, or accompanying an ambassador on a helicopter to Tel Aviv or even crossing into Israel on a bus. A military plane headed to Cairo had an empty seat, but it went to someone else. Finally, a hired driver took Kerr over the Lebanon Mountains and across the Syrian border to Damascus, then on to Amman, Jordan. It felt like an escape.

"I'm fearful that all this uncertainty and inconvenience, not to mention even a sense of physical danger, has not done Steve's image of Beirut much good, and in his present mood he wonders what any of us are doing here," his father, Malcolm H. Kerr, the president of the American University of Beirut, wrote to other family members that day in August 1983.

A few months later, Malcolm Kerr was shot twice in the back of the head outside his university office.

Steve Kerr was eighteen then, quiet and sports-obsessed. He was a lightly recruited freshman at the University of Arizona, before it was a basketball power. It took a vivid imagination to see him becoming an NBA champion as a player and a coach, now leading the Golden State Warriors.

But perhaps it should be no surprise that, at fifty-one, Kerr has found his voice in public discourse, talking about much more than basketball: heavy topics like gun control, national anthem protests, presidential politics and Middle East policy. With an educated and evenhanded approach, he steps into discussions that most others in his position purposely avoid or know little about, chewing through the gray areas in a world that increasingly paints itself in bold contrasts.

In many ways, he has grown into an echo of his father.

"The truly civilized man is marked by empathy," Malcolm Kerr wrote in a foreword to a collection of essays called *The Arab-Israeli Confrontation of June 1967: An Arab Perspective*. "By his recognition that the thought and understanding of men of other cultures may differ sharply from his own, that what seems natural to him may appear grotesque to others."

In a sometimes emotional interview this fall, Kerr spoke about the death of his father and his family's deep roots in Lebanon and the Middle East. Some of the words sounded familiar.

"Put yourself in someone else's shoes and look at it from a bigger perspective," he said. "We live in this complex world of gray areas. Life is so much easier if it could be black and white, good and evil."

Providing commentary on the state of today's politics and culture is not a prerequisite for Kerr's job. There are sports fans, maybe the majority of them, who wish athletes and coaches would keep their non-sports opinions to themselves—stand for the anthem, be thankful for your good fortune, express only humility, and provide little but smiles and autographs.

Kerr understands that. Sports are a diversion for most who follow them, "only meaningful to us and our fans," he said. In a sports world

that takes itself too seriously, that perspective is part of the appeal of Kerr and the Warriors. They won the 2015 NBA championship, were runners-up last season and remain a top team this season. They seem to be having more fun than anyone else.

But Kerr also knows that sports are an active ingredient of American culture. He knows, as well as anyone, that players are complicated, molded by background, race, religion and circumstance.

And Kerr is, too: a man whose grandparents left the United States to work in the Middle East, whose father was raised there, whose mother adopted it, whose family has a different and broader perspective than most. The Kerrs are a family touched by terrorism in the most personal way. Malcolm Kerr was not a random victim. He was a target.

That gives Steve Kerr a voice. His job gives him a platform. You will excuse him if he has a few things to say.

"It's really simple to demonize Muslims because of our anger over 9/11, but it's obviously so much more complex than that," he said. "The vast majority of Muslims are peace-loving people, just like the vast majority of Christians and Buddhists and Jews and any other religion. People are people."

He delved into modern Middle East history, about the Second World War and the Holocaust and the 1948 creation of Israel, about the Six-Day War in 1967, about peace accords and the Israel–Palestine conflict and the Iraq War and the United States's scattered chase for whatever shifting self-interest it has at any particular time.

"My dad would have been able to explain it all to me," Kerr said. Instead, he absorbed it as a boy and applies it as an adult. "He at least gave me the understanding that it's complex. And as easy as it is to demonize people, there's a lot of different factors involved in creating this culture that we're in now."

Malcolm Kerr was a professor at UCLA for twenty years, and the sprawling ranch house where the family lived in Pacific Palisades, California, has a flat driveway and a basketball hoop bolted to the roof above the garage. Steve Kerr spent countless hours in the driveway practicing the shot that would give him the NBA record for career three-point percentage that still stands. But not all memories in the driveway are about basketball.

"I remember when the Camp David Accords happened," Kerr said, recalling the 1978 peace talks between Menachem Begin of Israel and Anwar el-Sadat of Egypt, shepherded by President Jimmy Carter. Kerr had just entered his teens.

"One of my best friends was a guy named David Zuckerman, a Jewish guy, and his father was an English professor," Kerr said. "Mr. Zuckerman and David drove me home from baseball practice or something, and we pull up in the driveway and my dad sees us and comes running out. Mr. Zuckerman's name was Marvin, and my dad said, 'Marvin, Marvin! Did you see the picture today of Begin and Sadat?' It was the biggest thing. It would have been the equivalent of the Dodgers winning the World Series. He was so excited for that moment because that is what he really hoped for: Middle East peace. That was his dream. That day, I'll never forget it."

Kerr paused.

"And then it was only a short time later that Sadat was killed," he said.

The Sadat assassination was in October 1981, just twenty-seven months before Malcolm Kerr was killed.

"WE WERE THE GOOD GUYS"

Malcolm Kerr's parents, Stanley and Elsa Kerr, were American missionaries who met in the Middle East after the First World War. He worked for American Near East Relief in Turkey during the slaughter of countless Armenians (detailed later in his memoir, *The Lions of*

Marash). She had traveled to Istanbul to study Turkish and to teach. They married in 1921 and moved to Lebanon to run orphanages. They went on to teach at the American University of Beirut for forty years.

Malcolm was one of their four children. He went to the United States for prep school and graduated from Princeton before he returned to AUB for graduate school. It was there that he met Ann Zwicker, an Occidental College student from California spending a year studying abroad.

Beirut was a cosmopolitan, sun-kissed city on the Mediterranean, a mix of Christians and Muslims seemingly in balance, if not harmony. AUB was founded in 1866 as a bastion of free thought and diversity, welcoming all races and religions. As wars and crises suffocated the Middle East in recent decades, it has often felt like an island, protected by prestige and open-mindedness.

Malcolm and Ann married and raised four children: Susan, John, Steve and Andrew. The first three were born in Beirut. Malcolm Kerr took a teaching job at AUB, but the Kerrs settled in California when Steve was a toddler. Malcolm Kerr's tenure at UCLA was sprinkled with sojourns and sabbaticals that persistently pulled the family back to the Middle East.

Steve Kerr spent two separate school years in Cairo. There were summers in Beirut and Tunisia, another year in France, and road trips circling the Mediterranean in a Volkswagen van. Steve "was not always thrilled," he admitted, to leave friends and the comfort of California. He hated to miss sports camps and football and basketball games at UCLA, where the Kerrs had season tickets.

In hindsight, though, his family's long history in the Middle East, beginning nearly one hundred years ago, shaped him in ways that he only now realizes.

"It's an American story, something I'm very proud of, the work that my grandparents did," Kerr said. "It just seemed like a time when

Americans were really helping around the world, and one of the reasons we were beloved was the amount of help we provided, whether it was after the First World War, like my grandparents, or the Second World War. I'm sort of nostalgic for that sort of perception. We were the good guys. I felt it growing up, when I was living in Egypt, when I was overseas. Americans were revered in much of the Middle East. And it's just so sad what has happened to us the last few decades."

Kerr was in high school when his father was named president of AUB in 1982. It was Malcolm Kerr's dream job. But the appointment came as Lebanon was embroiled in civil war. Yasir Arafat's Palestine Liberation Organization, expelled from Syria, had its headquarters in Beirut. Iranian Shiites, followers of Ayatollah Ruhollah Khomeini, had moved into Lebanon and given voice to the impoverished Shiite minority there. The Christian population was shrinking, and Lebanon was in the middle of a tug of war between Israel and Syria.

"I bet there's a fifty-fifty chance I'll get bumped off early on," Malcolm Kerr told his daughter, Susan, in March 1982, she recalled in her memoir, *One Family's Response to Terrorism*.

He accepted the job the next morning. The Israeli invasion of Lebanon, and the countermove by Iran to send its Revolutionary Guards there through Syria, began in June 1982, weeks before Malcolm Kerr was to start the new job. In the chaos, Iran-backed militants were organizing and would eventually become Hezbollah.

Malcolm Kerr was kept in New York until things settled, but AUB's acting president, David Dodge, was kidnapped in July, and AUB was in need of leadership. Malcolm Kerr arrived in August, expressing hope that the destruction and death closing in on the campus could be kept outside its walls. (Dodge, who was released by his captors after a year, died in 2009.)

Back in California, Steve began his senior year and starred on the basketball team.

"I wanted him to be at games, but I knew that he was doing what he loved," Kerr said of his father. "And when you're sixteen or seventeen, you're so self-absorbed. You just want to play and do your thing."

Malcolm Kerr wrote letters home almost daily. They detailed tense meetings with political leaders, the latest assaults on Beirut, the assassination in September 1982 of the Lebanese president-elect, Bashir Gemayel, the interviews with foreign journalists. Most were filled with optimism and good humor.

"The thought of being in Pacific Palisades for Christmas is more appealing than I can say, and I wouldn't miss the chance for anything," he wrote in one. "Hopefully I'll get there in time to catch a few of Steve's basketball games and watch Andrew wash the cars."

That December, the Kerrs posed at their California house wearing matching AUB sweatshirts.

Steve Kerr went with his mother and brother Andrew to Beirut in the summer of 1983, before he went to play at Arizona for first-year coach Lute Olson. A few months before, militants had bombed the United States embassy in Beirut, killing sixty-three, including seventeen Americans. But the visit fell during what felt like a lull in the war.

"We went hiking in the mountains above Beirut and swimming in the Mediterranean," Kerr said. "The house where they lived was on campus—the presidential house, the Marquand House. It was beautiful. It was surreal. There was a butler. We didn't have that back home. But now he was living the life of the president. We had a great time during the day, and then we played cards after dinner outside."

The trick was leaving. Ann Kerr went with Steve to the airport in August.

"There was some question about whether flights would be going out because of everything that was happening," Kerr said. "We were in the terminal, and all of a sudden there was a blast. It wasn't in the terminal but on the runways. The whole place just froze. Everybody just froze. People started gathering, saying, 'We've got to get the hell out of here.' My mom grabbed me, and I remember running out of the terminal and through the parking lot. It was really scary. I remember thinking, This is real."

The Kerrs pondered options for getting Steve out. They learned that a private plane of diplomats was going to the United States Marine base and there might be an available seat on the flight back out. Steve spent hours waiting, talking to Marines. In the end, there were no seats. The Kerrs eventually made arrangements for a university driver to take Steve over the mountains, through Syria to Jordan. (The driver, a long-time friend of the family, was killed by a sniper in Beirut in 1985.)

On an early morning in October 1983, a truck bomb destroyed the four-story Marine barracks. Among the dead were 220 Marines and 21 other service members.

"I remember looking at all the photos afterward," Kerr said. He started to cry. "I see all these, the nicest people, who I met and they were showing us around the base and just trying to do their jobs and keep the peace. And a truck bomb?"

Kerr said he recognized some of the faces of the dead.

"There is a chaplain who had come over and kind of taken us under his wing," he said. "The nicest guy. And I saw his face . . ."

Kerr wiped his eyes and took a deep breath. "What has it been, thirty years? And it still brings me to tears."

In December, John visited his parents in Beirut. They had a videotape of Steve's first game for Arizona a couple of weeks before. The picture was fuzzy, shot without sound from a camera high in the gym, and they could not always tell which player was Steve. It did not matter.

"I think he scored three baskets, and we must have watched each of them ten times, rewinding the tape over and over again just to relish every detail," John wrote in an entry for a family scrapbook made on an anniversary of Malcolm Kerr's death. He called it "Dad's and my high point as sports fans."

In the middle of a night in January 1984, Kerr got a call in his dorm room from Vahe Simonian, a family friend and a vice president at AUB who was based in New York. Simonian told Kerr that his father had been killed.

The assassination, on January 18, 1984, was international news, including on the front page of *The New York Times*. Malcolm Kerr, fifty-two, had stepped out of the elevator toward his office in College Hall and was shot in the back of the head. The two unknown assailants escaped. A group calling itself Islamic Holy War took responsibility later that day.

"Dr. Kerr was a modest and extremely popular figure among his 4,800 students and faculty, according to his colleagues here," *Times* reporter Thomas L. Friedman wrote from Beirut that day. "He was killed, his friends insist, not for being who he was, but because now that the Marines and the American Embassy in Beirut are smothered in security, he was the most vulnerable prominent American in Lebanon and a choice target for militants trying to intimidate Americans into leaving."

Andrew Kerr, who was fifteen at the time, heard about his father's death on a radio in a shop near AUB's campus. Ann Kerr learned about it while waiting at a campus guardhouse, out of the rain, for a friend. She ran to College Hall, to the second floor, where she found her husband "lying on the floor, face down, his briefcase and umbrella in front of him," she wrote in her memoir, *Come with Me from Lebanon*.

A memorial service was held a few days later. John came from Cairo and Susan came from Taiwan. Steve was the only one of the children who did not attend. He missed another one at Princeton, but attended a third in Los Angeles.

"It sounds bad," he said. "Obviously, the basketball wasn't more important. But the logistics were really tricky. And it was cathartic for me to just play."

He had a breakout-game in a victory over rival Arizona State two nights after his father's death. The Wildcats had been 2–11, but won eight of their final fourteen games. The next year, they reached the NCAA tournament on their way to becoming a lasting national power.

Four years later, Kerr was the target of pregame taunts at Arizona State. A group of students shouted, "PLO, PLO," "Your father's history," and "Why don't you join the Marines and go back to Beirut?"

"When I heard it, I just dropped the ball and started shaking," Kerr said at the time. "I sat down for a minute. I'll admit they got to me. I had tears in my eyes. For one thing, it brought back memories of my dad. But, for another thing, it was just sad that people would do something like that."

WHERE THE VISION COMES FROM

Ann Kerr-Adams is eighty-two, wears Keds and keeps her hair in a chin-length bob. She is the longtime coordinator of the Fulbright program at UCLA and oversees a class called "Perceptions of the United States Abroad." She is also an emeritus trustee at AUB and usually goes back to Beirut once a year for meetings.

She remarried in 2008. She and Ken Adams share the California house that she and Malcolm bought in 1969.

The stately living room, with a grand piano and views of the Pacific Ocean, is neatly decorated with treasures of a well-traveled life, like etchings of Cairo and Ann's framed watercolors of Tunisia. The mantel has an oval-framed photograph of Steve and Andrew in a field of flowers in Morocco.

"I would say Steve's intellectual interests really blossomed in the last ten years," she said. "But I don't think of Steve being like Malcolm."

They shared a passion for sports (the children's hour-a-day limit for television did not apply to sports) and an irreverent sense of humor. But Steve is more diplomatic than his father, she said.

A nearby guest room was where the three Kerr boys slept. The bunk beds that Steve and Andrew shared are gone, but there is a painting that Steve did as a boy—a self-portrait of him in a UCLA shirt and a Dodgers cap, his blond hair hanging past his ears. The bathroom has a painting of poinsettias he did when he was nine, and a closet contains his screen prints of boats in Cairo.

"Here's a picture of Steve, the ornery teenager," Kerr-Adams said on a recent Sunday afternoon, stopping in a hallway lined with family photographs. "He was always snarling in pictures. Now he has to smile for photos. The irony of it all."

Across the hall is the room that Malcolm used as an office. His children harbor happy memories of the sound of his typewriter clacking and the smell of the popcorn that he liked as a snack.

The backyard, with wide ocean views that test the flexibility of the human neck—from Los Angeles on the left, to the Santa Monica Mountains on the right—features a broad patio. On Sunday afternoons, it was frequently filled with professors, neighbors, visiting dignitaries and friends from around the world. It was the family's connection to the Middle East that made his childhood unique.

"It would be totally different without that," Kerr said. "Totally different. I wouldn't be exposed to not only the travel and the interaction with people, but I wouldn't be exposed to the political conversations at the table and at barbecues about what was going on in the world."

But talk around the house was more likely to involve the Dodgers or Bruins. Malcolm was a good athlete, a basketball player growing up and an avid tennis player until the end. He and Steve spent a lot of time at the high school hitting and fielding, and Malcolm sometimes joined Steve in the driveway.

"He was a lefty and had a nice hook shot," Kerr said with a laugh.

Kerr credits his father for his demeanor on the sideline as an NBA coach: calm and quiet, mostly, and never one to berate a player. Kerr was not always that way.

"When I was eight, nine, ten years old, I had a horrible temper," Kerr said. "I couldn't control it. Everything I did, if I missed a shot, if I made an out, I got so angry. It was embarrassing. It really was. Baseball was the worst. If I was pitching and I walked somebody, I would throw my glove on the ground. I was such a brat. He and my mom would be in the stands watching, and he never really said anything until we got home. He had the sense that I needed to learn on my own, and anything he would say would mean more after I calmed down."

His father, Kerr said, was what every Little League parent should be. The talks would come later, casual and nonchalant, conversations instead of lectures.

"He was an observer," he said. "And he let me learn and experience. I try to give our guys a lot of space and speak at the right time. Looking back on it, I think my dad was a huge influence on me, on my coaching."

Kerr played for some of the best basketball coaches in history—Olson at Arizona, Phil Jackson with the Chicago Bulls and Gregg Popovich with the San Antonio Spurs among them. By the standards of basketball coaches, they were worldly men with interests far beyond the court.

"I remember Phil talking to the team about gun control, and asking the players, 'How many of you have guns? How many of you know that if you have a gun in your house you're more likely to have a fatality in your house?'" Kerr said. "It was a real discussion, with guys saying that we need to have some level of protection, because we are vulnerable in many ways, too.

"And I remember one presidential election, it was probably 2000, I was with the Spurs and we did two teams shooting—the silver team against the black team or whatever," he said, referring to a drill run by Popovich. "Pop was like, 'OK, Democrats down there, Republicans down here.' I think it was about twelve against two at that point, so he had to even up the teams a little bit. He would just make it interesting."

Kerr—who has three children, all young adults, with his wife, Margot—has never talked about his father in front of the team, and Warriors players have only a vague notion of Kerr's family history. It is context, mostly, an unstated part of his background.

"I really realized from Pop and Phil that I could use my experience as a kid and growing up to my advantage as a coach," Kerr said. "And connect with players and try to keep that healthy perspective. Keep it fun, and don't take it too seriously."

It was during Kerr's tenure with San Antonio that the family, after years of reflection following the 1996 passage of the Antiterrorism and Effective Death Penalty Act, decided to sue Iran. The Kerrs came to believe that Iranian-sponsored Hezbollah had targeted Malcolm.

"I didn't need revenge, I didn't need closure," Steve Kerr said. "So I was indifferent to the lawsuit. But then I recognized that it was important to a couple of members of my family, my sister and my younger brother, in particular."

When it came time to testify in United States District Court in Washington in December 2002, Kerr was with the Spurs, in the last of his fifteen seasons in the NBA. He did not want to miss games.

"There's nobody better than Pop to talk about something like this," Kerr said. "I told him, 'I don't really want people knowing what it is.' I didn't want the attention. But I also don't want people thinking I'm injured. So Pop said, 'You missed two games for personal reasons. Big deal. Your reputation precedes you. Nobody is going to question what's going on with you.' And he was right. I told my teammates and nothing ever really came of it."

He testified in a nearly empty courtroom, missing two Spurs' road games on the West Coast. The Kerrs learned two months later that they had won the suit—millions of dollars that they may never see. But money was never the point.

"It provides a structure to enable people to channel their feelings through justice and the rules of law, rather than become vigilantes," his sister, who is now known as Susan van de Ven, said in a phone interview from England, where she is involved in politics as a county councillor. "It gives a very focused approach to people who are rightly and insanely aggrieved. That's the kind of culture we should have. We shouldn't be responding with violence. I'm sure that's why Steve talked about guns. It's all related, isn't it?"

Her book detailed the family's experience with the lawsuit.

The night before the Warriors visited President Obama to celebrate their 2015 NBA championship, Steve had dinner with Andrew, who works for an architectural design and residential builder in Washington. They discussed what Steve might say to the president. Andrew recommended complimenting him on his efforts toward gun control. Kerr did.

In June, at the end of a podcast with Bay Area sports columnist Tim Kawakami, Kerr asked if he could raise one more topic. Our government is "insane," he said, not to adopt stronger background checks on guns that most Americans agree upon.

"As somebody who has had a family member shot and killed, it just devastates me every time I read about this stuff, like what happened in Orlando," Kerr said, referring to the June massacre at a Florida nightclub. "And then it's even more devastating to see the government just cowing to the NRA and going to this totally outdated Bill of Rights, right to bear arms. If you want to own a musket, fine. But come on."

Since then, Kerr has become a go-to voice in sports for matters of bigger meaning. It surprises his family in some ways, knowing that he was probably the quietest of the siblings as a child.

"He's carrying around the family business in another discipline," said John Kerr, a professor of community sustainability at Michigan State. "There was no way he would do anything for a living that didn't involve sports. No way. And now that he's at the pro level, he has the opportunity to speak out. He's smart enough to realize he can do it."

NBA training camps began just as debate swirled over the decision by Colin Kaepernick, the San Francisco 49ers quarterback, not to stand for the national anthem, in protest over the killing of unarmed black men by police officers. Amid the divisiveness, Kerr was a nuanced voice in the middle.

"Doesn't matter what side you're on on the Kaepernick stuff, you better be disgusted with the things that are happening," Kerr said.

He added, "I understand people who are offended by his stance. Maybe they have a military family member or maybe they lost someone in a war and maybe that anthem means a lot more to them than someone else. But then you flip it around, and what about nonviolent protests? That's America. This is what our country is about."

In November, after the presidential election, Kerr was among the NBA coaches, including Popovich, who criticized the state of political discourse in the age of Donald J. Trump.

"People are getting paid millions of dollars to go on TV and scream at each other, whether it's in sports or politics or entertainment, and I guess it was only a matter of time before it spilled into politics," Kerr said. "But then all of a sudden you're faced with the reality that the man who's going to lead you has routinely used racist, misogynist, insulting words."

It is no surprise, then, that Kerr also has opinions on the Middle East. Like his father decades ago, Kerr said he believes that American policies have muddied the region. The heart of the problem, he said, stems from the lack of a two-state solution for Israel and Palestine. The Iraq War made things worse.

"To use Colin Powell's line, 'If you break it, you own it,' and now we own it," Kerr said. "And it's, like, 'Oh, my God, wait, it's so much more complicated than we thought.' Everybody looks back and thinks we would have been way better off not going to war. That was really dumb. But history repeats itself all the time. We didn't need to go into Vietnam, but circumstances, patriotism, anger, fear—all these things lead into war. It's a history of the world. It just so happens that now is probably the scariest time since I've been alive."

In Beirut, AUB still thrives. On its campus overlooking the Mediterranean is a new College Hall, a virtual replica of the one where Malcolm Kerr was killed, the building destroyed by bombs in 1991. There is the dignified Marquand House, where Malcolm Kerr lived when he was a young professor and returned to when he became president.

In an oval garden between College Hall and the chapel, there is a banyan tree that Malcolm Kerr climbed as a boy and carved with his initials, now high out of sight. Under the tree is a Corinthian column that the family chose in the days after his death to mark the spot where his ashes were buried.

"In memory of Malcolm H. Kerr, 1931–1984," the engraving reads. "He lived life abundantly." Those were the words that Susan wrote on a piece of paper that marked the site until the stone was etched. The paper is still there, on a plaque that also features an excerpt from Kerr-Adams's book. "We are proud that our dad and husband came to AUB," Susan wrote, in words that are now faded with time.

Steve Kerr has never seen it. He has not been back since his father was killed. But, more and more, he hears the echoes.

POSTSCRIPT: Steve Kerr continues to coach the Warriors, leading them to five consecutive appearances in the NBA Finals, and remains outspoken on issues of politics, social justice and gun control.

17

A FOOTBALL COACH, A TORNADO AND A MURDER

Parkersburg, Iowa

I. SAVING TRADITION AMID THE DEBRIS

Ed Thomas stood in the ruins of Room 214 at the high school, where the clock face on the wall was stuck in time: 4:56.

"Yeah, that would be about right," Thomas said.

There was a school here, for decades, but it was turned to rubble on May 25 by the strongest tornado to scour Iowa's gentle landscape in thirty-two years. Three-quarters of a mile wide and with winds over 200 miles an hour, it touched down on the southwest end of this 1,900-person town and stayed down for thirty-four seconds, by one account. It spun mercilessly eastward until it knocked down 220 houses, 22 businesses, City Hall and Aplington–Parkersburg High School. Eight people died, and students from the school helped dig their graves.

The tornado also wiped out Ed Thomas's football program. And Ed Thomas is not the type of man to stand for that.

That is why, minutes after emerging with his wife, Jan, from beneath the basement steps to find their house on Conn Street and all the ones around it virtually erased from their foundations, Thomas walked—his two cars were destroyed, too—the few blocks to school. And he started to rebuild the past thirty-three years.

Thomas is fifty-seven years old, and for most of his life, Room 214 served as his classroom for teaching government and economics, his headquarters as the athletic director and his office as coach of the football team.

Three of the room's cement-block walls had been lined with framed photographs of all-conference players, hundreds of them. Some were in black and white.

Most are gone. There is a hole to the sky where the roof was, and the floor is covered in fallen white ceiling tiles, turned to mush by rain. Fluorescent light fixtures, ductwork, books and computer equipment— a mouse here, a keyboard there—are part of the mucky piles. So are broken pictures of football players.

Thomas's teams have won two state championships, had four runner-up finishes and made the playoffs eighteen times. Improbably, for a school of about 240 students, four former players are in the NFL: defensive end Aaron Kampman of the Packers, defensive end Jared DeVries of the Lions, center Casey Wiegmann of the Broncos, and center Brad Meester of the Jaguars.

But the biggest game in school history, as far as Thomas is concerned, is the one scheduled for September 5 against West Marshall. It is the home opener. And Thomas is determined, with a lot of help from friends, former players and the NFL, to play it on the field that bears his name.

"It would be such a positive uplift, that would be a form of normalcy for our people," Thomas said. "Friday nights are such a big thing at A–P."

Recovery will be difficult. The sod on the field, nicknamed the sacred acre, has to be replaced. Tiny bits of debris littered the grass, and

countless pieces of broken wood, two-by-fours mostly, speared the field like javelins.

"The field was like a pincushion," Thomas said. One piece of wood was embedded so deep it had to be sawed off.

The electronic scoreboard lay crumpled in one corner. The goal posts, now removed, had been twisted into corkscrews. One set of bleachers was so damaged it was hauled away. Another, where the press box was ripped from its perch, may be condemned. Lights dangled from the poles that had not fallen. A fence surrounding the new-but-ruined polyurethane track that circles the field—itself scarred by punctures and tears—was torn out. Even the weight room, in a separate building next to the school, is gone, although a couple of the weight machines remain, like pieces of outdoor sculpture.

The wreckage of the high school will be scrapped, and a new school will be built in its place. No one knows how long that will take. Graduation was held at the school a week before the tornado, and next year's students will squeeze into the middle school in Aplington, about five miles away. Some middle-school students will shuffle to the elementary school, which sits near the high school but was spared the storm's fiercest wrath.

Yet Thomas wants the football field back in less than three months. His mind sees seventy players taking the field in the familiar red pants, jerseys and helmets of the Falcons. Tradition says that every player, even the freshmen, dresses for every varsity game, even if it takes three buses to get to road games. His mind sees freshly mowed grass and bright lights. It sees cheerleaders and bleachers full of people crying tears of joy.

"If Ed Thomas wants it, Ed Thomas will make sure it gets done," Mayor Bob Haylock said.

Thomas looks like a coach. He has a military-style crew cut. He wears metal-rimmed glasses and walks with a forward lean, as if perpetually pacing a sideline. One day last week he wore shorts and a gray sweatshirt that read FALCON FOOTBALL in red letters.

But his eyes welled up when the questions struck a certain memory, and his confident coach's voice paused occasionally to gather strength. He sobbed one day last week when a coach from another team brought a bus of kids to help with the cleanup.

The day after the tornado, Kampman, who grew up in nearby Kesley and whose in-laws live down the street, arrived in town and bear-hugged Thomas.

"I won't forget that too soon," Kampman said. "It was a nice moment to share some pain with him."

Kampman and the other former A–P players, during phone interviews, described Thomas in near-identical terms: a great coach who saw larger life lessons in everything. Now he has a lesson that cannot be matched.

"I told the kids, you're going to be better people because of this," Thomas said. "Other people don't get these situations. You're living this. We're going to be a better school and a better community because of this."

On Sunday, May 25, Thomas was in his office when he heard the town's sirens go off. It was raining, but there was little urgency, since warning sirens are just part of the summer soundtrack here. Thomas drove home. His wife screamed for him from the basement.

She had brought two pillows down there, and the couple huddled under them beneath the steps. They soon heard the shattering of glass, the shredding of wood. When the noise subsided, they walked up the stairs into daylight. Part of one interior wall was the only thing standing of a three-bedroom home where they had raised two sons. Everything else was heaped in a pile or strewn somewhere in a field to the east.

The floors—linoleum where the kitchen was, hardwood in the living room—were all that remained last week. The pillows were still at the bottom of the basement steps, floating in muck.

The town was a hive of activity. Dump trucks moved back and forth. As Thomas stood on his property, new telephone lines were strung overhead from new poles. But the devastation was still staggering. Streets, now passable and identified by spray painted plywood signs, were lined with giant piles of debris. Trees not toppled stood as ghoulish sentries; shorn of their leaves, bark and all but the biggest of their branches, they looked like skeletons under surrender.

Ed and Jan Thomas say they will rebuild their house on the foundation. For now, they live in an apartment over the hardware store downtown, which was spared. But Ed Thomas seemed more concerned with the school and the football field.

"I probably wouldn't tell my wife this, but I don't know what hurt worse—my school or my home," he said. "The school was kind of my safe haven. I was at school as much as I was at home."

Thomas surveyed the damage in the roofless gym, where buried near the top of one pile was a large piece of cloth. It was a state championship banner, once hanging from the rafter, left in the rubble like discarded laundry.

A moment later, Thomas's cellphone rang. "Sure," he said. "I'll send a few players over." He hung up.

"They need some help digging a couple more graves," he said. The clock over his head, like the other one, was stopped: 4:56. But time marched on.

II. PERFECT RECOVERY

The surrounding cornfields where the tornado cut its deadly path last May have since grown tall, yielded their crop and withered to a faded brown. But this 1,900-person town, its south side cleaved by one of the biggest tornados on record, has defied the dying days of fall and reversed the cycle. It sprouts with life.

Some signs are as obvious as buzzing saws and pounding hammers. Others are as subtle as the sod on the graves that many of the football players from Aplington–Parkersburg High School helped dig for some of the eight people killed by the tornado. The grass has sown itself back to the earth, like healing scars.

The house of the football coach, Ed Thomas, at the corner of Conn and Johnson, has been rebuilt, among the first of the 222 houses destroyed to become a home again.

The rubble that was the high school is gone, replaced by the ascending brick walls of next year's classrooms.

The football field, which was speared by debris, is again lush green, lined with stripes and mowed perfectly. The mangled signs of 205-mile-an-hour chaos are gone, replaced by new bleachers, light towers, goal posts and a short chain-link fence behind which restless men and children watch the games. A new scoreboard stands in a corner. A rumpled metal piece of the old one, proclaiming this to be

Falcon Country, hangs as a twisted memorial where the players take the field.

"You get beat up, battered, but you get back up off the ground," Thomas said.

The Falcons, beyond reasonable expectations, are 10–0 and ranked number one in Iowa's Class 1A, for small schools but not the smallest. There is no high school here, not anymore and not yet, but there is a team. And those who never dreamed of such destruction now imagine a recovery that includes a championship.

Aplington–Parkersburg opened the state playoffs with a 42–0 victory against St. Ansgar on Wednesday night at Ed Thomas Field. As people gathered in the chilled twilight before the game, many stopped at the orange construction fence to look at the school being resurrected. They saw backhoes and dump trucks. They saw a horizon filled with houses and businesses in various states of construction. When asked about May 25, some of them cried.

Then they filled the new bleachers and cheered.

"We're just happy to help out the town," said Alex Hornbuckle, a junior running back who scored five touchdowns Wednesday and is one of three 1,000-yard rushers on a team running an old-school wing-T offense. "Whether it's building houses or playing football, we're just happy to help," he said.

The tornado was an EF5—the top of the Enhanced Fujita scale, the state's strongest in at least a generation—and it demolished City Hall, the gas station, the grocery store and the high school. It uprooted families and hundred-year-old trees. Neighbors found one dead woman on her lawn. Her husband, with a neck brace, goes to the football games, like just about everyone else.

Four assistant coaches lost their homes. So did about eight players. One lost his grandparents, too.

Thomas and his wife, Jan, emerged from their basement that day to find their possessions scattered over the fields to the east. He walked to the high school, the first to arrive at the wreckage. He vowed to rebuild the thing he knew best: the football program.

Thomas has been the coach at Aplington–Parkersburg—"A–P" to everyone here—for thirty-four years. The Falcons won state championships in 1993 and 2001, and four former players are in the NFL: Packers defensive end Aaron Kampman, Lions defensive end Jared DeVries, Broncos center Casey Wiegmann and Jaguars center Brad Meester.

But the tornado forced the Falcons to rebuild, literally. The first day, they pulled countless pieces of lumber—pieces of homes—that the tornado had thrown into the field like darts. On the day they played their first home game in September, the scoreboard went up.

In between, a temporary locker room was carved from a building constructed as a bus barn. Musco Lighting, based in Muscatine, Iowa, donated and installed the lights—about $150,000 worth, Thomas said. Turf experts advised Thomas on rehabilitating and reseeding the field. A man put in a concrete floor in part of his barn to create the team's weight room. A new track, replacing the one gouged with debris, is nearly complete.

On Wednesday, a school assembly was held at the middle school in Aplington, where the 240 high school students have squeezed in. In the hallway was a hand-painted sign: "We can't be knocked down," it read. "Falcon Pride is stronger than the EF5."

Thomas accepted a $16,332 check from Varsity Gold, a fundraising company that solicited and matched donations from rival high schools. All told, about $300,000 has been donated, not including the lights. About $175,000 has come from the NFL's Youth Football Fund, with a matching program for players. The rest has come mostly in small increments.

"Sometimes I catch myself thinking, Did this really happen to us?" Thomas said.

But thoughts of the "sixty seconds of horror," as the high school principal, Dave Meyer, called it, are never far away. The school held a tornado drill two weeks ago, as Iowa requires, though it was euphemistically called a shelter drill. Some students needed counseling, and some were excused from taking part.

Parents said that many children would not sleep upstairs in their bedrooms, away from the relative safety of the basement.

"We still have kids on our football team, if there's bad weather, especially wind, it gets to them," Thomas said. "They want to be home."

During the game Wednesday, Dawn Wiegmann, the wife of an assistant coach and mother of a starting safety, recalled the warm afternoon when the family's house was destroyed. Her daughter and son Coy were in the basement with two of Coy's teammates, including Hornbuckle. Her husband, Jon, was not home.

As the children screamed at her to get downstairs, she was frozen by the sight of the approaching black twister. Only when the eighty-year-old tree in the yard was ripped from the ground did she scurry to the basement, under the pool table, with the children.

She remembers the noise—"It hurt," she said—and how the back half of the house lifted and fell back on its foundation, three times, with a bang and a shudder.

The Wiegmanns have lived divided since. On Sunday, they hope to move into their rebuilt home, sleeping under the same roof for the first time since May.

And on Monday, they will be back at Ed Thomas Field, where Aplington–Parkersburg plays St. Edmond (9–1) from Fort Dodge.

There are times during practice when Thomas senses that his players are distracted. He will stop and have them look around, at the part of town that was wiped away and is being rebuilt. That is their motivation.

Before the game Wednesday, Thomas paced inside the makeshift locker room. The players, all seventy-four of them in uniform, were silent.

"I think you've understood since day one that this wasn't some ordinary season," Thomas said. He reminded the boys of the first game, on the road, when the visiting bleachers were filled with Aplington–Parkersburg fans an hour before kickoff.

"That's what you guys have meant to this community," he said. "We've been playing for a lot of people. Tonight is no different."

The Falcons soon ran underneath the battered sign salvaged from the old scoreboard. The people in the bleachers stood and cheered. Just behind them, in the twilight behind the construction fence, a school was rising again.

III. BOND OF TWO FAMILIES IS UNBROKEN DESPITE KILLING IN A SMALL TOWN

The body of the football coach lies under a rectangular patch of dirt, slowly being covered by creeping clover and crabgrass. But there is no doubt among people here that his soul is somewhere high above. A tombstone for Ed Thomas should be in place this fall.

The body of the coach's former player is in a county jail. But there is no doubt among people here that his is a soul lost. An insanity defense for twenty-four-year-old Mark Becker is expected when his murder trial starts next month.

For more than thirty years, the Thomas and Becker families were bonded by school, church and the communal raising of boys in this small town about a hundred miles northeast of Des Moines. Then their worlds collided in a fury of gun blasts.

And Parkersburg, a town of 1,900 people and no stoplights, was left to piece itself together, again.

It was Mr. Thomas who emerged from the basement fifteen months ago to find his house, along with 220 others, blown away by the biggest tornado to scrub Iowa in decades. He walked two blocks to the demolished high school where he had taught and coached for more than three decades, and vowed to patch Ed Thomas Field and the football program together in time for the season opener.

Mr. Thomas pointed Parkersburg toward normal. And it followed.

It was Jan Thomas, his wife, who was the first volunteer paramedic to arrive at the high school's temporary weight room early on June 24. The police chief stopped her at the door. It's Ed, he said. Mrs. Thomas had arrived in time to say goodbye.

That night, she called Joan and Dave Becker. And a small-town murder, as unexpected and unexplained as any other, had its most important answer. A violent death cannot shatter a town if it does not divide friends.

Unlike the aftermath of so many other killings, where the focus shifts quickly to a cry for justice, the Thomas family has made empathy the overriding emotion in Parkersburg.

"When I think about Ed, I can't help but think of Dave and Joan Becker," said Tom Teeple, the town's barber.

Mr. Teeple closed his eyes and puffed his cheeks, as if to keep grief from spilling. "Jan, at least, has some kind of closure," he said. "But those people, it's going to go on and on and on."

It was thirty-year-old Aaron Thomas who set the public tone on the day of his father's killing with two sentences uttered amid a three-minute statement.

"We also want to make sure we express our concern and our compassion for the Becker family," Mr. Thomas said. "We ask that people pray for them as well, and that people take the time to comfort and be with them through this, as they are also going through a lot."

At a time when no one knew what to feel, they had one thing to do: Remember that two families were grieving.

"That's something my mom and I had talked about before I went up there," Mr. Thomas said last week. "With the Becker family, Joan and Dave, we knew what they were going through as well. They were suffering and hurting. The last thing we wanted to see was a big upheaval toward them over something that they . . ."

He did not finish the sentence. The implication was clear. It was not their fault.

The Aplington–Parkersburg High football team started practice last week, under the direction of two assistants, Al Kerns and Jon Wiegmann. There was a space in the breeze where Ed Thomas's bellowing voice used to be. From across the street came the din of construction, the beeping and growling of machinery. School starts Monday.

The first football game is August 28. ESPN will televise it. Starting at offensive tackle will be Mark Becker's younger brother, Scott, a senior and a favorite of Ed Thomas's.

Dave Becker is a quiet bear of a man, residents said, who played football for Ed Thomas in the 1970s. Joan Becker was a radiant cheerleader. Their three boys played for Mr. Thomas, too. Both families are members of the First Congregational Church, where Mr. Thomas was an elder and taught adult Sunday school, often to the Beckers.

At church on June 21, Ed Thomas asked about Mark, a star linebacker in high school. He had been arrested the night before, part of a baffling string of run-ins with the law. He was said to have damaged a home with a baseball bat and then led the police on a car chase. Ed Thomas prayed for Mark Becker.

Three mornings later, the police said, Mark Becker walked into a cavernous red shed—last season's locker room, this off-season's weight room, now a maintenance barn—and shot Mr. Thomas several times.

"Right after I heard it, I wanted to find the person who did it," said Alex Hornbuckle, a senior running back who was not among the twenty or so students in the weight room at the time. "Then I heard it was Mark. I used to really look up to him."

No one else was hurt. Mr. Thomas, fifty-eight, died about the same time that Mark Becker was arrested in the driveway of his parents' home.

Mr. Becker pleaded not guilty to first-degree murder. The trial is scheduled to begin September 15. Thomas family members are not sure how much of it they will attend.

Mr. Becker's public defender, Susan Flander, said she would use the defense of insanity and diminished responsibility. People in Parkersburg presented a tidier diagnosis: Mark Becker got into drugs. Fell into the wrong crowd. Lost his way, and took Ed Thomas with him.

"It's truly a double loss to our family," Joan Becker said in a phone interview.

The Beckers declined to comment further except through a statement that acknowledged "the mercy and grace the Thomas family, our church family and our entire community has shown to our family."

The day before the funeral, as thousands lined the sidewalks and waited hours to pay respects, the Thomas and Becker families had a private viewing.

"They had a huge history," the Reverend Brad Zinnecker said. "So they needed some time to be together."

Sunday mornings at church, Jan Thomas and Joan Becker can be seen sitting side by side. Last Thursday morning, Mrs. Thomas was in her yard, hanging a wind chime on the back porch. A woman of deep faith and a firm handshake, she wants to let her two sons do the talking that her husband used to do.

In July, Aaron Thomas left a job at a bigger school in La Porte City, Iowa, and took on his father's role as activities director at Aplington–Parkersburg. He and his wife and their three little boys have moved in with Jan Thomas—into the three-bedroom home rebuilt where the tornado swiped the old one—until their own house is built nearby.

"He really wanted to coach my three kids," Aaron Thomas said of his father. "He thought he could make it through that, could last that long."

The second Thomas son, Todd, twenty-eight, and his wife are moving to Parkersburg, too, from Cedar Falls. A financial planner, he will coach the offensive line. That was always his father's specialty.

Together, huddling close with their mother, they are pushing Parkersburg forward, toward a "new normal," as Aaron Thomas called it.

Until not long ago, that was Ed Thomas's job.

POSTSCRIPT: *Aaron Thomas became principal and basketball coach at Aplington–Parkersburg High, where the football field is named for his father. Mark Becker is serving a life sentence.*

18

THEY HEARD THE HELICOPTER GO DOWN. THEN THEY PRAYED.

Calabasas, California

I t began as just another Sunday at a little church along Las Virgenes Road, on a quiet edge of suburban Los Angeles. The Church in the Canyon is an unremarkable box of a building, with a flat roof over glass front doors.

It was about 9:45 a.m. The Sunday worship service was an hour away. A ceiling of low clouds obscured the tops of the bare, brown hills across the road.

You cannot always see the moment that the world is about to change.

Elizabeth Howland Forrest had just arrived from Santa Monica, mesmerized along the way by the low-flying helicopter that she followed west for several miles on Highway 101. It weaved so masterfully with the bends in the road, she thought, until she lost sight of it ahead of her. She got off at the Las Virgenes exit, hit green lights at the strip center and the apartments, and parked at the church. She checked her makeup in the rearview mirror.

Scott Daehlin, who lives in a GMC Safari in the parking lot, had prepared the sanctuary's sound system for choir practice and stepped outside to get something from his van. Jerry Kocharian, a church member and maintenance worker, stood with his coffee on the opposite side of the building.

Pastor Bob Bjerkaas was inside, teaching Sunday school to teenagers, focused on Genesis. What does the ancient book say about the life we live now?

Pastor Bob, the congregants call him, heard a low helicopter through the church walls. That was not unusual on the edge of Los Angeles, where so many copters—news copters, traffic copters, police copters, search-and-rescue copters, private copters catering to those rich enough to fly over traffic instead of drive through it—provide a thwap-thwap-thwap backbeat to daily life.

But this one sounded really low.

Outside, Daehlin tried to trace the sound moving through the clouds. His body felt it—a persistent percussion, "like a kick drum"—but his eyes could not spot the helicopter, invisibly gliding away from him.

"Oh, no," he muttered. "It's too low."

On the other side of the church, Kocharian caught a vague glimpse, a dark phantom in the murky clouds. It crossed Las Virgenes.

"It didn't circle like it was trying to land," Kocharian said. "It was moving."

Out of a corner of her eye, from the driver's side window, Howland Forrest saw a flash that spun her head toward the hills. The men outside heard it less as a boom and more as a thud—abrupt, a quick beat of shattering parts, and utter silence.

It burst through the walls of the church.

"Oh, dear Lord," Pastor Bob said. "Something happened."

There was no explosion, no Hollywood-style fireball. The helicopter struck the earth about a half-mile from the Church in the Canyon, on high ground scorched by the massive Woolsey fire in November 2018.

Fifteen months ago, the mountains burned, all the way to Malibu, but the fire spared the church. The story was everywhere but there.

Not this time. By topographical luck, the church had the only real vantage point of the wreckage. The best view was from the church marquee along the street. Neighbors ambled there immediately, mingling with the churchgoers. No one in the growing crowd knew what to make of what they saw.

There were flames, but no inferno. Witnesses described something like flares, at least for a while. Pale smoke rose into the low, gray clouds.

Daehlin called 911. Within minutes, patrol cars zoomed past, toward Malibu Canyon, then spun around. They pulled into a driveway at the Las Virgenes Municipal Water District, a smattering of buildings at the base of the hills directly across from the church.

Fire engines of various shapes and types came next. Television trucks followed. Emergency medical workers scampered up the hills, on trails usually used by dog walkers and mountain bikers, with all the best intentions.

Sunday services at the Presbyterian-affiliated Church in the Canyon begin at 10:45. About seventy-five worshipers came on Sunday, chattering about the commotion outside. They filed into the small sanctuary, with rows of padded chairs under a low ceiling lined with fluorescent lights. The budget is tight, but Pastor Bob hopes to upgrade the lights by Easter.

Pastor Bob is fifty-one, with red hair and a red goatee flecked with gray. He is legally blind in one eye and does not drive. He is married with four children—three boys and a girl, aged fifteen to twenty. He has a big laugh.

Many call him Coach Bob because he has coached lacrosse for

decades, including at a high school. Pictures of past teams fill the walls of his office.

No one calls him by his last name, Bjerkaas. He spelled it, with a plea.

"Do not spell it a-s-s," he said. "It's bad enough to have 'jerk' in there."

Pastor Bob's planned Sunday sermon was about Job—"the suffering of a righteous man, and how we make sense of it," he explained in his office on Wednesday.

"It was unusually apt," he said. .

A strange morning turned surreal. At the start of the Sunday service, Pastor Bob was passed a note from Howland Forrest, the church member who had glimpsed the crash from her car. He glanced at it. Reading is hard for someone who can wave his hands near his face and not see them.

The note said that Kobe Bryant was in the helicopter. It was forty-five minutes before TMZ first broke the news to the world.

Someone in the parking lot, working for a local television station, had passed that rumor to Howland Forrest. Soon she saw a black SUV pull in. The driver got out, wearing a dress shirt with dark pants and dark jacket, she said. Visibly upset, he walked across the street, spoke with the authorities, and came back to the church lot.

He had been at Camarillo Airport, Howland Forrest said the man told her, waiting for a helicopter from Orange County. He planned to drive Bryant, his daughter and seven others to Mamba Sports Academy in Thousand Oaks.

"He said, 'I got a quick call to come here,'" Howland Forrest said. She prayed with him, she said, and he left.

Pastor Bob did not dare share such information, unverified and unreported. But he steered his sermon toward the unfolding events outside.

"At the end, in my appeal, I said, 'We've had a very powerful reminder that life is uncertain,'" he said. "'Just as Job experienced great tragedy, very suddenly, something really shocking happened here today. It could happen to any one of us.'"

At 11:32, during the sermon, TMZ broke the story: Kobe Bryant was dead, killed in a helicopter crash. A man in the congregation stood to share the news from across the road that was now pinging around the world. It could not be more local or global.

As planned, the congregation concluded with an African American spiritual, "He's Got the Whole World in His Hands."

The service ended at noon. The crowd outside was multiplying. A sheriff's deputy came into the church. They were closing roads in the area and wanted those in the church to know.

"This is going to get crazy, really fast," the deputy said.

At the Mamba Sports Academy, fifteen miles west down the 101 in Thousand Oaks, there was no slow reveal. There was no evolving storyline. The news of a helicopter crash and Kobe Bryant's death came together, in one wicked blow.

A house of worship, a cathedral of sport, separated by a strand of highway, suddenly connected by the irrationality of happenstance.

"The whole room suddenly went silent," said Jennifer Miller, who had two sons, aged eleven and thirteen, playing on teams from Fresno in a weekend tournament. "Basketballs dropped."

The academy, the size of a Costco, squats in an industrial complex in Thousand Oaks. It once housed workers for Amgen, the pharmaceutical giant with a sprawling campus nearby, but was gutted and remade into a mega-gym a few years ago. Bryant became a partner in 2018, a couple years after his retirement from the NBA.

On this foggy morning, the academy was filled with excited boys and girls, their parents and coaches, the din of chatter, the thump of balls, the squeaks of sneakers, the bleats of whistles.

One of the five courts was cordoned off Sunday. It was where Bryant would coach the team of his thirteen-year-old daughter, Gianna, just as he had on Saturday. They had games at noon and two. Everyone knew that. People spent much of the morning watching games while sneaking peeks to see if Bryant had arrived.

News of the crash rippled quickly. Games were stopped. Miller got a stream of text messages. This isn't true, right? He's there with you, right?

There were sobs and circles of prayers. That is another thing the Mamba Sports Academy had in common with Church in the Canyon. Prayers.

At the church, people came. At Mamba Sports Academy, most people left. There was nothing else to do.

"It was surreal stepping out of that building and into, maybe, a different world," Miller said.

Strange, the string of destruction and attention that has come recently to this normally quiet stretch of suburbia in Conejo Valley, with its landscaped streets and strip malls, manicured yards and swimming pools. The area feels designed to get away from the kinds of things that have plagued it recently.

Times like these can test faith. Pastor Bob had eased people through the fright and destruction of the wildfires, fifteen months ago, that had driven out his family, too. He prayed with people affected by the mass shooting at the Borderline bar in Thousand Oaks on the eve of those fires, when twelve people died, plus the gunman.

This was different—as out of nowhere as a meteor, just outside the church doors.

Someone stopped him after church. What are you going to do?

"I have no idea," Pastor Bob said. There is no action plan for unimaginable events.

Images beamed from satellite trucks and photographers parked outside the church's front door had quickly ricocheted around the globe. People raced to the source of those pictures, crowding to see something they just had to see for themselves.

"I thought, what's the nicest thing we can do right now?" Pastor Bob said. "We spent Sunday trying to be nice, in the name of Jesus."

They let people park. They brought out water and coffee. They opened the restrooms. Television trucks and reporters crowded in. Fans soon flocked, like a pilgrimage.

"There was not a single problem," Pastor Bob said. "Not a single piece of litter. A couple of guys were smoking marijuana in front, and I said, 'You wouldn't smoke marijuana in your grandma's front yard, would you?' And they said, 'Oh, we're sorry, Reverend.'"

He laughed.

"Life has a little bit of good and bad in it," Pastor Bob said. "And on this side of heaven, we should always cultivate the good."

Midway through the afternoon, when the crash's death toll was confirmed at nine, Pastor Bob used his coach's voice to get everyone's attention. There would be a prayer service at 6:30, he said.

Eighty people came. Most were faces Pastor Bob had never seen. There was a broad range of ages and ethnicities crowded into the little sanctuary that night, under the flicker of the fluorescent lights. Most wore Kobe Bryant jerseys. One teenager was named Kobe. Another was named Bryant.

"There are a lot of things we all have in common," Pastor Bob said on Wednesday. "Sometimes when these difficult things happen, we're reminded of that."

Every day since has felt more normal than the day before. On

Wednesday, a few television trucks remained. A shrine of flowers and balloons and notes was piled around a light post on the sidewalk. Sheriff's deputies remained stationed across the street, to guard the area from the overly curious, while others patrolled the hills on horseback and all-terrain vehicles.

A constant swirl of a couple of dozen people stood by the church marquee. A young man from Van Nuys. A Caltrans worker on his lunch break. A man in a business suit. Two friends taking selfies. A woman with a dog.

They stood together, their backs to the church, staring at something they could not quite see. They just knew that the world had changed somehow, and this was the place it happened.

POSTSCRIPT: *There were no plans for an official marker at the helicopter's crash site, though it remains visible from the church if you know where to look.*

19

CHILDREN OF THE CUBE

Salt Lake City, Utah

There were three worthwhile vantage points for "Max Park vs. the World," an exhibition featuring seven of the globe's fastest speedcubers. That's the moniker for the growing faction of people who solve Rubik's Cube-style puzzles at mind-bending speeds. Six of them formed a relay against Park, an autistic sixteen-year-old from California who is breaking most of their records.

One good spot was from the audience, joining hundreds of (mostly) young people gazing up at the celebrities of speedcubing the way NBA fans crowd sidelines to watch Stephen Curry warm up.

Eyes and phones were up. Mouths were open. My son was in the crowd, somewhere.

On stage was Feliks Zemdegs, a twenty-two-year-old Australian who holds the world record in the 3 by 3, the six-sided, three-layer configuration of the original Rubik's Cube, which bestows an illusion of brilliance on those who can solve it. Zemdegs has done it in 4.22 seconds. Earlier in the day, hundreds lined up for his autograph.

Around him were other record-setters, all famous in this world, each smiling behind a mixed-up cube of a different size: a 2 by 2, a 3 by 3, all the way up to a 7 by 7.

"The team assembled by Feliks to take down Max Park!" an emcee said through a microphone.

Park sat at a nearby table alone, with cubes of all sizes in front of him. He owned world records in the 4 by 4 (18.42 seconds), 5 by 5 (37.28 seconds), 6 by 6 (1 minute 14.86 seconds) and 7 by 7 (1 minute 47.89 seconds).

I wondered if a better vantage point was behind the stage, the same view that the competitors had, directly into the awed faces of their fans. Most of those in the audience had qualified to compete at CubingUSA's nationals, too, alongside their fast-fingered heroes, over three summer days inside a convention center.

But I settled for the third spot to watch—off to the side, neither competitor nor fan, but merely a parent trying to make sense of it all. Among the spectators, expressions of wonder tilted like sunflowers atop the craned stalks of their necks, aimed toward the bright light of speedcubing's stars, was my son, Joe, competing at his first nationals.

He is sixteen, straddling the moat between childhood and adulthood. He has spent most of his years trying to fit in but usually being pushed out. We learned he had attention-deficit hyperactivity disorder in kindergarten, and some symptoms often associated with autism continue to vex doctors and psychologists as he approaches his junior year of high school.

His biggest issue remains socialization. Joe's a smart and tenderhearted kid, but like the cubes he carries everywhere, he can be hard to decipher and solve. Most don't give him the time.

When not at the skate park, he's usually home at the piano, practicing the Mozart pieces he learned from YouTube, or studiously putting together jigsaw puzzles, or practicing his cubes with a timer. I forget the last time he was invited somewhere.

Yet there he was, fitting in as never before. Like everyone else, he held a plastic cube, both a security blanket and a badge. He had a lanyard around his neck identifying him as one of about six hundred competitors, a special collective.

He had found acceptance by doing nothing more than being himself. Funny that it would come in a place where he could leave all the reinvention to the familiar 3 by 3 object in his hands, the one that has 43 quintillion possible configurations but that he and all the others could solve in seconds.

The crowd hushed. The race began. In little more than five minutes, Max Park solved all six of the puzzles, leaving the world behind.

"A valiant effort from the dream team," the emcee said.

I walked away with no doubt about the best view—that of a parent, watching a child find his place.

Max Park's parents, Schwan and Miki, knew something was different with their son when he was a baby. He seemed to live in his own world. For a time they wondered if he was deaf.

Doctors told them it was autism, the developmental disorder that can show itself in a range of symptoms from a young age—among them, the delayed use of spoken language, a lack of eye contact or inter-est in engaging with others, repetitive sounds or mannerisms, a hyper-focus on certain activities.

Another issue can be fine-motor skills. Max's therapists and parents put the boy through all kinds of exercises to improve his dexterity—picking up coins and placing them in the slot of a piggy-bank, for example. When he was seven or eight, Max was handed a Rubik's Cube.

"He fell in love with it," Schwan Park said at a competition in Berke-ley, California, a couple of months ago. "And he practiced all the time."

The Parks were just glad to find therapy that did not feel like a chore. Soon, Max could solve a 3 by 3 cube in about the time it takes to read this sentence aloud.

Just about everyone knows what a Rubik's Cube is. Invented in 1974 by a Hungarian architect named Erno Rubik, it had its first big moment in 1980 and 1981, when it was named Toy of the Year by people who confer such awards.

But fads fade, and by the end of 1982, even *The New York Times* declared it dead. The cube remained famous, in a nostalgic way, but as a fascination it lay mostly dormant for twenty years.

These days, most people fall into two camps. One is filled with those who remember Rubik's Cube as a pop-culture relic, as evocative of the 1980s as leg warmers and Duran Duran. They have no idea that cubing is having another moment.

The second camp is filled with speedcubers.

The World Cube Association, formed in 2004 to approve events, track times and provide order to all the high-speed twisting, says more than 100,000 people have competed officially. Popularity has grown exponentially in recent years. The number of first-time competitors in 2017 was about 24,000, five times more than in 2012.

Cubing's resurrection began slowly about fifteen years ago. The

2003 world championship was the first since 1982. Cubing clubs cropped up at college campuses, from Cal–Berkeley to Rutgers, spreading the gospel by holding open competitions.

The internet, particularly YouTube, slingshotted the rebirth. A puzzle that once seemed impossible was demystified in how-to videos. Cubers long ago figured out that the clunky Rubik's Cube was not built for speed, so other manufacturers jumped in, mostly Chinese companies like MoYu and Gan, engineering slick-moving variations of all conceivable shapes and sizes.

They show up in packages on my porch with startling regularity, in exchange for my son's allowance and savings account.

Joe gets them for birthdays and Christmas, too—polyhedrons of all sizes, including an 11 by 11 cube, tetrahedrons (pyramids), dodecahedrons (12 sides) and some with so many sides that I can't figure out how to count them, never mind turn their parts. There are single-color cubes where the moving parts are not square; they shift into incomprehensible shapes when they are scrambled, and back to a cube when solved.

Besides the puzzles in his backpack (usually a dozen) or scattered around the house (who knows), they are displayed on an Ikea bookcase in his room, bought specifically for that purpose. He tells people that he has two hundred puzzles in his collection. I'm scared to count, lest my brain compute the dollars spent.

Sometimes a new cube will arrive that looks just like a dozen others he already has, but Joe assures me that it's way better. I long ago got past the horror of entering his room to find his latest puzzle shattered into a pile of hundreds of plastic parts. He puts them back together after lubing them and inspecting the inner workings—usually. He could create a cubing junkyard with spare parts in his desk.

The persistent clicking of cubes being solved is a soundtrack of our family. I worry when I don't hear it coming from behind his bedroom door.

The puzzles are sold at online customization shops and retailers like the Cubicle, which has emerged as the sport's cultural trendsetter. It sponsors most of the world's top cubers, putting them in team jackets and paying travel expenses to competitions. It supplies contest purses, including the $23,200 at stake during last month's nationals. Top cubers are on the verge of making full-time livings solving puzzles.

That is the growing world that Park, speedcubing's latest star, now inhabits and dominates.

Like a lot of parents of modern-day cubers (including me), the Parks didn't know that cubing competitions were a real thing until their child asked to go to one. Max was eleven, without many friends at home. They went.

"He knew everybody," Schwan Park said. "He knew all the other cubers, their names, their times. We thought, oh, this will be a great place for him to socialize."

The Parks used cubing to reinforce other lessons—how to sit down correctly, how to make eye contact with a judge and say, "I'm ready." His cubing times weren't the point.

"To us, it felt like free therapy," Schwan Park said.

At his second contest, Max won the 6 by 6 event. These days, he holds the world records in 4 by 4, 5 by 5, 6 by 6 and 7 by 7. He won the 3 by 3 and the one-handed 3 by 3 events at last year's world championships in Paris, but does not hold those records—not yet, anyway.

"He is breaking cubing," said Phil Yu, twenty-eight, chief executive of the Cubicle and still a world-class competitor. "He is physically really strong. And his turning speed is out of control."

Part of what the Parks practice with their son now is how to handle the fame and attention: the autograph hounds and photo seekers, the glad-handers and back slappers, the people who may misread Park's autism as aloofness and walk away disappointed in their hero.

Yet Max Park fits in, too. He's adored by the cubers who want to be more like him, and liked and respected by the older cubers whose records he's now breaking.

"This group is really accepting," Schwan Park said. "A lot come from the same situations, people looking to fit in. We meet a lot of parents, and we all want the same thing for our kids."

At my son's first cubing competition, in Berkeley nearly two years ago, he averaged 48.43 seconds per solve in his attempts at the 3 by 3, still cubing's glamour event. Now at nationals, he averaged 19.91—a "sub-20," considered an elusive breakthrough just a couple of years ago, speedcubing's four-minute mile.

His average would have put him in the top ten in the world in 2004. Now it didn't crack the top 500 at nationals.

But his goal was personal bests, and he got them in 3 by 3, Pyraminx (a pyramid) and Skewb (a cube with pyramid-shaped corner pieces).

The highlight, though, was just being there.

"It's the story I hear nonstop," said Kit Clement, the executive director of CubingUSA. "Cubing initially can feel antisocial—you do it alone, no one understands you. Then you come to a competition and suddenly there are eight hundred other people just like you."

Cubing competitions are mostly a quiet parade of competitors unscrambling puzzles against an automated timer (forty of them at nationals) in front of a judge. They are more about data collection than spectacle.

Most time is spent waiting. At nationals, competitors sat at large round banquet tables. They practiced their own puzzles and borrowed others and spun them constantly in their fidgety fingers. Even if there was no conversation, there was the comfort of someone clicking and clacking alongside.

It felt like a never-ending lunch in a school cafeteria, where every table was the cool kids' table.

"We're all on the same wavelength here—we all speak the same language," said Brandon Harnish, a longtime competitor who, now twenty-two, oversees competitions as a World Cube Association delegate.

He looked around. Round tables were filled with children.

"All these people sitting together, hanging out, feeling comfortable?" Harnish said. "That's not a goal. It's a result."

My son has been to eleven competitions now, and I've talked to children and parents at most of them. Not all speedcubers come from the same mold, of course, but most seem to have interests in computers, science and math, often music. A few even mentioned origami.

Not all are shy, but a lot of them are, at least at home, where their fascination with cubes is a quirky curiosity, not a binding trait. I am far from the only parent in awe of how much my son comes out of his shell when he enters a room about to hold a cubing competition.

The trickiest puzzle is figuring out why only about 10 percent of speedcubers are female. (At nationals, where the median age was sixteen, 41 of 634 competitors were female.) Some suggest that the issue is a self-fulfilling one; girls see few other girls and stay away. The World Cube Association wants to add female delegates, who run sanctioned competitions, to provide role models to younger girls.

At the airport gate in San Francisco, while waiting to board the plane to Salt Lake City, my son excused himself. Maybe he heard the clack of cubes the way a dog picks up a scent, but he sat down next to Sameer Aggarwal, a slight, bespectacled thirteen-year-old from Bellevue, Washington, playing with a cube. He was on his way to his first nationals, too.

The boys struck up a conversation and fidgeted with puzzles as strangers nearby watched in wonder. Sameer's parents and I shared smiles and shrugs.

Manish and Rakhi Aggarwal later described their son as a studious middle-schooler, excelling in math, science, Spanish, violin and piano—and now cubing. He qualified for nine events at nationals, and did so well that he made the semifinals in three of them.

"We're on top of the world, actually," Rakhi Aggarwal said on the last day.

Adults tend to be most amazed by speedcubing—I can tell by the reaction of strangers watching my son twiddle away in public. It's probably a generational perspective, one ingrained from the original era of Rubik's Cube, when solving it felt virtually impossible.

I never came close to solving a Rubik's Cube as a child. But alone in the hotel one night during nationals, excited that my son was out to dinner with new friends, I followed an online tutorial narrated by Yu, the Cubicle chief executive, that has been viewed nearly 10 million times. In an hour, after some hiccups and playbacks, one of my son's 3 by 3s went from chaos to order.

"What makes you and me different," Yu told me, "is thousands and thousands of practice hours."

I haven't practiced since. But my son rarely puts the cubes down. On the plane ride home, he tried solving a 3 by 3 cube blindfolded, one of the many hard-to-fathom variations of speedcubing. He stared at a scrambled cube and examined the pattern of the colors. After a couple of minutes, he covered his face with his hat and took a deep breath.

I watched as my son's fingers rotated the layers at an incomprehensible speed. They paused sometimes as his brain tried to conjure the current position of the colors, to tell his fingers what to do next. I quietly recorded with my phone.

In a minute, the six sides of the cube went from kaleidoscope to nearly solid. He opened his eyes. Only a couple of pieces were in the wrong spot.

So close, I said, amazed and proud.

He smiled. "We can go again next year, right?" he said.

POSTSCRIPT: *We went again the next year.*

20

THE GIRL IN THE
NO. 8 JERSEY

Novato, California

I was on the sideline of a soccer field two Saturdays ago, watching my twelve-year-old daughter and her Novato teammates. I don't remember much about that game, but Novato won, and one of the goals was scored by the smallest girl on the team, a quick and feisty forward who wears a long ponytail and jersey number 8. We whooped and cheered her name. I found out later that her parents weren't there that afternoon. They were in Las Vegas for a getaway weekend.

About thirty-six hours later, I was on my way to Las Vegas myself, rushing to join my *New York Times* colleagues to cover the latest mass shooting, maybe bigger than them all. I hadn't covered one of them since 1999, when I was in the wrong place at the right time and rushed into the aftermath of Columbine.

A colleague of mine and I checked into a massive suite at Mandalay Bay Resort and Casino, eleven floors directly below that of the shooter. It had the same view of the concert ground across the Strip, where investigators in the daylight were picking through the carnage of the night before. That was about when my wife sent me a text. That little soccer player's mom was at the concert the night before, she said. She's missing.

But Stacee Etcheber was not my story. The gunman was. I spent a week mostly about one hundred feet below where the shooter committed mass murder, trying to solve the mystery of what he'd done. I talked to people, followed every lead and wrote stories. It's what reporters do. It was a news story, as horrific as they come, and we're trained to keep our emotional distance from the things that we cover.

Late that night, I stood in front of the window, just like the one that a madman broke eleven floors above and used as a perch to shoot hundreds of people he did not know. The body count was on its way to fifty-eight. I thought about home.

Stacee's family soon announced that she had died. My wife and I didn't really know Stacee much—obviously not well enough to notice that she was not among the few dozen people at a rec-level girls' soccer game. But some of our closest friends were dear friends of hers, and our town is small enough that there was probably no more than two degrees of separation to the family.

My family was among the hundreds of people, friends and strangers, who crowded onto the grounds of an elementary school and held candles aloft during the vigil. My daughter was one of the dozens of kids who solemnly held roses in her honor, and she hugged her classmate and teammate when it ended. She and a couple of friends made a cake and delivered it to the Etchebers' house the next day.

Orange was Stacee's favorite color, and on Friday, after people bought as much orange ribbon as they could find at all the local craft stores, an army tied ribbons all around town, from the trees on downtown's Grant Avenue to the posts in front of Pioneer Park. My wife and her friends tied them around the trees in front of the middle school where Stacee's daughter goes to school, along with mine.

I missed it all. I was as close to the site of the shooting as you could get, and yet felt fully disconnected from the effect of the tragedy. One night I walked to the memorial that sprang up in the median of South

Las Vegas Boulevard, the kind of now-familiar post-shooting memorial that I saw at Columbine almost two decades before, with balloons and flowers and candles. I found a photo of Stacee that had been placed in the middle of it all, and took a picture and sent it home.

In Las Vegas, Stacee was just one in a crowd, part of a list. But she and her family were all anyone talked or thought about back in Novato, and that is where I got my news. I heard that Stacee's husband, a San Francisco police officer, was running with Stacee through the barrage of gunfire when he stopped to help someone; he told his wife to go on and never saw her alive again. I heard that television news trucks were parked in front of the house. I heard stories of friends pulling over in their cars to cry at the weight and nearness of it all. There were beautiful and crushingly sad Facebook posts in Stacee's honor, the kind you see after every tragedy, except these were written by people I knew well.

I heard my wife, who grew up in a nearby town, tell me that she had never been more proud to call Novato home.

I checked out of that Mandalay Bay suite on Saturday morning, excused from reporting duties, and flew home in the hopes of making my daughter's soccer game. I found the red rose from the vigil, starting to fade and wilt, in a vase on the kitchen counter. When we got to the game, we and the other parents were somewhat surprised to see Stacee's husband and extended family there, too. Warming up with the girls was number 8, with her long ponytail.

We all wore orange ribbons, attached by safety pins, including the girls on both teams. The Novato team wore orange armbands with the initials "S.E." Before kickoff, both squads came across the field to the spectator side and lined up in straight lines. Our team's coach asked the parents to stand for thirty seconds of silence. And then two of the league's better teams played a rather meaningless soccer game, only this one felt about as meaningful as anything I've ever watched.

And it was late in the second half when the ball suddenly swung from one end to the other, and Stacee's daughter gave chase through three retreating opponents and beat them all to the ball. And in one blink-and-you-missed-it moment, she booted the ball into the corner of the net for what held on as the winning goal.

Her teammates chased her and swarmed her, and they and she looked as free and happy as girls can be on a sunny fall Saturday afternoon with their friends. The parents jumped and cheered as loudly as I've heard parents cheer at a kids' soccer game. Behind my sunglasses, I was bawling. It was the first time I'd cried all week.

POSTSCRIPT: *Three years later, there are still a few faded orange ribbons clinging to trees in my town.*

ACKNOWLEDGMENTS

I am eternally proud to call myself a reporter for *The New York Times*—saying it out loud or handing out a business card still makes me feel like an impostor.

I have been fortunate to work for imaginative, smart, patient sports editors: Tom Jolly, Joe Sexton, Jason Stallman and Randy Archibold. They are the ones who have let me do whatever it is I do. I am grateful for their guidance, trust and ongoing friendship.

And I thank all the colleagues who were part of telling these stories, from the photographers on the road to the copy editors in the office. So many people work behind the scenes to get every story published. My name goes at the top, and I get too much credit when a certain story resonates. I know that. I don't know how to rectify it other than to tell my colleagues—my friends—how proud I am to work with them.

I thank Matt Weiland, my book editor, and all the good people at W. W. Norton. Their belief and investment in me will never be taken for granted.

I thank my literary agent, Luke Janklow, for his enthusiastic encouragement and guidance. He sees things in me that inspire me to think beyond the next deadline and reach for more. And I thank Luke's patient assistant, Claire Dippel, whose cheerful voice is one I always hope to hear when I call.

My thanks and love go to my wife and my children, who recognize the faraway look I get when I'm working, and only tease me a little for it. And to my parents, who worry that large gaps between stories mean that my job is not going well, and who hustle out to buy a paper copy of *The New York Times* whenever they hear I've published another one.

And, of course, my enduring thanks to the people in these pages who let me into their lives. I never know what compels people to trust a stranger who wants to pry into their world, sometimes at the most difficult moments, to tell a story for a million other strangers, but I have not forgotten any of you. I hope some of our readers feel the same way.

CREDITS

PART I. CLIMBING AND FALLING

p. 1: "Snow Fall: Avalanche." Photo by Ruth Fremson. Copyright © 2012 by the New York Times Company.

1. SNOW FALL
"Snow Fall: The Avalanche at Tunnel Creek" by John Branch. Copyright © 2012 by the New York Times Company.

2. THE DAWN WALL
" 'Battling' Up a Sheer Yosemite Face, Seizing a Dream, Not a Rope" by John Branch. Copyright © 2015 by the New York Times Company.

"Hanging Out 1,200 Feet Up (Yes, Downtime)" by John Branch. Copyright © 2015 by the New York Times Company.

"Abduction. Lost Finger. Now, a Rock Climber's Tallest Hurdle" by John Branch. Copyright © 2015 by the New York Times Company.

"After Brutal Traverse, Climber Looks Upward" by John Branch. Copyright © 2015 by the New York Times Company.

"Climber Yearns for the Summit, and a Shower" by John Branch. Copyright © 2015 by the New York Times Company.

"Pursuing the Impossible, and Coming Out on Top" by John Branch. Copyright © 2015 by the New York Times Company.

p. 59: "Caldwell led the last pitch of the Dawn Wall as Jorgeson belayed." Photo by Max Whittaker. Copyright © 2015 by the New York Times Company.

p. 82: "Tommy Caldwell, left, and Kevin Jorgeson after completing their 19-day free climb of the 3,000-foot Dawn Wall on El Capitan in Yosemite National Park." Photo by Max Whittaker. Copyright © 2015 by the New York Times Company.

3. LOST BROTHER
"Lost Brother in Yosemite" by John Branch. Copyright © 2015 by the New York Times Company.

p. 87: "Dean Potter BASE jumping in Yosemite National Park in 2007." Photo by Drew Kelly. Copyright © 2015 by the New York Times Company.

PART II. WINNING AND LOSING

p. 95: "Summer Ball, center, listens to coach Tonya Lutz during a break in the Carroll Academy Lady Jags home game against McKenzie High School." Photo by Ruth Fremson. Copyright © 2013 by the New York Times Company.

4. ON LEAGUE NIGHT, A 300 GAME LIVES
"Bowlers Honor Man Who Died After His First Perfect Game" by John Branch. Copyright © 2008 by the New York Times Company.

5. PERFECTION IN THE HORSESHOE PIT
"Perfection in the Horseshoe Pit" by John Branch. Copyright © 2012 by the New York Times Company.

6. WHERE DRIVERS AND DANGER MEET
"Danger and Excitement Intersect at Figure Eight Racing" by John Branch. Copyright © 2010 by the New York Times Company.

p. 108: "Drivers competing in the world championship of figure-eight racing at the Speedrome in Indianapolis. Cars must pass by one another at the crossover in the middle of the racetrack." Photo by AJ Mast. Copyright © 2010 by the New York Times Company.

7. ENDURING TRADITIONS
"Two Hopi Traditions: Running and Winning" by John Branch. Copyright © 2015 by the New York Times Company.

p. 114: "The Hopi High assistant coach Juwan Nuvayokva near his childhood home in the Hopi village Oraibi." Photo by Nick Cote. Copyright © 2015 by the New York Times Company.

8. WHERE CREATIVITY WAGS ITS TAIL
"Where Creativity Wags Its Tail" by John Branch. Copyright © 2020 by the New York Times Company.

9. A LAST HURRAH FOR HOLLYWOOD PARK
"A Last Hurrah for Hollywood Park" by John Branch. Copyright © 2013 by the New York Times Company.

p. 126: "Hugo Rousseau, a waiter who has worked at the track for 13 years, watched a race on a quiet Saturday afternoon." Photo by Monica Almeida. Copyright © 2013 by the New York Times Company.

10. THE LADY JAGUARS
"'It Ain't About the Record'" by John Branch. Copyright © 2012 by the New York Times Company.

"'We're Not Really Bad Kids'" by John Branch. Copyright © 2012 by the New York Times Company.

"'Bad Decisions, Good Intentions'" by John Branch. Copyright © 2012 by the New York Times Company.

PART III. HIDING AND SEEKING

p. 250: Cover image from "Deliverance From 27,000 Feet." Photo by Dawa Finjhok Sherpa / Seven Summit Treks. Copyright © 2017 by the New York Times Company.

p. 285: "Last Respects." Photo by Josh Haner. Copyright © 2017 by the New York Times Company.

p. 287: "Goutam Ghosh." Photo by Josh Haner. Copyright © 2017 by the New York Times Company.

PART IV. DYING AND LIVING

p. 289: "Orange ribbons were tied all around Novato, Calif., in remembrance of Stacee Etcheber." Photo by Peter DaSilva. Copyright © 2017 by the New York Times Company.

16. SEEING THE WORLD BEYOND THE COURT
"Tragedy Made Steve Kerr See the World Beyond the Court" by John Branch. Copyright © 2016 by the New York Times Company.

p. 293: "Photos of Malcolm H. Kerr, in the room he used as an office at the family's home in Pacific Palisades, Calif." Photo by Emily Berl. Copyright © 2016 by the New York Times Company.

17. A FOOTBALL COACH, A TORNADO AND A MURDER
"In Iowa, Saving Tradition Amid the Debris" by John Branch. Copyright © 2008 by the New York Times Company.

"Football Team Helps Storm-Damaged Town Bounce Back" by John Branch. Copyright © 2008 by the New York Times Company.

"Bond of Two Iowa Families Unbroken Despite Killing" by John Branch. Copyright © 2009 by the New York Times Company.

p. 310: "The school will be torn down and rebuilt." Photo by Stephen Mally. Copyright © 2008 by the New York Times Company.

p. 320: "An Aplington-Parkersburg High football player passed a tribute to coach Ed Thomas on Aug. 13 in Parkersburg, Iowa." Photo by Jim Slosiarek. Copyright © 2009 by the New York Times Company.

18. THEY HEARD THE HELICOPTER GO DOWN. THEN THEY PRAYED.
"They Heard Kobe Bryant's Helicopter Go Down. Then They Prayed." by John Branch. Copyright © 2020 by the New York Times Company.

19. CHILDREN OF THE CUBE
"Children of the Cube" by John Branch. Copyright © 2018 by the New York Times Company.

p. 332: "Joe Branch competing at the CubingUSA nationals." Photo by Alex Goodlett. Copyright © 2018 by the New York Times Company.

20. THE GIRL IN THE NO. 8 JERSEY
"The Girl in the No. 8 Jersey" by John Branch. Copyright © 2017 by the New York Times Company.

p. 343: Photo by John Branch.

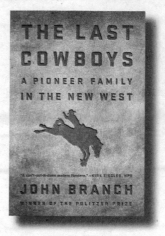
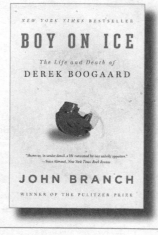